# History After Lacan

MW00813876

This is the story of a social psychosis. It begins by recovering Lacan's neglected theory of history. Contrary to received views, Lacan was not an ahistorical poststructuralist. Rather, he argues that we are in the grip of an ego's era – an era that begins in the seventeenth century and climaxes in the present, leaving us all fairly mad.

*History After Lacan* draws on psychoanalysis, political economy and feminism. It argues that the psychical fantasies analysed not only by Lacan but also by Freud and especially Melanie Klein are microcosms of the macrocosmic process at work in the ego's era. Brennan brings these different psychoanalytic theories together in her concept of the 'foundational fantasy'.

In the ego's era, the foundational fantasy, which founds 'subjects' through splitting and repression of the mother, is acted out. It is acted out in relation to nature. Thus the fantasized attacks on the mother's body described in psychoanalytic case histories can also be read as a description of the dynamics underlying attacks on the natural environment.

To explain the relation between microcosm and macrocosm we need appropriate theories of space and time. Brennan starts to develop these by showing how profit requires an ever increasing spatio-temporal speeding up of natural production, a requirement which, in its turn, alters the physis we inhabit.

**Teresa Brennan** teaches at the University of Cambridge. She is the editor of *Between Feminism and Psychoanalysis* and author of *The Interpretation of the Flesh*.

Feminism for Today
General Editor:
Teresa Brennan

**The Regime of the Brother**
After the Patriarchy
*Juliet Flower MacCannell*

**Feminism and the Mastery of Nature**
*Val Plumwood*

# History After Lacan

Teresa Brennan

London and New York

First published 1993
by Routledge
11 New Fetter Lane, London EC4P 4EE

Simultaneously published in the USA and Canada
by Routledge
29 West 35th Street, New York, NY 10001

© 1993 Teresa Brennan. The moral right of the author has
been asserted.

Typeset in 11 on 13 point Garamond by EXPECT*detail* Ltd,
Southport
Printed and bound in Great Britain by
Clays, St Ives plc

*British Library Cataloguing in Publication Data*
A catalogue record for this book is available from the British
Library.

*Library of Congress Cataloging in Publication Data*
Brennan, Teresa
History after Lacan/Teresa Brennan.
    p.   cm. — (Opening out)
    Includes bibliographical references and index.
    1. History—Philosophy.   2. Lacan, Jacques,
1910–81   .   – Contributions in philosophy of history.   3.
Political Economy. Title.
II. Series.
D.16.8.B7167   1993
901—dc20   93–17237

ISBN 0–415–01116–7 (hbk)   ISBN 0–415–01117–5 (pbk)

*For Susan James*

# Contents

# Series preface

Feminist theory is the most innovative and truly living theory in today's academies, but the struggle between the living and the dead extends beyond feminism and far beyond institutions. *Opening Out* will apply the living insights of feminist critical theory in current social and political contexts. It will also use feminist theory to analyse the historical and cultural genealogies that shaped those contexts.

While feminist insights on modernity and postmodernity have become increasingly sophisticated, they have also become more distant from the *realpolitik* that made feminism a force in the first instance. This distance is apparent in three growing divisions. One is an evident division between feminist theory and feminist popular culture and politics. Another division is that between feminism and other social movements. Of course this second division is not new, but it has been exacerbated by the issue of whether the theoretical insights of feminism can be used to analyse current conflicts that extend beyond feminism's 'proper' field. In the postmodern theory he has helped build, the white male middle-class universal subject has had to relinquish his right to speak for all. By the same theoretical logic, he has also taken out a philosophical insurance policy against any voice uniting the different movements that oppose him, which means his power persists *de facto*, if not *de jure*. Currently, there are no theoretical means, except for fine sentiments and good will, that enable feminism to ally itself with other social movements that oppose the power networks that sustain the white, masculine universal subject. *Opening Out* aims at finding those means.

Of course, the analysis of the division between feminist and other social movements is a theoretical question in itself. It cannot be considered outside of the process whereby feminist theory and women's studies have become institutionalized, which returns us to the first division, between feminist practice and feminism in the academy. Is it simply the case that as women's studies becomes more institutionalized, feminist scholars are defining their concerns in relation to those of their colleagues in the existing disciplines? This could account both for an often uncritical adherence to a postmodernism that negates the right to act, if not speak, and to the distance between feminism in the institution and outside it. But if this is the case, not only do the political concerns of feminism have to be reconsidered, but the disciplinary boundaries that restrict political thinking have to be crossed.

Disciplinary specialization might also be held accountable for a third growing division within feminism, between theoretical skills on the one hand, and literary analysis and socio-economic empirical research on the other. Poststructuralist or postmodern feminism is identified with the theoretical avant garde, while historical, cultural feminism is associated with the study of how women are culturally represented, or what women are meant to have really done.

*Opening Out* is based on the belief that such divisions are unhelpful. There is small advantage in uncritical cultural descriptions, or an unreflective politics of experience; without the theoretical tools found in poststructuralist, psychoanalytic, and other contemporary critical theories, our social and cultural analyses, and perhaps our political activity, may be severely curtailed. On the other hand, unless these theoretical tools are applied to present conflicts and the histories that shaped them, feminist theory itself may become moribund. Not only that, but the opportunity feminist theories afford for reworking the theories currently available for understanding the world (such as they are) may be bypassed.

None of this means that *Opening Out* will always be easy reading in the first instance; the distance between developed theory and practical feminism is too great for that at present. But it does mean that *Opening Out* is committed to returning theory to present political questions, and this just might make the value of theoretical pursuits for feminism plainer in the long term.

*Opening Out* will develop feminist theories that bear on the social construction of the body, environmental degradation, ethnocentrism, neocolonialism and the fall of socialism. *Opening Out* will try to cross disciplinary boundaries, and subordinate the institutionalized concerns of particular disciplines to the political concerns of the times.

*Teresa Brennan*

# Preface

This book continues an argument on energy and exploitation begun in my *The Interpretation of the Flesh*, which deals with the formation of femininity and energetic exploitation at the interpersonal level. *History after Lacan* addresses the relation between energy and exploitation at the socio–historical level. It does so after outlining a theory of history identified in (or with) Lacan's writing. Lacan's theory of history occupies Part I of this book. The theory of interpersonal exploitation is summarized briefly early in Part II. Apart from that the overlap in content between this book and its predecessor is slight. It is not necessary to have read *The Interpretation of the Flesh* to read this book.

However, I do want to note that both books were conceived at the same time and as part of the same overall project; they owe their conception to the same inspiration. The unity is obscured by their exegetical fixations on Freud and Lacan respectively. In the first instance, these two books were drafted as one, without their current fixations. They were also drafted in a propositional mode; I shifted to the secondary mode in executing them, for reasons which are not all bad, except that too marked a preference for the secondary mode, and a reliance on established names in writing, are products of the social trend which my books were meant to analyse.

As I think others doubt their inspiration, or lose their nerve, in a similar way, I will use this preface to enter a few notes on how the social trend I analyse affects the writing process. It is a trend in which we depend more and more on established fixed points, or recognized reference points, for legitimation. Now of course there is more to the secondary mode than dependence on social approval and security. After all, it dispels unfounded ideas of originality. For that matter, it often combines with primary research. And from the communicative standpoint, the secondary mode has this advantage: it helps the reader to situate the discussion and find familiar reference points from which to depart. The problem occurs only when these reference points take on a function of legitimation over and above that of communication and acknowledgement, when a preference for the secondary mode is set not only by the love of learning.

The issues might be plainer if I summarize my theory of fixed points. In *The Interpretation of the Flesh*, I wrote that the ego depends on fixed points because it depends on its identifications with others, and ideas, to maintain its sense of its individual distinctness, or identity. These identifications involve the image the ego receives from the other, an image which remains still or constant in relation to the movement of life. Psychically we need these fixed points, but they also hold us back (we are all familiar with the friends who do not wish us to change). In this book I argue that the fixed points of the psyche are parallelled and reinforced by the construction of commodities in the social world: psychical fixed points block the mobility of psychical energy; the technologically fixed points of commodities, unless they are constructed with care, block the regeneration of nature and natural energy. The key word in the last sentence was 'reinforced'. In an interactive understanding of energy, the barriers that we erect between thought and matter, individual and environment, are precisely socially constructed ones. What happens on the socially constructed outside has energetic consequences for the psyche.

This is why, if my general thesis in this book is correct, if the history of modernity is the acting out of a fantasy and a psychosis by a technology and economy in which fixed points proliferate, if the fixed points on the inside are strengthened by this proliferation, then it should be harder to write in anything other than a secondary mode. It should be that much harder to go beyond an existing idea, a familiar category, for these constitute points of reference for identity, or the ego. We are more likely to lose confidence in saying anything that is not familiar, to need confirmation for what we do say from the other. We are also more likely to only affirm that which affirms us as we are.

Whatever the content of an inspiration, carrying it through requires the confidence to proceed in the propositional mode. This is a style of thinking and writing that seems to be tolerated more in the French academic world than outside it. Within the English-speaking academies, one does not proceed propositionally, one proceeds critically. Creditable academic work consists of research, exegeses and critiques. On the other hand, the confidence required by the propositional mode can easily veer into mania. A certain kind of confidence is as much a symptom of the ego's era as the diffident dependence on the other's social approval. The ego can be original, but if the ego alone governs writing, it will demand that the reader do all the work required to understand what it writes. Either the ego trusts that the other's (like the mother's) main aim in life is to understand it, or the ego believes in and defers to an ideal other with whom it identifies as an imaginary part of itself. These attitudes are two sides of the same coin.

So for that matter is the intellectual division of labour between France and the English-speaking world, a division of labour in which both sides prop each other up. On the face of it, it seems easier to write in the propositional mode if one writes in France, while those who do not instead write secondary works elucidating, praising or damning the propositions. We write on Lacan, Derrida, Foucault, Kristeva, Irigaray; a decade ago we wrote on Althusser, Lévi-Strauss and, if we are getting very old, or were very precocious, Sartre and Merleau-Ponty. They have the insights, we fill them out, gain PhDs, and have something to say at conferences. The number of unsung genii in the English-speaking academic world who could not risk the primary mode because it would have meant bad scholarship, or worse, immodest claims, is a matter for the benighted historians of late twentieth-century thought. (Pity them, reader, as they attempt to tabulate intellectual histories based on computer print-outs and telephone bills.) By the same token, the historical fate of those who have had ideas, but been poor in attending to the other in communicating them, has also yet to be determined.

The question of course is how to combine the propositional and secondary modes and thus transcend them. To combine them is to regard yet disregard the other, to regard the right to understand, and thus communicate, to disregard the desire for recognition, and thus risk going beyond the fixed points governing social approval at the time of writing. It is to balance confidence and context, the movement of ideas and fixed points. And that can only be done if one gives out more than one takes in.

Part I of this book is in the secondary mode. Part II is in the propositional mode. While I have wondered why these different modes dominated at different times, it is only as I end this project that I can see its writing has been affected by a broader social trend, which counters the generation of life and ideas. I have not dwelt in this book or its predecessor on how this trend affects the process of writing and thinking, nor do I want to suggest that writing, of itself, will counter the ego's era. The idea is simply that writing in a more propositional style goes against that era, to the extent that it shifts the fixed points on which the ego depends. This is something to bear in mind when labouring against these points becomes onerous.

Cambridge
February 1993

# Acknowledgements

Earlier versions of parts of *History after Lacan* appeared in *Economy and Society* (August 1990) and *Paragraph* (March 1991).

Many people have kindly commented on or in other ways assisted with this book. John Bechara and Barbara Mikulski provided critical support in its inception. Kwok Wei Leng and Philipa Rothfield helped prepare the first draft; Sarah Green's and Sarah Wragg's indefatigable intelligence dragged the second draft into the light. Wonderful Woden Teachout and Diana Grivas also helped – a lot.

I benefited from the intellectual generosity of Con Coroneos, Max Deutscher, David Held, Terry Eagleton, Lesley Goldmann, Sarah Green, Geoff Harcourt, John Henderson, Jane Humphreys, David Lane, Elisabeth Lissenberg, Juliet MacCannell, Michael Moriarty, Suzanne Raitt, Morag Shiach, Janet Soskice, Gayatri Chakravorty Spivak, Evelien Tonken, Benno Werlen and Edmond Wright, all of whom read and responded to one or both parts of the manuscript. Especial thanks to Gayatri Spivak, who did me the honour of publicly responding to a presentation of Part I, and whose insight sharpened it. Much gratitude as well to Malcolm Bowie, Joanna Hodge, Anthony Giddens and Fredric Jameson for encouragement and very detailed comments. Judith Butler's and Jonathan Rée's various interventions over the last few months kept me thinking; their support was much appreciated, as was that of Gillian Beer, Wendy Brown, Drucilla Cornell, Carol Gilligan and Alice Jardine. My pleasure in recording all these debts is great, but it is with particular satisfaction that I thank Peter Lambley, for reminding me that there are purposes other than writing, Daphne Lambert, who was the condition of reversing modes, Janice Price, for insisting I finally publish; Sourayya Azim, for providing another home base; and the three whose friendship saw this production through: Bice Benvenuto, an exile in the Roman tradition – my psychoanalytic interlocutor;

Ingrid Scheibler, American after Dos Passos – who knows about matters of spirit; Susan James, English in good faith, who pre-empted some of my worst mistakes - in the text.

May they all be acquitted of any guilt by association, and the errors, which are solely mine.

# Texts and translations

To avoid the anachronistic comedy of the Harvard reference system, I have modified it: the original date of publication or, in Lacan's case, presentation is the date given in the text. This is the first date in the list of works cited; the date of the edition used is listed at the end of the entry where it differs.

I have made use of translations where available. Unless modifications are serious, they are silent. About a third of Lacan's writings have been translated. Lacan's seminar *Encore* is still untranslated, although two chapters from it, 'A love letter' and 'God and the jouissance of the woman', are translated by J. Rose in J. Rose and J. Mitchell (eds) *Feminine Sexuality*. Where the reference to *Encore* is to a translated chapter, both the French and English references are given in the text. Unattributed translations are mine.

# Part I

There is, therefore, a single ideology of which Lacan provides the theory: that of the 'modern ego', that is to say, the paranoiac subject of scientific civilization, of which a warped psychology theorizes the imaginary, at the service of free enterprise.

(Miller 1977, p. 137)

# Chapter 1

# The problem

This is the story of a social psychosis. Its central character is the ego, an ego which is just as social and collective as the psychosis it underpins. The story has its point of departure in the theory of Jacques Lacan, who thought that the psychosis, which is apparently with us now, begins with an ego's era, which in turn begins in the seventeenth century. Like Max Weber, Lacan makes the psychological conditions under which capital could gather steam pre-date its social dominance, although he does so with a very different understanding of 'psychological conditions', one which is centred on the ego.[1] But although the ego's era begins before the advent of capital, it is accelerated by it. Or rather, with that advent, the ego begins its progress to the centre from the wings, seeking to make over all that exists in its own image. If so far this totalizing process has canvassed at least four centuries, it has not yet reached a natural limit.

Lacan implied that the ego would act as if there were no limits, pushing off into outer space on the strength of its imperative to expand. But presently, 'the everlasting nature imposed condition of human existence' (Marx 1867, p. 82) is making itself felt. It pushes against a technology that, for Walter Benjamin, severs modernity from the 'powers of the cosmos' (Benjamin 1925–6, p. 103). The powers of

---

1 Max Weber's *The Protestant Ethic and the Spirit of Capitalism* is qualified in ways that are underappreciated when it comes to the question of economic or religious priority in determing social change. As Tawney puts it, for Weber 'The question is why [the rationalist] temper triumphed over the conventional attitude which had regarded the *appetitus divitirum infinitus* – the unlimited lust for gain – as anti-social and immoral' (Tawney 1930, p.I(e)). Weber's answer was the religious revolution of the sixteenth century, but it was an answer, he specifically stressed, which should be viewed as part of a two-sided approach: 'it is, of course, not my aim to substitute for a one-sided materialistic an equally one-sided spiritualist causal interpretation of culture and of history. Each is equally possible, but each, if it does not serve as the preparation, but as the conclusion of an investigation, accomplishes equally little in the interest of historical truth' (1920, p. 183). See also the discussion in Giddens (1971, p. 119ff.).

the cosmos certainly seem very distant in an era riddled with pre-millennial tension (PMT), from which it tries to escape under various 'post' designations: poststructuralism, postmodernism, all of which signal the end of something, without signalling the anxiety that accompanies the uncertainty of what is to come. This anxiety, the genesis of which will be one of our main themes in this book, is also evident in the reluctance to trace a pattern from which some sense of future direction might emerge.

The sense of ending and loss has of course been with us for some time, but it is now being formalized in relation to nature. Various analysts of the present have defined a new epoch accordingly. For Strathern, this is the epoch 'after nature' (Strathern 1992). For Jameson, it is 'postmodernism', which he redefines as 'what you have when the modernization process is complete and nature is gone for good' (Jameson 1991, p. ix). Yet while Lacan himself did not dwell on nature, his theory suggests that the ego can only make the world over in its own image by reducing the lively heterogeneity of living nature and diverse cultural orders to a grey mirror of sameness. And it can only do this by consuming living nature in producing a proliferation of goods and services whose possession becomes the *sine qua non* of the good life. Of course, if nature is endlessly consumed in the pursuit of a totalizing course, then that course is dangerous for living; it constitutes a danger to one's own survival, as well as that of others. That, approximately, is the technical, legal definition of psychosis.

Aside from the threat to survival, psychosis has of course other, less dangerous symptoms. One of the lesser symptoms of psychosis, like neurosis, is the inability to concentrate for very long, to constitute memories in a temporal sequence or to follow an argument. This means that, if this is a psychotic era, the contemporary efflorescence of critiques of metanarratives sits nicely with the shorter attention spans such an era would induce. This is not to dismiss these critiques out of hand. Grounds for doing so have yet to be established. It is, however, to enjoin the reader's tolerance in following an account with its own speculative logic, which this book will become, while those grounds are explored.

As with concentration, so with history, which after all requires a memory. When Lacan discusses how a social psychosis comes into being, he reveals a historical dimension to his theory of the imaginary, and the historical consciousness is something a social psychosis would obliterate.[2] Over the past twenty years it has become exceedingly difficult to think about how broad history intersects with the psyche, because a poststructuralist or postmodern sensibility berates generality. It has also become difficult to apply theory in explaining concrete exploitation. Currently, the wish to take account of 'gender, race and class' is muttered mantra-like at the beginning of every academic paper, but the wish remains too often unfulfilled. There is what I will call an applicability gap between theory and explanation, which sentiment alone will not bridge. We can do local research, specific genealogies, we can think about little alterations in time and space, micro-historical shifts, but the applied understanding of exploitation, together with the generality necessary for tracing a guide to action on a larger scale, is inhibited. The inhibition is founded in a variety of good and bad arguments, with which I will not engage very much.[3] Even the good reasoning about 'the inhibiting effects of totalitarian discourses' and the notion that 'the attempt to think in terms of a totality has in fact proved a hindrance to research' is grounded in a critical dissective mode of reasoning (Foucault 1980, pp. 80–1); it takes apart the existing disreputable master narratives, but this focus on dismemberment makes it more a reaction to the mistakes of Marxism; it is more the antithesis of Marxism than its own thesis (cf. Barrett 1991). As writers under the sway of the Foucauldian antithesis do not proceed propositionally, they cannot construct a propositional theory which would explain, amongst other things, why so many intellectuals are suddenly susceptible to the notion that the attempt to explain the whole is a mistake.[4] The abruptness of the acceptance of the idea that totalizing theories are a mistake, the wariness about using the term 'history'

2 cf. Horkheimer and Adorno: 'Just as every book which has not been published recently is suspect, and the idea of history outside the specific discipline of history makes modern men nervous, so the past becomes a source of anger. . . . History is eliminated in oneself and in others out of a fear that it may remind the individual of the degeneration of his own existence – which itself continues' (Horkheimer and Adorno 1972, p. 216, trans. mod.).
3 Strictly the inhibition of generality in the human sciences has a longer history than the designations 'poststructuralist' or 'postmodern' indicate. See Quentin Skinner (1985). I have used the word 'generality' in preference to 'totality', and while this distinction echoes one made by Foucault, it should be clear that the generality I have in mind concerns historical dynamics which are cumulative.
4 Other attempts at taking account of poststructuralist insights while believing that any theory that is to serve as a guide to action has to be a theory of general historical dynamics include Fredric Jameson, throughout his work, but especially (1984); Gayatri Spivak (1987); Terry Eagleton (1988). Ernesto Laclau and Chantel Mouffe (1985) also belong here: they posit that 'radical democratic politics should avoid the two extremes represented by the totalitarian myth of the Ideal City, and the positivist pragmatism of reformists without a project' (p. 190). See also Dews (1987).

(outside the discipline of history) that prevails, suggests that this acceptance is not only founded in critical thinking, but that it is also partly unconscious. If this is so, then the historical dynamics informing this psychical response deserve consideration. And of course they can only be extended this courtesy in the most cursory way if one holds to the *a priori* position that historical generalization is a mistake.

In other words, the position that we should not generalize historically is a position that inhibits its own historical investigation. It has also pre-empted a possibility recognized by Foucault, but not the Foucauldians: 'if we limit ourselves to . . . always partial or local enquiry or test, do we not run the risk of letting ourselves be determined by more general structures of which we may not be conscious, and over which we have no control?' (Foucault 1984, p. 47). In turn, to recognize that there is a more general trend at work is not to deny the significance of the local. Specific genealogies need not be posited as an *alternative* to narratives. A totalizing trend obviously intersects with specific genealogies. On the one hand, this means that the history of any given period or region cannot be rendered in terms of the totalizing trend alone. On the other, to focus solely on the specific genealogy is to lose sight of the process whereby, as Adorno observed, the dissimilar is made similar, as cultural diversity and specific histories are covered over.[5]

The genial injunctions to avoid historical generalization do not abolish either speculation or concrete investigation. It is rather that they abolish the interplay between them. And this abolition, this self-conscious inhibition, means that contemporary critical and social theory, at one level, does no more than tell us that doubt is good, that difference should be celebrated, that essentialism and foundationalism should be avoided, that the subject–object distinction is a bad thing, that the subject is worse, that actually the subject is alright and even reproduces the social structures that produce it, and so on. Theory that did more might mean that the best are not left, after Marxism, like chastised puppies, trying to look sceptical as they advocate solidarity. The problem of course is developing a historical theory of the general which is other than Marxism, so plainly wrong in its industrial

5  While cultures are resilient, and fight back with claims about specific national identities, the very fact that these identity-conscious statements now need to be made may itself signal an intersection between the relatively local context and the ego's era: these identity statements may reflect a sense of what is being lost, as well as a concern with personal identity which, in psychoanalytic terms, is a concern of the ego's.

premises and centralized conclusions, but which approximates Marxism's explanatory reach in a way that begins to bridge the applicability gap.

Lacan's theory of the ego's era and perspective on history deserves some attention because it contributes a little to the development of such theory. It provides us with a lever (not an elaborated theory of history, not at all) but a lever for thinking through the trajectory of modernity. Part of its potential stems from the fact that, while it stresses psychical factors, it does so in a way which makes the psychical into a material or, strictly, a physical force which is at the same time cultural. More of that in a moment. There is also the more textual reason for attending to Lacan. The prejudice against general 'totalizing' theories has contributed to a serious misreading of Lacan in which he is too readily assimilated to the poststructuralist grain. The existence of the historical side of Lacan's theory of the imaginary, let alone its implications, has been ignored or at best mentioned in passing.[6] The very fact that Lacan's historical theory has been neglected reveals much about the power of the secondary source in structuring received views, and the power of the secondary source in today's academic institutions is also, in part, a product of the ego's era. A few words on this neglect.

Lacan's theory of history has been neglected because of an over-emphasis on the notion, which possibly derives most from Lemaire's early exegesis, that 'his views . . . on humanization are structuralist' (Lemaire 1977, p. 81). This is true, but partial. Jameson, publishing in the same year that Lemaire was translated, suggested that what was really innovative in Lacan was the interleaving of dialectical (Hegelian) thinking and structural analysis, but his observations did not affect the common preconception that Lacan is ahistorical (Jameson 1977, p. 104). That preconception prevails even though much of Lacan's theory of history is embedded in texts that have been readily available – much of what follows is based on the *Écrits* – and even though his historical side is crystallized in an aspect of his work which has received considerable attention: his critique of ego psychology. But the trend is

---

6 In general, the French Lacanian exegetes have been as neglectful as the English-speaking ones. Concerning the latter: aside from Juliet MacCannell (1986), who demonstrates that Lacan is a cultural thinker, there is a brief discussion of Lacan's historical dimension in Ellie Ragland-Sullivan (1986). But while the theory attributed to Lacan here has not been developed, his Hegelianism has received some attention: from Anthony Wilden (1968), in the original English translation of the Rome report, and notably from Fredric Jameson (1977). David Macey (1988, pp. 4–5) also discusses how Lacan's commentators have denied his debt to the past, particularly 'Kojève–Hegel'. See too Borch-Jacobsen (1991).

to concentrate on Lacan's polemic against ego psychology (and other 'sciences') while neglecting his polemic against the social order which produces them. As Gallop points out, Lacan 'does not limit his attacks to American psychoanalysis. There is a more general attack against the "American way of life"' (Gallop 1985, p. 57).

As I have suggested, then, despite his almost postmodern aspersions on grand theories of history (Lacan 1953b, p. 51), Lacan has a fledgling one nestling in his work. It builds on the Hegelian master–slave dialectic. Like Marx, Lacan reverses some of Hegel's implications. But he does not stand Hegel on his head. Rather, he turns him back to front. If history led anywhere, it was to the 'ego's era'. Lacan discards any Hegelian optimism about progress to higher moments as history unfolds, or the 'appeal to any tomorrow' (Lacan 1953b, p. 80). For Lacan, 'the problem is knowing whether the Master–Slave conflict will find its resolution in the service of the machine. . .' (Lacan 1948, p. 27). There are evident parallels between Lacan's theory of history and Adorno's conclusion that while there is 'No universal history' leading 'from the savage to humanitarianism . . . there is one leading from the slingshot to the megaton bomb',[7] just as there are parallels between Lacan's theory and that of Benjamin. The parallels between Lacan's thought and that of the early Frankfurt School, in which Adorno was prominent and to which Benjamin loosely adhered, suggest that a sense of a totalizing destructive historical course is in the air. At the same time, the difficulties in describing both the course and its mechanism, the fact that so much of this description is allusive rather than argued, is of itself symptomatic, as if the very process that needs to be described robs those who would describe it of the words to say it.

This is particularly true of Lacan. But let us continue with what he does say. Lacan points both to some social ramifications of the master–slave dialectic and, more crucially, to a dialectic working between space in the environment and in the psyche.[8] The aggressive imperative involved in making the other into a slave, or object, will lead to spatial expansion (territorial imperialism). This is because the objectification of the other depends on establishing a spatial boundary by which the other and the self are fixed. But this fixing of the other leads to the fear

---

7  Theodor Adorno (1947, p. 320). There is also a parallel between Lacan's argument on the 'closed thinking' of the ego, which will figure below, and Adorno's critique of 'common sense'.
8  Dialectical particularly in its search for 'essential levels of reality beneath apparent ones', a search which Jay opposes to Foucault's affinity with positivism, apparent in Foucault's disdain for any such search (Jay 1984, p. 522).

that the other will retaliate, which in turn leads to a feeling of spatial constriction. Moreover, the feeling of spatial constriction is related to the physical environment. These changes have physical effects on the psyche, which in turn alter the psychical perception of the environment, and of one's own boundaries. With spatial constriction, one's boundaries are threatened, and the resultant fear increases the need to control the object. The aggressive territorial imperative is or has not been confined to the West, although for Lacan the West is evidently where it happens.

Lacan's spatial dialectic bears on territorial colonization, urbanization and war, and in principle his account can be extended in a dialectical discussion of the relation between the ego's need for fixity and technological domination. By a further extension, Lacan's theory can explain, or, more accurately, can help explain, the environmental degradation that the ego's era trails in its wake. Lacan's theory can explain these things because the 'in principle' extension his theory needs means exploring how an ego's era plays itself out over long time and large space, how it is that we can speak of an 'ego's era' at all, how an ego's era began.

Some Lacanian epigones hold views that bear on this, in so far as they attribute the social psychosis, the outcome of the ego's era, to the demise of the 'psychical fantasy of woman'. The 'psychical fantasy of woman' is Lacanian shorthand for a process whereby women are split into two types, good and bad, mother and whore, and idealized and denigrated accordingly. The fantasy is meant to be as universal and transhistorical as the symbolic order itself; for by splitting women into two types the man is able to situate himself as subject. The demise of this fantasy, to the extent that it is in fact demolished, is meant to bring on social psychosis because girls are no longer girls and boys are no longer boys (or something like that). Feminism is meant to aid and abet the social psychosis because it puts sexual difference in jeopardy. As recent feminism has stressed sexual difference almost to the point of irritation, this Lacanian view is of course based on a caricature, prevalent amongst those who formed a fixed view of feminism *circa* 1971 and have done no reading since. Lacan himself, as we will see, had more complex opinions on the origins of the ego's era and its social psychosis. Nonetheless, the psychical fantasy of woman is a running motif through the story that is to follow; some of the story hangs on whether this fantasy is the cause or the cure for the ego's era.

Chapter 2 of this book outlines Lacan's historica  theory. Part II turns to the 'extension' it needs, which might more accurately be described as theses, around which Lacan's allusions can take on a consistent and narrative shape. In the next section of this introduction, I shall briefly summarize the direction of Chapters 3, 4 and 5, outlining the main theses of the book in the process. The theses outline is condensed, and is intended as a recapitulation of the argument, as much as a guide to it. As these theses are dense, the reader who is not in that kind of mood may prefer to proceed directly to the next section.

The most obvious problem with Lacan's theory is the apparent anthropomorphism in the idea of an ego's era. How can the definition 'psychosis', which is only applied to individuals, be applied to an era, and the era designated as that of the ego (an apparently individual entity)? Moreover, the mechanism by which a subjective malady makes itself felt on the larger social scale has to be established. The short answer to the first question is that knowledge of the ego's antics and psychotic symptoms can be treated as knowledge gained by looking down a telescope the wrong way. It is knowledge safeguarded by the genre of the individual case study, insofar as that genre assumes that the dynamics and symptoms it studies are individually self-contained. To demonstrate that they are not, Part II begins with the analysis of the desires encapsulated in a commodity. The commodity is a point at which the social and psychical converge. But to reach that point, to make this idea plausible, we need to postulate some other energetic mechanism of connection or refraction between psyche and social order. Psychical factors have to be conceived in energetic, physical terms. The relation between physical and social determination has been conceived as a one-way street, when it should allow for a two-way traffic. The social actually gets into the flesh, and unless we take account of this, we cannot account for the extent to which socio-historical realities affect us psychically, and how we in turn act in ways that produce and reinforce them (cf. Freund 1988 and Frank 1990). We also need to address the problem of how we come to experience ourselves as contained entities, contained in terms of our energies and affects.

All the prejudices of Western thought since the Renaissance reinforce this notion. To allow that my feelings physically enter you, or yours me, to think that we both had the same thought at the same time because it is literally in the air, is to think in a way that really puts the subject in question. In some ways, the truly interesting thing is that this

questioning has begun, and not only in this book. The suppos
contained subject has been and is questioned in popular culture, as we
shall see below. In fact the real question in some ways is why the
academy has been so slow, Deleuze excepted, to entertain the idea that
the subject is not self-contained at the material level of energy. But, to
borrow an old adage of Gramsci's, it is always the case that practice
marches ahead of theory.

The short answer to the second question, how it is that psychical
processes are acted out over time and large space, lies in economics. To
a considerable extent, Part II is preoccupied with political economy. We
shall see that the extension of the ego's era in time and space is in fact a
process whereby time, meaning the natural cycles of generation, is
replaced by space, and how this process eventually impinges on time as
the sense of history. Focusing on this dimension will also enable us to
begin overcoming the applicability gap, to indicate ways in which this
psychoanalytic theory connects with the realities of exploitation.

But my argument on economics in turn relies on clarifying the
psychical well-springs of the ego's era, and the idea of beings as
contained entities. These things are related, and the relation is made
explicit in the first thesis I will introduce. This thesis is about a
foundational fantasy.

*Thesis 1: The subject is founded by a hallucinatory fantasy in which it
conceives itself as the locus of active agency and the environment as
passive; its subjectivity is secured by a projection onto the environment, apparently beginning with the mother, which makes her into
an object which the subject in fantasy controls.*

This and the next thesis rest on a synthesis of Freud and Klein, as well
as Lacan. Lacan believes that the subject is always split, and that the
splitting is tied to the death drive, and the enactment of the internal
master–slave dialectic. Freud's theory allows us to conceive the split in
the subject in terms of hallucination, in turn prompted by the pleasure
principle, and the desire for instant gratification.

Freud is especially useful here, because his theory of the (un)pleasure
principle has a reference point in physics; it points to how the
foundational fantasy produces rigidity, and alters the relation to time
and space. The production of rigidity is essential in understanding the
objectification which is the hallmark of Lacan's ego, and the ego's era. It
also allows us to define the nature of objectification more precisely than
did Lacan or Heidegger whom he follows on this issue. It does this

because it sees objectification as an energetic event, in which the projection of a passive image literally 'fixes' the subject and its object in place. It thus allows us to conceive of a distinction between subject and object in a particular way.

Klein's theory means we can specify the content of objectification in yet more detail. By her account, the processes I tie to objectification are also tied to the drive for knowledge. It is not difficult to leap from here to Foucault's analysis of the drive for knowledge as a drive to power, a jump facilitated by the similarity, or indebtedness, of Foucault's theory to Heidegger's. For Heidegger, metaphysical knowledge is always tied to control. But Klein argues too that the death drive working within results in the envious desire to poison, fragment and destroy the mother's body. By this book's argument, these desires are also critical in the process of control and objectification, but the process is not confined to the mother's body, nor did it necessarily originate in relation to it.

*Thesis 2: The foundational fantasy is the basis of the subject's conceiving itself as contained in energetic terms. To the extent that the fantasy dominates the subject's psyche, knowledge or experience of energetic connections between beings and entities is foreclosed.*

Critical here is the understanding of how energy is bound in psychical life. I argue that a particular form of this bondage produces the ego; and that that form is affected by the subject's environment. Hallucination splits the subject because it divorces an imagined world from the world of sensory connection and sensory experience. But the split is cemented by the repression of the hallucination, which binds energy. By the power of hallucination then, the discreteness of the ego begins in two ways. It begins to be separate from unrepressed energy in real terms; its repressed energy is subject to another law. The ego can also imagine that things are other than they are. One can imagine a pleasure which relieves the unpleasure experienced when wishes or needs are not gratified. But this distinctively human power of hallucination, also visualization in general, focuses on entities precisely as discrete, in such a way that underexplored sensory connections between the subject and the others and the living environment overall are blocked out.

Visualization, whether in the form of hallucination or visual perception, observes difference rather than connection. In addition, focusing on a particular image means cutting oneself off from the flow of information from the other senses. For instance the sense of smell might convey information which conflicts with the hallucinatory wish, and this sense might connect it with the mother, or other factors in its environment, in an unbroken chain, in which the distinctness of the infant or the other as a discrete entity is not secured.[9] The more the 'spatial dialectic' takes hold, the more the fantasy takes hold, the less the subject has knowledge or experience of any energetic connections with others. We will suggest that this is because energy is bound in commodities and the technology that produces them, in a manner that parallels its bondage in hallucination. The two levels of bondage reinforce each other.

This adds a dimension to the existing feminist critiques of the mind–body distinction, critiques based on the subject–object distinction. These critiques are a recent development in feminist thought. Like this argument, they are often grounded in psychoanalysis, and the idea of a split between the mental subject from the bodily object. Such a split is contradicted by a variety of evidence and experience: for instance, psychosomatic disorders show how the division between mind and body is artificial. The problem with these critiques so far is that they are ahistorical; they allow for no variation in the power of the 'mind–body distinction' at any given time. Partly for this reason, they usually stop short at exhortation, exhortations to the effect that we need sciences and theories which are not governed by this distinction. But the only way such theories could come into being is by specifying how the mind–body distinction is produced. As I have indicated, this we will attempt to do, and the attempt indicates that the power of the distinction is precisely historical.

> *Thesis 3: Before the advent of a Western technology capable of fulfilling the desires embodied in the foundational fantasy, it is contained. The advent of that technology is prompted by the fantasy and represents an acting out of it on an increasingly global scale, an enactment that reinforces the psychical power of the fantasy.*

We have sound reason for supposing that the foundational fantasy of objectifying and dismembering that on which we depend is an ancient one in the West. This means that the psychical fantasy pre-dates its technocratic acting-out on the large scale. Yet in drawing out the

---

9 Senses which connect subjects one to another are severed. Relevant here is Freud's link between the defeat of the sense of smell and the rise of a certain form of unhappy sexuality. (Freud (1929) *Civilization and Its Discontents*, SE, vol. 21 pp. 105–6 *n*.3).

relation between the psychical fantasy and technology, Klein's 'mother's body' has to be correlated with living nature. It is this correlation that is the condition of recognizing that the process Klein helps describe is a microcosm of a large-scale assault, a psychical fantasy writ large. The large-scale acting-out represents the fantasy's spatial and temporal extension. Instead of the length of an individual's lifetime, or the years of their madness, 'the ego's era' spans a few centuries. Instead of megalomanic fantasies that are dreamed, technologies that make them come true, increasing their coverage of the earth's surface and corruption of its temporal parameters in the process.

Having denied that the 'object' has any will of its own, the foundational fantasy also denies the effects of the object upon the subject. These effects become far more significant as developing technologies permit the subject to construct a world of objects which fulfil its fantasies. When the world is actually turned into a world of objects, when living nature is consumed in this process, the power of the fantasy, the extent to which it takes hold psychically is reinforced. Lacan's spatial dialectic gestures to this process of reinforcement, but we are able to specify it further in terms of time and energy, as well as space. As the repressed hallucination and the technology applied to commodities alike bind energy, they increase rigidity and fixity, and this in turn increases the need to project a fixity felt as a constraint that slows the subject down. This makes the question of culpability in relation to the origin of the fantasy complicated. Ingredients of the foundational fantasy have been discerned in psychoanalytic theories about the infant, but the infant is also affected by its environment. The more fixed its environment, the more the infant projects.

While the foundational fantasy is reinforced, and could in theory be negated by historical circumstance, it is itself in some ways a historically, culturally specific product. An analysis of some of its ingredients (the idea that the subject is contained in terms of energy, thought governed by a subject–object split) indicates that the fantasy is specifically Western. So, in its origin, is the technology that currently produces commodities in which the foundational fantasy is most readily discerned.

The idea of a Western fantasy that is technologically reinforced is very similar to Heidegger's notion of a metaphysical mindset, which is also reinforced by technology. This notion needs more comment before I go on to the next thesis. Apart from anything else, this will draw out the difference as well as the similarity between this argument and Heidegger's.[10]

Heidegger locates the origin of the metaphysical mindset in Platonic and post-Socratic philosophy, which puts the subject's relation to present space at centre stage of its concerns; the environment begins to be conceived or objectified as an environment or background in which the subject is central. While Heidegger calls this mindset metaphysical, foundational is probably a better term. Condemning metaphysics, as Rée argues, has been a popular philosophical pastime for over two hundred years (1987, pp. 2–3).[11]

And as I have indicated, Heidegger uses the term metaphysics in a specific way. He situates metaphysics as a privileging of space over temporality, and argues that this privileging results in a repression of the historical process. He sees technology as a force which threatens to make this repression absolute. In part it does so because technology confines human experience within a rigid frame, which closes off forms of connection with the world other than those based on a relation between the human as subject and the world as object. This rigidity results in a loss of flexibility, which Hodge (1994) terms a 'disambiguation', in turn produced by the need for technical exactness. Manifold meanings are excluded in the name of one, for one clear meaning is a condition of control. But for Heidegger, unlike some of his ambiguous followers, the analysis of this control has a central focus in the analysis of technology and the process by which technology and rapid technological shifts compress time, and the collective human experience of historical time, in favour of space.

I am about to argue too that technology compresses time for space, but will do so on slightly different premises. The first difference is that Heidegger confines the metaphysical mindset, prior to its technological enactment, to philosophy, to philosophical metaphysics which proceeds from a disembodied, subject-centred standpoint. I am locating the foundational fantasy as a general psychical event, general in the West at least. It is a fantasy that philosophy formalizes, but over which it has no monopoly. However the analysis of that fantasy and its technological reinforcement should contribute something to a synthesis of Freud and Heidegger, especially on the question of rigidity. On the other hand, the concrete specification of the contents of the foundational fantasy will

10 The similarity is due in part to Lacan's indebtedness to Heidegger, which is discussed in Part II.
11 And Derrida and Rorty are only the last knights in the 'holy war' against metaphysics (Rée 1990, p. 31).

lead us to more concrete conclusions on the mechanism by which 'time' is compressed for space, conclusions which rest on the idea that natural energy is bound in profitable commodities in a manner comparable with the repression of energy in hallucination. These conclusions make profit synonymous with control.

We reach these conclusions not only by spelling out the contents of the foundational fantasy, but by hypothesizing about what comes before the fantasy, the stuff out of which it is made. This is an appropriate point to explain why I am writing of a foundational fantasy, which I will do before discussing the actual foundations I assume exist. To talk of a foundational *fantasy* is to draw on two streams of theory which have been opposed: the Derridean and the Lacanian, deconstruction and psychoanalysis. But it is a use that both, deconstruction especially, would have difficulty accommodating. Derrida's critique of anti-foundationalism is a critique of a self-presencing subject. I have called the fantasy foundational because I am in full agreement with this critique, as far as it goes. By this critique, the subject always assumes it is present in some form as a subject from the beginning. It is present in that it is the source of meaning, the origin of both meaning and meaningful signification. By Derrida's account the subject is born into a play of signification, and does not found it. Against the idea of the foundational present subject is the play of difference. But the foundational fantasy, as I will describe it, requires a different kind of foundation. It requires a foundation before the foundation, a foundation which is conceived in non-subjective terms.

> *Thesis 4: The foundational fantasy is not fantasmatic because there are no foundations. It is fantasmatic because of the illusory founda-tions it structures and proceeds to make material, which overlie the natural generative foundation with which it competes.*

Derrida's position, like Foucault's, stops short after uncovering the basis of the subject's illusions about itself. It does not go on to postulate an alternative source of the meaning to which the subject lays claim. I will challenge this by postulating a three-stage rather than a two-stage process. That is to say, in the (Derridean) two-stage process, the foundational present subject of meaning is counterposed to a play of difference in which there is no meaning or inherent conation. Derrida accepts the subject's illusions, insofar as he accepts that conation is the subject's invention. In the three-stage process, which conceives a foundation before the subjective foundation, the subject's construction of its illusory priority is both an active appropriation and a theft. In this act, the subject invests itself with the properties that animate the generative logical chain of nature, at the same time as it denies the existence of logic or reason in anything beyond itself. In assuming that the generative chain of nature is logical and conative I follow Spinoza. The point here is that it is possible to think of a logic that is not subject-centred, not divorced from matter or the flesh, and in this not transcendental.

If the critique of foundationalism is as antithetical as the Foucauldian critique of generality, this may be because of the Heideggerian lineage shared by Derrida, as well as Foucault and Lacan. Heidegger is revered by all three as the point of departure for the illusion of mastery that makes itself present and thinks in totalizing terms. I am inclined to doubt that Heidegger's thought rules out a foundation which is not subject centred. Despite Derrida's certainty that it does, I suspect the debate is only beginning (cf. Scheibler 1993, Hodge 1994). Enough to say that Heidegger's level of abstraction lends itself to conclusions that go either way. My practical difference from him lies in the rejection of an overarching abstraction in the concept of Being, an abstraction which means that the conclusions which follow from it might lead anywhere (cf. Lacoue-Labarthe 1987).

However, I have not dwelt on the differences between the following argument and Heidegger's. I have merely tried to indicate some of the overlaps, while grounding myself on Lacan and Freud. Thus Heidegger, in this book, is a little like the butler. He comes on and off at the beginning and end of every chapter, he is obviously crucial although he does not star, and he probably did it. On the other hand, as I have indicated, beginning with a concrete specification as to the nature of the foundational fantasy means that the speculations that follow from it also have concrete implications.

*Thesis 5: The means by which time is compressed for space is identical to the process of producing profit. In this process, distance takes the place of the time of natural reproduction, for overall profit depends on binding natural substance and energy in commodities at a faster rate than nature can reproduce.*

The extent to which the foundational fantasy can be enacted on the larger scale depends on the limits imposed on the fantasy's aspiration: (a) by the available technology; (b) by the dominant social discourses, particularly religion, and (c) by the forms of economic and political organization. Thus for some time in the West the fantasy was held in check by feudalism, where the available technology meant that nature imposed its own balances. We may diminish nature in the construction of the built and technological environment if this construction takes place without regard for replenishment. Thus the technological and economic modalities governing this construction are critical, for they determine whether any allowance for replenishment is made. It is of course possible to have technology which *could* exhaust natural reserves but which does *not* do so because there is no economic imperative in this direction. The foundational fantasy makes itself come true globally because an economic profit imperative overrides all political, social and religious constraints in its deployment of a technology capable of satisfying the desires of the foundational fantasy with some precision.

In essence, the economic argument of Part II is this. The speed of technological changes, not only their spatial but their temporal effects, changes with capitalization. It does this in these ways. To make a profit, capital has to produce commodities at a faster rate than the time taken by living nature to reproduce itself. As the only substances out of which commodities can be produced are those supplied by living nature, this means that the profit factor tends to exhaust natural resources. It also results in a territorial imperative (the quest for new natural reserves) and a quest for any means by which the rate of reproduction of living substances can be increased. This applies to human beings as much as to other features of living nature. In part, this process was theorized by Marx. The distorting factors in Marx's analysis were his adherence to the subject-object distinction which meant he grouped living nature with technology as the 'object'. The human was the 'subject'. He restricted his analysis of how the time factor contributed to profit by focusing on the differential between the time taken to reproduce *human* labour power and the value human labour added in production within a given time, and neglected how this time differential was relevant to all natural substances. Marx also projected back from an environment in which materialism became a, and some times the, crucial determining factor in an ahistorical manner. The great materialist, paradoxically, did not take the physical changes wrought by capitalization seriously; by this argument, these changes reinforce the psychical fantasy that aims at instant gratification, and this gratification in turn is provided by commodities.

Despite this, Marx's value-theory remains the best place to begin in analysing the mechanism by which the foundational fantasy makes itself global. Marx was the only classical political economist who identified the 'two-fold nature' of a commodity. He began *Capital* by stressing it. A commodity has both use-value and exchange-value. As I will show, use-value refers to the level of energy and substance, while exchange-value refers to the level of (social) time and space. Read without the form of subject–object distinction he adopted, Marx provides us with the basis of a theory of how the natural temporal order must be made over and dominated by the order of space so that a profit, or surplus-value, can be extracted from living nature. This allows us to grasp the relation between time and energy in a way which accounts for how the foundational fantasy makes itself global, covering ever greater distances under its own law of speed.

This approach also enables us to consider questions to do with environmental economics, scale and strategy. It does this because a value-theory without the subject–object distinction makes questions of space integral to the production of surplus-value, and shows that there can be no profit without large-scale spatial expansion. It also shows that the ideal polity for capital is a state which facilitates spatial expansion while it abolishes the restrictions imposed by natural time.

In the light of this agreement, the traditional Marxist analysis, which endorses economic centralization, cannot hold. Of course, Marxism is untenable for other reasons. Even if it had not been abruptly dropped in the academy, it would have been hard to sustain after the collapse of Eastern Europe had revealed that illusions about socialism's ultimate appeal were precisely that.[12] 'State socialism' did not have the economic success its founders anticipated.[13] Nor did it prevent the eruption of demands that embody the foundational fantasy; however reasonable and appropriate they are, they still embody it. And while state communism held these demands in check, it is difficult to gauge the extent or length of the resentment directed against it for doing so.[14] On the other hand, precisely because state communism set limits on this fantasy, it draws attention to the role the state plays not only in restricting or facilitating the range of choice etc., but also in regulating

12  While there have been attempts to explain 'economics' from a Foucauldian or poststructuralist standpoint, these attempts focus on the story-telling aspect of economic discourse: deconstructing the relevant metaphors and so on (McCloskey 1985). They are critiques only; they do not try to advance a theory of how a political economy would look or work if a (or the) binary opposition, so central to poststructuralism, were removed. Their concern is with the existence of the oppositions as such.

13  See Mandel (1972, p. 514 *n*.36) for a discussion.

14  The idea that the collapse of Eastern Europe represents a victory for capital is well propounded in Callinicos (1991).

time and distance. The state regulates the speed of gratification, as much as production and distribution on the macro level. All those photographs of all those queues, the very media obsession with queues in Eastern Europe, constitute a symptomatic recognition of the state's role in the spatio-temporal regulation of the economy.

The economic argument in this book is its most speculative part; it grows out of its own logic rather than the literature in the field, and I am including it for the reason that some new economic speculation is essential to clarify the relation between the foundational fantasy and the macrocosmic ego's era, in terms of time, space and energy. If nothing else, it might move debates on the environment along, through the critical process that the discussion of its errors will entail.

> *Thesis 6: As the foundational fantasy is enacted on the large scale, as more and more objects are constructed in reality, the balance of energetic power, in relation to the generative chain of nature, has to shift. It shifts in terms of a paradox. While the world appears to get faster and faster, it in fact gets slower and slower.*

This thesis again rests on an assumed homology as well as a connection between the mother's body and the natural order; it assumes that they are governed by logical connections which move more rapidly than the subject–object connections which frame human communication and technological constructions. This will be evident in the last chapter, where we note that alterations in the physical environment alter perspective. They do so as we alter the time–space relations and therefore the *physis* of the environs and ourselves. On this basis we can account for how individual boundaries are both shaped and broken, for increasing fragmentation, and altering perceptions of energy, and even the carry-on over identity, all of which become issues as the social psychosis makes itself global. For by this point I have suggested that capital supplies the means for making the original foundational fantasy global. It does this by increasing the accumulation of 'fixed points' or commodities in, and as part of, the built environment. As these artifactual fixed points function after the manner of hallucinations then, although capital appears to speed things up, the actual result is a world which physically becomes slower relative to the speed of nature. This slower world, because it is a constructed fantasy world, also affects styles of thinking. It favours thought which emphasizes metaphor and abstraction, for these modes of thought are at one remove from felt experience, just as the fantasmatic yet material coverage of the natural world is at one remove from living nature.

As the fantasmatic coverage of a natural living reality with a socially constructed overlay of a different material order severs connections to the living reality, referents in real felt experience carry less weight in any argument. It is easier to carry a chain of reasoning through on the abstract level than it is to tie it back to the material level, partly because the 'nature' of 'material reality' is confused; it becomes a mixture, of the generative natural chain, and the subject–object constructions that overlie it.

One perspicacious critic of an early draft of this book asked me how I could write about a natural reality as if its character was unproblematic. The answer is: I cannot; I assume that a living natural reality exists, and that knowledge of it is confused by the fantasmatic material overlay, just as the living reality itself becomes confused. I also assume that one result of the social coverage is to make one doubt the existence of an unchanging reality, precisely because connections with that reality are severed and reality is changed. But even if the world becomes an 'as if' fantasmatic world, it does not follow that this is the only possible world.[15] The fact that an 'as if' world is constructed, a world which accords with the 'at-one-remove' style of thought embodied in abstraction, does not mean that the constructed world of fantasies cannot be differentiated in principle from a living reality. The constructions might make metaphors more substantial, but they do not make metaphors the only reality, although they may aim to do so. I am tempted to say the matter is undecidable, except for this: what follows depends on its explanatory force, its applicability, and on how far it brings together some otherwise competing insights which are split and scattered amongst alternative cultures and the academy.

I have summarized the main argument of this book in thesis form, but these theses are heavily indebted not only to Lacan, Freud, Klein, Marx, and Heidegger to an extent, also Derrida, but to the feminist context in

---

15 It does not mean that there has never been a world which 'is' (Derrida 1974). Whatever subtleties and insights this argument contains, the argument against the existence of the 'is' could be as much a product of a world in which 'as if' fantasies are materially constructed as a correct view in itself.

which they were synthesized. These theses were influenced by two lines of thought forefronted in feminist theory. The first is about the concept of psychical fantasy. The second, as I have indicated, is a series of convergent arguments criticizing the subject–object distinction, and with it the split between mind and matter. The question of psychical fantasy came on to the feminist agenda mainly but not only because of Lacan, and the claim made by some Lacanians that certain of the fantasies and structures of the unconscious were universal. This was an issue for feminism (as it had been for anthropologists and Marxists) because of its ahistoricism. It was also an issue because the claims for universality were at the same time claims for the universality of patriarchy. From Freud and Lévi-Strauss to Lacan, or rather certain interpretations of Lacan, universal claims have been made about how the laws of psychical structure will invariably determine human behaviour, irrespective of history. They are still being made. Those who are dubious about historical grand theory may refrain from generalizing, but some contemporary Lacanians show no such reticence. Thus the 'psychical fantasy of woman' is meant to be a universal condition of the patriarchal centre holding. But the issue became the concept of a transhistorical psychical fantasy as such. If transhistorical psychical fantasies exist, the question for feminism appeared to concern their content. For instance, if the content of a transhistorical fantasy makes patriarchy inevitable, assumptions about that content have to be investigated. At the same time, the concept of transhistorical psychical fantasy is an interesting one. It gives the psychical some autonomy in history. It allows for a tension between psychical factors and socio-historical ones.[16] It also suggests that the extent to which a psychical fantasy takes hold depends on how far it is reinforced or negated by socio-historical circumstances. But until we know if a fantasy is transhistorical it is best to limit the purview implied by its label. However ubiquitous such a fantasy may be, whatever its historical persistence, to term it 'transhistorical' is to impute an immutability to it, when we simply do not know if it is immutable, and exempt from historical scrutiny. It is possible to keep the idea that a psychical force can persist through other massive historical changes, that it can be

16  I was beguiled completely by this tension for a while, and reached the conclusion that a transhistorical psychical fantasy could be identified, but that it was not the fantasy of woman (Brennan 1991). I am grateful to those colleagues, numerous, but especially Linda Nicholson, who pointed out that this hostage to fortune should be ransomed. In my enthusiasm, I missed a more accurate designation for the objectifying fantasy that founds the subject, which is that the fantasy is precisely *foundational*.

reinforced or negated by historical factors, without granting it exemption from historical let alone cross-cultural enquiry (hence the term foundational, which ties the fantasy to the West, and probably to the Socratics).

The central idea in the foundational fantasy, that an objectifying projection is a condition of subjectivity, evidently overlaps with the work of Irigaray, Kristeva, and that stream of feminist critiques of science (largely American based: Chodorow, Gilligan, Fox Keller, Jessica Benjamin) which situate the subject–object distinction in infancy. In fact one of the interesting things about this line of thought is its independent appearance in a variety of feminist contexts. And the feminist arguments provide a basis on which existing arguments on the subject–object distinction (Hegel, Husserl, Merleau-Ponty), and a subject-centred world-view in which instrumental objective reason dominates nature's needs and ends (Adorno, Horkheimer), as do visual means of control and knowledge (Heidegger, Foucault), at the expense of the other senses (Merleau-Ponty, Deleuze, Lyotard), can be synthesized and developed: these arguments falter because they take no account of how the split between subject and object is connected to the early fantasmatic relation to the mother, nor/or of how this split in turn severs the connections between individual and environment, in a manner which means both that these connections are overlooked and that the physical effects of the socially constructed environment are denied. In addition, these thinkers are frequently victims of the escalating tendency to abstraction. By my argument, the tendency to abstraction is also, in part, a product of the acting out of the fantasy on the larger scale.

If we confront a social psychosis governed by an ego with a vested interest in flattening everything that exists into a grey mirror that reflects it, if it can only effect this mirage by fragmenting knowledge of its totalizing dynamics, so that the picture it constructs is impossible to piece together, *if*, indeed, it means that abstract and 'as if' thought increases as sensory ties are severed, then any theory which makes fragmentation and discontinuities a virtue and metaphor a blessing accords with the ego's dynamics. At the same time, it has to be stressed that whenever the theoretical avant-garde voices any tendency of the social psychosis, and celebrates it as a virtue, it at the same time expresses an opposition to this tendency. In fact it is this dual expression of opposites that I think defines the avant-garde. It is always first in identifying with the next turn in the social psychosis; it is always first in opposing it. Thus for instance, in the late 1960s, various theories of sexual liberation advocated free love without ties, restrictions or commitments. It was only in retrospect that it became clear that this advocacy was consistent with objectifying and commodifying women. Instead of being tied down to one man, a woman was to be freely exchanged amongst many. Nonetheless, these same sexual liberation theories also contained the beginnings of the critique of patriarchal norms. In a future retrospect on our present, something similar might be said about the emphasis on metaphor, and especially about the critique of totalizing theories. The critique of totalizing theories might partake of a fragmenting process through its emphasis on discontinuity, but it also reflects an awareness of the destructiveness totalization imposes. The misinterpretation of Derrida's statement that 'there is nothing outside the text'[17] reflects the extent to which the world is becoming nothing more than a text – a text which can only be understood in terms of what its metaphors suppress, in order to maintain an illusion of presence.[18]

In a moment, we shall discuss Lacan's theory about how the ability to make connections declines at the same time as a historical consciousness fades, a fading in which the demise of the psychical fantasy of woman is meant to matter. At this point, I want to note another factor which might contribute to that decline. If you have read this far, your concentration span is considerably greater than that catered to by popular television, film and the tabloid press. There is an ongoing debate as to the cause of abbreviated attention spans, but no doubt that they are shorter.[19] By this argument, aside from the question of literacy, the abbreviation of attention comes into being by this means: episodes, like entities, are focused on as discrete; the connections between them are sidestepped; I have indicated that visualization aids this process, and the ego's era is pre-eminently visual. While the effects of visualization have been much discussed in poststructuralist writings, while there are also arguments on severing sensory connections, the problem these arguments encounter is that they are unable to postulate

17  The original statement is 'Il n'y a pas de hors-texte': 'there is no extra text'.
18  Yet as befits the two-edged nature of the intellectual avant-garde, while the 'as if' is emphasized, the sensory severance that leads to that emphasis is recognized in other contexts. The fact that the primacy of sight and visualization over the other senses leads to the atrophy of the latter is stressed by Foucault, Derrida, Lyotard, Deleuze, Irigaray. The thing is, the recognition and the emphasis are not connected, even by Irigaray.
19  See the discussion of the eight-minute fix in Postman (1985, p. 100). For a more theoretical discussion of the media and ideology, see Thompson (1990).

a realm in which those sensory connections make sense. To postulate such a realm would be to postulate a foundation, and that these writers avoid at all costs. But postulating such a foundation is not a problem for popular culture. The New Age belief in energetic connections has extended well beyond the Arcana bookstores. It is reiterated in many blockbusters of the last fifteen years, from *Star Wars* ('May the force be with you') to *ET* ('Eliot feels his feelings'). After surveying Lacan's neglected theory of history, the first task for Part II of this book will be rethinking, or rather, recasting, this aspect of popular awareness in the light of critiques of foundationalism.

When finishing this Introduction a colleague now teaching in the United States rang me. She had just moved in with a New-Ager. They were having a house-warming party, and she phoned me from the kitchen, resigned to the improbable meetings that were taking place as their friends came together. 'At this moment', she said, 'a black-veiled psychic is in earnest conversation with a preppie writing a dissertation on Derrida.' 'What were they saying?' I asked. 'I am not sure,' replied my colleague. 'It sounded like, "Metaphors be with you".'

# Chapter 2

# The ego's era

Because for Lacan the 'psychical fantasy of woman' makes the idealization and denigration of women a transhistorical inevitability, because it
is a necessary offshoot of the symbolic order itself, because the symbolic
order, for Lacanians, is a universal condition of sanity, because any
necessary concomitant of it is as universal as the symbolic itself, this
fantasy has been the subject of intense debate, especially in France.[1]
Moreover, the idealized woman is the anchor of man's identity and the
guarantee of his 'Truth', the point from which and for which he can
reason. This means that the 'psychical fantasy of woman' is with us for all
time, or at least, with us for as long as we are sane.

Now, while it is evident that the claim that women are universally
split into two types is not valid cross-culturally, this ethnocentrism has
not troubled the Lacanians who uphold the fantasy, any more than the
limitations it imposes on women.[2] But we will begin with women.

Some Lacanian analysts are opposed to feminism because they feel
feminist demands imperil the psychical fantasy of woman. Alice Jardine,
in an accurate satire of their position, writes that according to these
Lacanians 'humanity must avoid the inevitable trauma of doing away
with "woman" as Man's symptom – if we are to avoid bringing the social
order, the order of language, crashing down' (Jardine 1985, p. 172). The
reasoning of these analysts (Lemoine-Luccioni and Montrelay are the
main offenders) seems to be that women should continue to act the part

1 See Marks and de Courtivron (1981, pp. 7ff.). Lacan's own position of idealization is complex.
  Idealization makes the 'lady' into something considerably less than a subject. (Cf. Lacan 1972–3, p.
  193.)
2 I am grateful to Marilyn Strathern and Henrietta Moore for numerous cross-cultural examples in
  which women are not categorized in terms of good and bad, the ideal and the denigrated. See
  below. The role of the idealized woman in relation to reason and truth is itself a historical one;
  woman replaces God with the emergence of courtly love: thus Lacan (1972–3, pp. 64–5). See also
  Philippa Berry (1989).

of the idealized or denigrated woman who features in man's fantasy if the
order of language, the symbolic, is to survive. By implication, the crash
they fear would be a psychotic crash. In effect they make acting the
feminine part the condition of avoiding it.

As I noted at the outset, Lacan himself saw the psychotic possibilities
in contemporary civilization in a more complex fashion. There is
support in his texts for the conclusions drawn by those who would
uphold the psychical fantasy of woman, and for the idea that changing
the 'cosmic polarity' between the sexes threatens the symbolic. But for
the most part, when Lacan discusses threats to the symbolic, he
concentrates on how a contemporary inflation of the ego results in the
'social psychosis'. It is when he discusses how the social psychosis comes
into being that he reveals the little known historical dimension to his
theory of the imaginary. Once this historical dimension is investigated, it
becomes plain that, far from being the bulwark against social psychosis,
'the psychical fantasy of woman' is a contributing cause.

While it might contain the social psychosis, the fantasy of woman also
encapsulates the foundational fantasy that gave rise to that psychosis.
This is not to say that Lacan himself gave the 'psychical fantasy of
woman' this determinate place in the social psychosis he attributed to the
ego's era, not for a minute. That argument has yet to be made. It only
becomes apparent after Lacan's theory of the ego's era is thought
through in the context of his theory of the 'psychical fantasy of woman'
and sexual difference. This thinking through has the further advantage
that, in addition to linking the psychical fantasy of woman to the ego's
era, it will point to connections between the ego's era, ethnocentrism in
the post-colonial context, ecological crisis, and the existence of ongoing
war (whose relatively localized scale, and for that matter shifts in locale,
renders its omnipresence less striking). That this theory has implications for making these connections (and Lacan thought making
connections in itself was a symbolic activity) should become evident,
although I do not pursue them all until Part II of this book. It should also
be evident that their pursuit is contingent on an analysis of the
foundational fantasy, and the economic mechanism by which time is
made over in favour of space.

Once Lacan's critique of ego-psychology is put in its context (which is
done in the next section), one can enquire into the origins of the ego's era.
It is Lacan's elliptical account of this which introduces the social
ramifications of the master–slave dialectic and, more crucially for Lacan,
the connection between the *physis* of space in the environment and the

psyche, a connection which presupposes that fantasy has a physical force in history.[3] But while these connections and extensions can be made, the determinate question of what brought the ego's era into being remains. This connection is implicit in Lacan's theory, but as I have indicated, it is exactly at this point that his own impulse to connect breaks down.

Yet Lacan's theory overall can also be used to explain his breakdown in this respect. For, as indicated already, Lacan's work also bears on making connections; this theme is constant throughout this chapter.[4] And as we shall see, when Lacan refers to making connections he says that the process is also one of 'rewriting history'. To avoid confusion, it should be emphasized at the outset that rewriting history, in the sense of making connections, is for Lacan an attribute of the symbolic. His theory of history is an account of how that symbolic activity, and a great deal else besides, is curtailed by the imaginary ego's era. In other words, Lacan is describing a specific era in history – that of the ego. But the era he is describing is one that curtails historical thinking.

Two caveats. Making connections is only a symbolic activity when it involves labour. It is easy enough, and can be psychotic in itself, to make connections on the basis of superstition, without any regard for consistency. Second (related), this is a reading of Lacan based on drawing out a common thread of reasoning in apparently disconnected remarks throughout his work. My belief is that there is more consistency in Lacan's *oeuvre* than he claimed, but certainly I have imputed much of this consistency. Felman says, of her exegesis of Lacan, that she 'is not absolutely sure that Lacan – as a subject of the signified – actually made all this entirely explicit to himself' (Felman 1987, p. 66) which is a polite way of observing that perhaps he did not know what he was saying. The same may be true for what is attributed to him here. But if what he was saying is what I think it is, the impossibility of saying it, while maintaining a masculinist identity, would have had to produce ellipses at critical points of connection. If 'No knowledge can be supported or transported by one alone' (ibid., p. 83) this is because the objectifying ego

3  Dialectical particularly in its search for 'essential levels of reality beneath apparent ones', a search which Jay opposes to Foucault's affinity with positivism, apparent in Foucault's disdain for any such search (1984, p. 522).
4  Critiques of 'making connections' and advocacy of empiricism have gone hand in hand since Francis Bacon first condemned the 'frantic search' to connect one event with another, in a panegyric to the values of studying the discrete that a contemporary Foucauldian could applaud.

censors knowledge.[5] By Lacan's account consistent connections that circumvent the ego – another name for them is logic – can only emerge or fail in a dialogue.

But as the Lacanian ego is always sexed, then in a dialogue with its own kind, its conclusions are more likely to maintain sexual identities as they stand. Its responses to reasoning are also more likely to be resistant, even hysterical in the clinical sense, when that reasoning puts those identities into question. We know that the dialogue that the ego, and any fixed sexual identity, needs is a dialogue with its others; and as Butler has argued so well, the other may be within it, as a possibility whose rigid repression leads to a general impoverishment of the being in question.[6] Butler is writing about what it means for someone maintaining a heterosexual or homosexual identity to repress and thereby exclude their homosexuality (or heterosexuality), together with other sexual possibilities, in order to maintain their identity as heterosexual, homosexual or some other form of sexual identity that means the person concerned has to take a position which certainly unconsciously, and very possibly consciously, inhibits them. What I want to do here is stress how a dialogue with the repressed or excluded also enhances logic. Logic has too summarily been assigned the role of a repressive force, and the way

5 In *Les Psychoses* Lacan briefly mentions the relations between thinking and the contemporary notion of a deconstructed subject, which he refers to as 'man [as] an open entity' or 'open being' (*être ouvert*). Those who 'really think, those who tell it, are meant to maintain themselves at this level' (1955–6b, p. 334). Lacan does not situate himself 'at this level'; it is not the level where analytic matters are explored. I think this is because the analytic level necessarily deals with how being is fixed.
6 Butler (1990) puts a general case on how identities are constructed in terms of heterosexist exclusion, and how the stability of identities depends on exclusion. She also stresses the significance of destabilizing identities. Her most recent work (Butler 1993) carries this project forward through showing how this destabilization would work in a psychically productive way; her argument differs so radically from Deleuze's, despite some apparent conceptual similarities, that I want to underline this considerable difference: Deleuze celebrates schizophrenic psychoses as an instance of where identity has failed, a celebration which means that the extraordinary psychical pain of psychoses, despite very occasional references to the notion that psychoses are not themselves the solution, is drastically downplayed. Butler's is not an argument against maintaining a coherent identity, but an argument for expanding it. The difficulty with the term 'stable identity' is that it can be taken two ways. It can be taken to mean a fixed and repressed identity, premised on exclusion and condemnation. Or it can be taken to mean an identity with relative peace of mind, in the sense that it is not at the mercy of the intrusive, instructing 'voices' that afflict the psychotic, pre-empting and overriding the judgement of the individual concerned. To live with or to observe this process for even a very limited period is to have no illusions about the 'liberatory' potential of psychoses: the psychotic is subject to the most authoritarian instructions from a nameless authority, 'the voice', who intervenes on the most trivial as well as the most significant of issues, from whether a person should get out of bed and/or put on their shoes, to whether they should move house. The now familiar debate in psychoanalysis and feminism about psychoses and the law of the father is of course relevant here, in so far as it is a debate about sanity. See Brennan (1989).

repression instead blocks logic has been neglected. This theme too will recur.[7]

## 'THE SOCIAL PSYCHOSIS'

It is time to place Lacan's theoretical critique of ego-psychology in the context of his historical theory of the imaginary. It is this account that ties the ego's excesses to the social psychosis. How the tie is effected should be clearer after recalling the broad outlines of Lacan's ego-psychology critique.

Lacan sets himself against Hartmann's American ego-psychology school, founded after many analysts emigrated to the United States in the 1930s.[8] He does so because 'ego-psychology' proposes to 'strengthen the ego'. The ego Lacan does not want reinforced is something other than the conscious subjectivity Freud has in mind when writing: 'where id was, there ego shall be'. The 'ego' Lacan is against is not reducible to the subject's experience of reconstructing and synthesizing its personal history in analysis (Ragland-Sullivan 1986; Lacan 1953–4, p. 232). The ego has more in common with the unconscious characteristics of narcissism; it does not want to know about what Lacan terms 'truth'. It is a 'carapace': a rigid construction harbouring the resistances to self-understanding, the defences against what the subject wants to conceal from itself. It is significant that one of Lacan's references to the ego as the centre of resistance has a historical cast.

> For us, whose concern is with present day man, that is, man with a troubled conscience, it is in the ego that we meet . . . inertia: we know it as the resistance to the dialectical process of analysis. The patient is held spellbound by his ego, to the exact degree that it causes his distress, and reveals its nonsensical function. It is this very fact that has led us to evolve a technique which substitutes the strange detours of free association for the sequence of the Dialogue.
> (Lacan 1953a, p. 12)

Note here that the reference to the capital-D Dialogue is a reference to Plato, who will concern us shortly. Note too that the implication of that

---

7   Moreover, if the ego's objectifying knowledge, as Lacan terms it, is tied to sexuality and the subject–object distinction, which by this argument it is, logical reserves have to be exhausted as the ego makes its subject–object world-view an actuality. See below.

8   H. Hartmann's theory is set out (in passionless prose) in Hartmann (1939).

reference is that whereas people may once have been able to reason after the manner of the Socratic dialogue, through questions and answers that reveal the truth through drawing out logical implications, that method is ruled out by the evasions of the ego: 'the characteristic modes of the agency of the ego in [small-d] dialogue', writes Lacan in another context, 'are reactions of opposition, negation, ostentation and lying' (Lacan 1948, p. 15).

In sum, Lacan does not want an ego strengthened when to do so is to increase its rigidity and resistance to truth. These lie at the heart of the paranoid 'social psychosis' (Lacan 1955–6a, p. 216). Rigidity and resistance do not only vary within the individual limits of an analysis. Lacan says these ego attributes thicken over time. On a social scale, they are worse now than they were a few centuries ago. And the place where they are absolutely worst of all is America.

This brings us to the historical context of ego-psychology. Lacan attributes it to the analysts' adaptation to their new home, and the influence of 'a cultural ahistoricism peculiar to the United States' (Lacan 1955, p. 115). In America 'history . . . finds its limit; [it . . .] is denied with a categorical will that gives the industrial corporations their style . . .' (ibid.). Now the notion that history 'finds a limit' evokes Hegel, and the evocation is not accidental. Hegel, Kojève's Hegel[9] especially, contributes to Lacan's perspective on history.[10] This will become more evident through considering another of Lacan's historical pointers. Here I will quote at length, breaking the quotation part way to comment.

The *moi*, the ego, of modern man, as I have indicated elsewhere has taken on its form in the dialectical impasse of the *belle âme* who does not recognize his very own *raison d'être* in the disorder that he denounces in the world.

But a way out is offered for the subject for the resolution of that impasse when his discourse is delusional. Communication can be

9  Alexandre Kojève's lectures had enormous impact on French intellectuals from 1933 onwards.
10 But while it will be argued that this historical perspective is not incidental to Lacan's theory, it is also true that Lacan's theory of 'the alienation of a subject who has received the definition of being born in, constituted by, and ordered in a field that is exterior to him, is to be distinguished radically from the alienation of a [Hegelian] consciousness-in-self. . .' Lacan's editor, J. A. Miller, draws attention to this unHegelian aspect of Lacan's theory after Lacan himself refers to Hegel with approval. J. A. Miller in Lacan (1964, p. 215). Lacan also stresses his difference from Hegel in the same context, but he nonetheless adapts Hegel's theory.

validly established for him in the common task of science and in the posts that it commands in our universal civilization; this communication will be effective within the enormous objectification constituted by that science, and it will enable him to forget his subjectivity.

(Lacan 1953b, p. 70)

The *belle âme* refers to Hegel's 'law of the heart and the frenzy of self-conceit': for Lacan, this is a process whereby the one judges the other.[11] This is a process of projection, which can lead to paranoia, where the ego fears that the other will do to it as it does to the other. But the ego is formed in this impasse, which returns us to the main thread. Lacan has 'indicated elsewhere' how the ego of modern man takes on its form, in his early texts particularly. What Lacan is referring to at this point is the outcome of that form.

If the subject did not rediscover in a regression – often pushed right back to the 'mirror-stage' – the enclosure of a stage in which his ego contains its imaginary exploits, there would hardly be any assignable limits to the credulity to which he must succumb in that situation.

(Lacan 1953b, p. 70)

I take 'credulity' as another word for delusion. Regression refers to part of the experience induced through analytic transference. In itself, the passage quoted alludes to analysis as an antidote to the social psychosis; it is not, I will infer later, the only antidote; there is another generated by the fact that only some, not all, human beings are identified with the dominant ego's standpoint. While analysis is an individual matter, the 'delusional discourse' is a mark of the times; something born it seems 'at the dawn of the historical era of the "ego" . . .' (ibid., p. 71). Ego-psychology is a product of its times. So was Freud's preoccupation with reality-testing and his mistaken emphasis on the 'perception consciousness system' which, like ego-psychology, stems from the 'mirage of objectification, inherited from classical psychology . . .' (Lacan 1948, p. 22).[12] That mirage is part of an 'enormous objectification' constituted in and through science. At another point Lacan suggests that positivism

11   I am not detailing Hegel's well-known master–slave dialectic at this point (I return to it below) or the law of the heart, Chapters 4(A) and 5(B/b) respectively of G.W.F. Hegel (1807). There is a discussion of the law of the heart in Wilden's extensive notes to the Rome Report (Wilden 1968). There is a concise statement of Lacan's understanding of the law of the heart in Lacan (1953a, p. 12).
12   Lacan took Freud's theories of perception more seriously, while relocating them, in his subsequent introduction of the category of the real. Cf. Lacan (1955–6b, p. 18).

forms part of this objectifying assault on reason through its focus on experimentation. Positivism reverses the tradition of 'true science' that psychoanalysis inherits. That is to say: in a social order that blocks off truth, psychoanalysts as 'practitioners of the symbolic function . . . return to a conception of true science whose claims have been inscribed in a tradition beginning with Plato's *Theaetetus*' (Lacan 1953b, p. 72).

The *Theaetetus* partakes of the broad Platonic rejection of surface, sensory reasoning, and is one of Plato's main works on epistemology (Plato c. 360 BCE). It also partakes of the Platonic equation of the good life with the love of reason, which in turn bears on Plato's idea that the soul's health lies in its curiosity and quest for knowledge. This quest for knowledge is essentially dialogic. It requires an interlocutor who enables the subject to move beyond the fixed meanings that constitute its present standpoint, and as Lacan makes plain at another point, it is the presence and position of this interlocutor that link the Socratic dialogue with the science of psychoanalysis.[13] But in terms of something that bears directly on Lacan's argument against positivism, the pithy-quotation-making-the-point is not to be found. It is in the earlier *Phaedrus*, of so much interest to Derrida, that Plato contrasts 'science' with 'mere empirical knack' (Plato c. 370 BCE, p. 89). Moreover science and reason (as distinct from unreason) seem to involve 'steeping oneself in speculation' (ibid.).

Despite the recent, frequent stress upon the visual connotations of the term 'speculation',[14] the word also connotes the art of wondering . . . about the connections between events, causes, origins, possible outcomes. Yet speculation, or some form of it, is the burden or blessing of paranoiac and intellectual alike. As Freud has it, in their delusions (which by definition have to be speculative constructions) paranoiacs find an outlet for their often 'acute perceptive and imaginative powers' that they cannot find elsewhere (Freud 1926, p. 99). Now if one were to offer a brief distinction between paranoid and non-paranoid speculation, it would be that the former is conducted from the standpoint of the ego: events and causes are speculated about in a self-referential way; any synthesis of the relation between those events and causes closes off knowledge of connections that jeopardize the ego's position.

13 There is another reference to the *Theaetetus* in Lacan (1964, p. 47), which, together with subsequent discussion of Plato in the same book (pp.230–1) highlights the importance of dialogue. Plato's emphasis on the search for knowledge and health is also consistent with Freud's assumption that curiosity is basic to psychical health. Cf. Toril Moi (1989).

14 The Greek word *theoria* refers to theory, speculation, and spectacle.

In non-paranoid speculation, this is not the case; speculation about the connections between things is open-ended. The point here is that it would be consistent with Lacan's social-psychosis hypothesis if speculation in the modern era were conducted solely from the standpoint of the ego, or *moi*. Thus, first, this standpoint is the 'reverse' of that of 'true science', and second, what can be known is restricted to what is acceptable to the ego. What is acceptable can nonetheless be unpleasant; for instance delusions of persecution are unpleasant, but they are acceptable in so far as the ego remains the focus of attention.

There will be more later on the relation between self-referential knowledge, and the positivism, the 'empiricist' objectification in knowledge that for Lacan marks science in the ego's era, but Lacan's notion of 'objectification' is always rather vague. What is it exactly? This has to be specified; we return to it in Part II of this book. But I can say here that if Lacan's remarks about objectification are read together with his theory of the ego, his critique of objectification echoes Heidegger's: it is more than the phenomenological insistence that the subject as well as the object has to figure in research, and that the grounds for the distinction between them should be questioned; it is also the idea that what is objectified is also dominated and controlled. This idea ties objectifying knowledge to the social processes of the ego's era. But more immediately, let us discuss the 'true science' Lacan counterposes to objectification in knowledge. In terms of the interpretation of Lacan (via Plato) offered here, it is a science where connections are made in a dialogic process. These connections are made through the symbolic; we could say that they are made from the 'position' of the 'I', which is the reverse of that of the *moi*.

At this stage a few lines on Lacan's view of individual psychosis might be helpful. For him psychosis not only consists of a default on the law of the father (an idea that is selectively emphasized by those who insist on maintaining the psychical fantasy of woman); psychosis also means that the subject has been unable to assume the position of 'I'.[15] Assuming this position means (among other things) that the subject seeks to know itself through the other, rather than to reduce the other to itself, as does the *moi*. Accordingly the range and accuracy of the connections made by the *moi* is curtailed by the limits of its own

15   The clearest discussion by Lacan of psychosis as a refusal of the name of the father is in his reinterpretation of Freud's case of the Wolfman (Lacan 1955–6b, pp.321 ff.).

standpoint ('what it can see with its own eyes', 'experimentation'), and its honesty in relation to those connections is restricted. On the other hand, the subject of the symbolic is meant to be able to make connections that increase understanding, even at the price of self-image.

Now analysts other than Lacan attest to the idea that making connections is basic to the psychoanalytic act. For Klein, and following her, Bion, 'attacks on linking' are prompted by the anxiety that underpins psychoses: these attacks also function as a psychotic mechanism in everyday life. They are the 'normal person's' response to anxiety and defence against insight (Bion 1962). But what Lacan makes clear, each time he refers to why it matters to 'make connections' (Lacan 1953–4, p. 67) or 'to link the subject to his contradictions' (ibid., p. 230), is, first, that this connecting process is one of seeking consistency; second, it rests on the subject's rewriting history. On the first point: in a remarkable treatment of the anamnesis in a case study by Michael Balint, the significant thing is that Balint's patient gives an account where things 'just don't fit together' (ibid., p. 228). In focusing on this, Lacan alerts one to a concern with logic that will figure again, especially in his interest in mathematics.

The logical process of seeking out contradictions and establishing consistency is obviously not limited to the historical accounts of the subject. But making connections, and filling in the blanks in the subject's story, is always and simultaneously an act of rewriting the past. Lacan stresses this at many points; I shall quote only one instance. In outlining the idea that there is a speech other than and beyond the empty speech of the ego, he writes that it is 'a speech which is to be reconquered since it is that part of the subject separated from his history' (ibid., p. 23).

His emphasis on the historical rewriting involved in making connections separates Lacan from those analysts he criticizes for reducing the dialogue to the *hic et nunc* of the analytic session (and Kleinians do so reduce it). It also formally separates him from Plato, who precisely privileged unmediated understanding over historical understanding.[16]

16 Indeed, it is tempting to compare Lacan's dual appeal to Plato and to history with a similar duality in St Augustine, who tried to reconcile the *fides historica* required by the church with the Platonic standpoint. That is to say, he tried to reconcile a faith about received views on what happened in biblical history with direct or unmediated knowledge of the divine. But where the comparison breaks down is that Lacan's idea of history is precisely not an idea of history as the past.

Lacan's idea of symbolic history is an unusual idea, signalled in the expression *rewriting* history. He puts the emphasis not on reliving, or even remembering. Rewriting, as opposed to reliving, takes the subject beyond the ego's *present* positi n. Thus

> the dimension proper to analysis is the reintegration of the subject of his history right up to the furthermost perceptible limits, that is to say, into a dimension that goes well beyond the limits of the individual.
>
> (Lacan 1953–4, p. 12)

Lacan is here writing of Freud's procedure. But he makes a similar observation on his own behalf, when discussing the necessity of distinguishing

> between the dual interpretation, in which the subject enters into an ego to ego rivalry with the analysand, and the interpretation which moves forward in the direction of the symbolic structuration of the subject, which is to be located beyond the present structure of the ego.
>
> (ibid., p. 65)

Yet how does this rewriting history, which moves forward from behind the past to beyond the present, how does it work? What is the connection between the history of the past and opening out of the present? Lacan's deeply Heideggerian answer to this question is 'the function of time' (ibid., p. 13). It is 'the time element . . . a dimension constitutive of the order of speech' (ibid., p. 243) that makes the symbolic historical, as much as 'tradition' (Lacan 1953–4, p. 54).[17]

In a manner that Lacan leaves obscure, the time element is affected by psychosis, whether this operates on an individual or a social level (but see Bowie 1991). Here, one can infer that if the social order blocks off truth through its intense imaginary affiliation with the ego's wish not to know, if the symbolic is under assault by a social psychosis, then the 'attacks on linking' (or more exactly, certain kinds of links) will increase, and the sense of historical moving time will be foreclosed. A contemporary sense of existing in an endless present, where space replaces time, has been observed by Jameson (Jameson 1991, p. xii). The correlative idea, that we are losing time and the sense of time,

---

17 The reference to tradition is only an allusion, but in view of the implication that the symbolic as much as the imaginary has a broad social dimension, it matters that the word is used.

belongs to Walter Benjamin (see Buck-Morss 1989), and it figures in much contemporary criticism. The notion that 'Time is being taken away from us, the time of our own becoming' has been captured exactly by Braidotti (Braidotti 1989, p. 158). She moreover situates the theft of time in terms of women having biotechnical decisions made for them. Her specific concern raises a question which will come to concern us more as this book progresses: whose symbolic time is being lost? Or to pose the same question from its other side, whose is the dominant ego?

Enough for now that, in the ego's era, symbolic time is stolen, and the 'symbolic' function of making connections suffers, in terms of rewriting history, and perhaps in terms of an increasing disregard for logical consistency as such. If one asks what the ego stands to lose in the face of making consistent connections, one can begin by noting that the ego desires to dominate and control, and that a means to domination and control is the fragmentation and disconnection of everything outside the ego, the reduction of everything different or other than itself to a scale the ego can manage, to a grey background of sameness – in order that the ego can stand out, in order that it does not disappear in the movement of living history, a temporal process where it might be able to identify itself by saying *that is I*, but where it cannot say *it is me*.

The ego is opposed to any historical understanding, including if not especially the understanding of its own course. It is also opposed to the history of anything different from itself. It is interested in difference only in so far as everything different from it provides it with a mirror for itself. In this respect, it will reduce all difference to sameness; if everything different is deadened and dominated in the process of becoming totally preoccupied with the ego, it loses the lively heterogeneous difference rightly celebrated in the postmodern *Zeitgeist*. The loss of this difference is not only signalled by my reading of Lacan; Lévi-Strauss also believed that the world will lose its diversity with modernization (cf. MacCannell 1976), and Benjamin, anticipating Lacan's formulation almost exactly, discusses the effects of the totalizing ego in a cultural psychosis (1939, pp. 58–9). But while the flattening process has its origin in the psychical dynamics of the ego's era, the postmodern insistence on difference refuses in general to identify a source for the trend to homogenization, under the mistaken idea that any such identification would partake of the logic of totalization.

Which brings me to a fundamental distinction. The symbolic

attributes of temporality, rewriting history and making consistent connections are *counterposed* in this argument to the totalizing, objectifying trends of the ego.[18] If the attacks on connections that go beyond the ego are increasing, if we are affected by a social psychosis, then it should follow that we are resistant to making the connections necessary to understanding the ego's era. And, as indicated above, it also follows that thought constrained by the process of objectifying knowledge is not coeval with logic; it is its simulating rival.

The idea that the ego is opposed to any historical understanding, and that the ego's era is psychotic, introduces another aspect of time in psychical life. This is the fact that psychosis is marked by hallucinatory, immediate perception, immediate in that it always takes place in the now. The idea that hallucinatory perception marks the ego's era is not suggested by Lacan, although he points to its obliteration of time. A few words on this are in order, which means a few words on Lacan's concept of the real are appropriate.

One of Lacan's most famous remarks on the real is that it 'always returns to the same place'. In his seminar *Les Psychoses* he is less abstract, and refers to the natural cyclical order as a timeless one in which, for instance, 'planets always return to the same place' (1955–6b). The real for Lacan is the arena of both the natural order and the realm of aberrant psychotic perception. Both the natural order and the aberrancies are known through the same perceptual apparatus and through language, whose chains of signification respect no distinction between these orders at the level of psychical investment. For language is always invested, meaning it is energetically cathected; this is, in part, why some signifiers have far more power than others. These signifiers act on immediate perception, in that we cannot name what we perceive without language. Of course the fact that language and signification run these realms together in the real does not mean that a natural cyclical

18  In Lacanian terms, totalizing theory can be read, as Jay notes, 'as the product of the illusory wholeness of the 'mirror' stage, before entrance into the 'symbolic stage' of language'. Jay also notes (critically) that this reading of Lacan informed the 'unremitting hostility to totality' of the major post-structuralist thinkers (Jay 1984, p. 515). At the same time, those thinkers overlook the extent to which making consistent connections in the context of seeking to understand what produced the present ('rewriting history') goes against the ego. The same contrast can be represented in Heidegger's terms. The total view is 'that for which man is prepared and which [. . .he] consequently intends in a decisive sense to set in place before himself. When the symbolic activity of rewriting history goes beyond the ego's present standpoint, it takes one by surprise' (Heidegger 1938, p. 129). Or, to put the issue in terms borrowed from Jay (1988), the 'epistemological vantage point' which *aspires* to broad knowledge of the whole is not identical with one which *claims* 'totalistic knowledge' (p. 5 and *passim*).

order and aberrant perception are themselves the same thing. What they have in common is that they are both without time: the natural cyclical order always repeats; it has no time in the sense that it has no history (although it does have a generational time). Aberrant perception is without time in that it is immediate.

Given that the connection between the ego and psychosis is one of standpoint, the question becomes: how does this in turn tie to hallucinatory immediacy? The answer is that because the ego reduces what there is to itself, it reduces it 'to the same place': one reduces it to one's own standpoint, and, in this sense, eliminates distance between one's experience and that of the other. By locating these experiences in the same place, by making them spatially identical, the ego's expansion thus eliminates the reality of distance. In turn, this means that the historical reference point that enables one to say that something is outside or beyond the self's present experience is also the reference point which would enable a line to be drawn between the here and now in perception, and images and memories that appear to be immediate but are not. It is this reference point that the ego's era erases.

## 'AT THE DAWN OF THE ERA OF THE EGO . . .'

But it is time to turn to the specifics of how the ego's historical era comes about. One can infer a date for it, in so far as Lacan says that the era's 'dawn' coincides with Pascal's *Pensées* (which, although he does not say so, was published in 1670). Pascal is the pre-eminent thinker of the spatial shifts that marked the beginnings of modernity. He is the philosopher of the terror – of the vast space in which an individual is nothing. He is also the critic of the new subject-centred outlook, in which the viewer's standpoint is made central. 'In painting, the rules of perspective decide the right place, but how will it be decided when it comes to truth and morality?' (Pascal 1670, p. 35). This is our first connection between space and the ego's era. At another point Lacan refers to the clock, which it seems marks the time of the critical historical turning point.[19] But how did the ego's era happen? Enough has been said about objectification in knowledge and its accompanying social psychosis to show that Lacan presupposes a process of historical change, but his indications as to the nature of its dynamic are brief. However, he did give some thought to this, especially in one of the

19 Lacan's reference to Pascal is in Lacan (1953b, p. 71).

earliest texts on aggressiveness in psychoanalysis, 'Aggressivity' (Lacan 1948).[20] There, it appears that the ego is affected by the social environment surrounding it; an environment it also affects. The link between the social environment's effect on the ego and the desire to shape the environment is space. Given that Lacan has emphasized that there is a relation between time and the symbolic, one might expect an explicit contrast between this link and that between the imaginary ego and space. Lacan does not make this contrast explicit. Once more we are left in the shadowy realms of inference. Yet the inference is strong, in that Lacan's comments on how spatial relations enter the ego's construction figure throughout his work, although the manner in which his discussions on space interlock with his historical theory of the imaginary has been neglected.[21] That neglect may be remedied by the recent outstanding translation of his relatively lucid *Seminar One*, which emphasizes the spatial dimension in the psyche (Lacan 1953–4).

From the beginning, Lacan had asserted that the 'lure of spatial identification' in the mirror-stage accounts for the *méconnaissances* that mark the ego in all its structures (Lacan 1949, pp. 4–6). The mirror-stage identification is an inverse one, in which the image is outside and opposed to the self; it is, so to speak, a 'reversal'. This spatial lure is an energetic formation which also structures the subject as a rival within itself. Subsequently, its energetic aspect will implicitly, as ever with Lacan who is always implicit, bear on the link between the ego and the environment. Turning here to the mirror-stage as an internal rivalrous structure: the key point here is that this structure not only constitutes the subject-to-be's identity. It is also a precondition for the subject's Oedipal rivalry with the other. Note that this means that an *internal* structure prefigures a similar *external* one. A psychical reality, or fantasy, pre-dates its subsequent acting out. The narcissism of the mirror-stage is inextricably bound up with aggressiveness against this 'other', and is the locus of the master–slave struggle for recognition that binds the ego as master and the ego as slave one to another. In steps that are not clear (and to which I return) Lacan discusses this

20 Stuart Schneiderman notes that the English equivalent of the French *aggressivité* is not 'aggressivity' (there is no such word) and distinguishes 'aggression' from 'aggressiveness' (1980, p. vii); I have taken this distinction into account.
21 By neglected I do not mean it has been ignored. Again, there is an excellent discussion in Jameson, (1977 (1988), pp. 85–7), (see also Jameson 1991) and in Jacqueline Rose (1981). It would be more accurate to say that the extent to which Lacan's discussions on space interlock with his thoughts on historical change has been ignored.

bondage and the aggressiveness it generates in the first four theses of 'On Aggressivity'. He introduces the fifth, final thesis by saying that

> Such a notion of aggressivity as one of the intentional co-ordinates of the human ego, especially relative to the category of space, allows us to conceive of its role in modern neurosis and in the 'discontents' of civilization.
>
> (Lacan 1948, p. 25)

The fifth thesis is avowedly 'social'. It is about aggression 'in the present social order' (ibid., p. 25). In it, Lacan indicates how the spatial dimensions of the environment and the ego intersect. He seems to be saying that aggression increases in the spatial restrictions of an urban environment. He explicitly refers to 'the dialectic common to the passions of the soul and the city' and to the effects of the 'ever-contracting "living space" in which human competition is becoming ever keener. . .' (ibid., pp. 26–7).[22]

For Lacan the city's spatial restrictions result in needs to escape on the one hand, and an increased social aggressiveness on the other. The apparent banality of Lacan's statement that 'overcrowding leads to aggressiveness' is alleviated in that his account gestures to why overcrowding leads to aggressiveness, and as we shall see, to a territorializing imperative whereby the ego seeks to make the globe over in its own image.

Aggressiveness motivates the drive to dominate not only the earth's surface but outer space through 'psycho-techniques' (ibid.). It is also part of a competitive Darwinian ethic which 'projected the predations of Victorian Society and the economic euphoria that sanctioned for that society the social devastation that it initiated on a planetary scale' (ibid., p. 26). It is with Victorian imperialism that the ego's era gathers steam. The Darwinian ethic, Lacan notes, presents itself as natural, although its true origins lie in the aggression generated by the master–slave dialectic.

In its entirety, 'On Aggressivity' suggests a fundamental connection

---

22 These 'passions of the soul and the city' remind us of Lacan's famous remark that the unconscious was resembled by nothing so much as Baltimore in the morning. In this connection one also thinks of Lewis Mumford's classic work on cities. 'The metropolis is rank with forms of *negative vitality*. Nature and human nature, violated in this environment, come back in destructive forms . . . . In this mangled state, the impulse to live departs from apparently healthy personalities. The impulse to die supplants it. . . . Is it any wonder that Dr. Sigmund Freud found a death wish at the seat of human activity?' (Mumford 1938, pp. 291–2).

between the spatial dimension of the ego and the spatial environment. However, the precise nature of this egoic/environmental spatial dialectic needs to be constructed from Lacan's allusions. There are some indications as to how this might be done. To begin explicating them, it is necessary to hark back to Lacan's comment on anxiety, and its intersection with the spatial dimension. Lacan's introduction of anxiety at that point in the text on aggressiveness appears somewhat *ad hoc*. Yet he has obliquely referred to anxiety earlier in the same text, through referring to Melanie Klein. Lacan's text is dated 1948, a time when Klein's name was associated with the view that anxiety and aggressiveness played a dominant part in very early psychical life.[23] Lacan refers to Klein in 'On Aggressivity' when discussing the 'paranoiac structure of the ego' and the 'especial delusion of the misanthropic "*belle âme*", throwing back onto the world the disorder out of which his being is composed' (Lacan 1948, p. 20). After referring to Klein's work, Lacan turns to aggressiveness and its relation to narcissism (ibid., p. 21). I take this mention of the *belle âme* as a signpost to the formation of the modern ego, given that Lacan referred to the *belle âme* when saying that he had 'indicated elsewhere' how the modern ego takes on its form.

Projection is a mechanism of the imaginary, and the subject who throws his disorder back into the world is engaging, evidently, in the act of projection. Klein was particularly concerned with the early operation of projection, whose force she linked to anxiety: for her, the extent of a subject's persecutory anxiety not only affects its ability to link; it also determines the degree to which it projects 'bad internal objects'. Projection is the mode for putting bad feelings and 'bad internal objects' (to which Lacan explicitly refers) (ibid., p. 21) outside the self: this projective process in turn generates feelings of persecution about bad objects returning, hence paranoia. This is not the only reference to this projective process in the text on aggressiveness. The projection of internal negativity is a mobilizing factor in war, as indeed is the need to dominate physical space (ibid., p. 28).

Taking physical pressure, its 'dialectical counterpart' in the physical environment and the aggressive anxiety they trigger into account, there are grounds for setting out how a historical, spatial dynamic might work. If, as Lacan says, the more spatially constricted the environment

---

23   There was controversy over Klein's work in the early 1940s, and subsequently in the British Psycho-analytical Society, and it ramified internationally. It centred (among other things) on Klein's taking Freud's concept of the death instinct seriously. See Brennan (1988).

is, the more anxiety and the aggressive desire to dominate space increase, then that desire and anxiety must increase as space becomes more constricted and more dominated. Yet as Lacan also says that this process produces an increase in aggressive competitiveness, his dialectic requires an economic, technological supplement.

The supplement should illuminate the ego's rigidity and desire for control. The rigidity, the basis of the ego's 'resistance to truth', is first formed in the spatial positioning of the mirror-stage. I want to suggest here that, just as there is a dialectic between the spatial dimensions of the ego and of the environment, so too might the ego's rigidity have a dialectical counterpart in the *things* the subject constructs. It is this dialectical counterpart which accounts for the temporal process at work in the foreclosure of the sense of time, and which explains why the sense of history is fading. As will be plain by Chapter 5, the 'things' constructed physically alter the perception of time. 'Things' means the whole technological apparatus by which the environment is controlled. The modern age 'begins that way of being human which mans the realm of human capability as a domain given over to measuring and executing, for the purpose of gaining mastery over that which is as a whole' (Heidegger 1949, p. 132).

Apart from the fact that the construction of things is one expression of the desire to dominate space, it is also consistent with Lacan's otherwise puzzling question as to whether the master–slave dialectic 'will find its resolution in the service of the machine'. It fits, too, with his suspicion of reality-testing. If the construction of things is one expression of what Lacan elsewhere refers to as 'the passionate desire peculiar to man to impress his image on reality' (Lacan 1948, p. 22) then reality-testing is suspect because the ego has constructed the reality it then proceeds to test.

As the point of departure for this supplement on how the ego's rigidity has a counterpart in the environment it constructs, it is worth recalling that Lacan ties both the ego's rigidity and the social psychosis to paranoia. The ego, in part, has a paranoid dimension because both the ego and the ego's objects are conceived of as fixed, and the ego wants them to stay fixed. Any unregulated movement or change in these objects poses a threat to the ego's concept of itself as fixed, in that its own fixity is defined in relation to them. Here we can locate the need to control the environment in an attempt to predict and regulate changes within it, to subject the irregularity of living things to a form of domination in which the ego closes off to itself the truth about itself, by making its dream of fixation come true. That is to say, at the same time as it closes off the truth on which its psychical health depends, it also, and in a parallel manner, restricts the regeneration of the natural environment on which it depends to stay alive.

This coupling of spatial shifts with technological expansion is repeated, although the emphasis is reversed in Marx's account. For Marx, the division of town and country is at one and the same time the basis of the accumulation of capital, which accelerates and requires the technological expansion necessary for winning in the competition of the marketplace. This does not solve the problem of what triggers aggressive competitiveness in so far as Marx himself continued to seek, and was unhappy with, his own accounts of the cause of the accumulation of capital; he sought them in a variety of places, from the relaxation of the church's laws restricting usury, to the shift whereby the merchant became an industrialist through employing small rural producers.[24] Marx's critics, notably Max Weber, have argued that he overlooked the extent to which substantial urbanization preceded capitalization (Giddens 1981, p. 109). Yet whatever the cause of capitalization, the technological expansion that accompanied it is the means whereby the ego is able to secure the 'reversal' in knowledge, as it makes the world over in its own image. It is also, and this is critical to the dynamics of the ego's era, a means of generating continuous economic insecurity and anxiety over survival in the majority, and guarantees their dependence on those identified with the dominant ego's standpoint.

In fact to say that the above points can be made in the form of an economic supplement is drastically to understate the case: the unelaborated relation between the economic dimension and the ego is the subjective flaw in Lacan's historical theory, because it is only through the elaboration of this relation that the mechanism by which the social psychosis could exist simultaneously in and around individuals will emerge. 'Aggressive competitiveness' is tied to imperialism (loosely) but the fact that this tie is also fundamental in the competitive profit motive is not followed through (despite, or perhaps because of, the Heideggerian allusions). This tie can be effected after the foundational fantasy is identified in more detail in Part II. And once this is done, the details of the mechanism by which the fixity or rigidity that Lacan so frequently refers to as a hallmark of the individual ego has a

24 Karl Marx (1894, pp. 323ff.; 593ff.). We return to Marx's political economy in Chapter 4.

counterpart in the *historical* ego's era will be apparent. So will another reason for scepticism about 'reality-testing'. Lacan refers to the ego's era approach to knowledge as paranoid, as it is based on a need for control. But he does not take account of how the ego technologically constructs an environment it can control, and how this, in turn, reinforces paranoia, precisely because the damage done to nature in the process makes the ego fear (rightly) for its own survival.

But the question for now is: how does Lacan's own argument on space bear on the social psychosis; its relation to the spiral of aggression needs amplifying. In one respect, an answer to this question has already been given. According to the Kleinians (and I have argued that this thesis is consistent with Lacan's account) anxiety increases the attacks on linking that underpin psychoses.[25] But why precisely do aggression and spatial conquests no longer work as safeguards against anxiety? Here, the answer is insufficient, until we take account of how aggression is used in the reconstruction of a threatening environment,

25  At this point a very relevant parallel between the arguments of Lacan's early and later work should be recorded, especially as it indicates that the notion of social psychosis was not superseded in his *oeuvre*. Lacan initially located anxiety in the imaginary, and later insisted it was due to 'lack over the representation of lack', which implies a failure of symbolic castration, an inability to break out of the imaginary. These successive accounts are thoroughly compatible. For in the first place he describes a spiral whereby the force of the imaginary increases; in the second he describes its consequence: it is that much harder to represent lack in an imaginary world, especially when representing it also involves rewriting one's historical subjectivity to move beyond the fixity of the present; an imaginary world is fixed in a perpetual spatial present (Lacan, unpublished seminar, *L'angoisse*). In fact, the complexity of Lacan's writing on anxiety reminds me that there are other interpretations of it which should be noted. One arises as a result of Lacan's observations on the ego's 'inertia', which Lacan refers to when discussing Melanie Klein's case study of Dick. Apparently because anxiety is produced in Dick after, and only after, the 'grafting on' of the symbolic through Oedipal interpretations, Felman (1987) concludes that anxiety is an affect associated with the symbolic. It may seem that this view puts my argument on the imaginary and the anxiety-related spiral of aggression into question. But the situation is complex. Consider the following quotation from an article Lacan wrote with Wladimir Granoff, in which Lacan and Granoff are discussing another case study, that of Harry: 'If Harry remains silent, it is because he is in no state to symbolize. Between imaginary and symbolic relationships there is the distance that separates anxiety and guilt' (Lacan and Granoff 1956). Unlike Dick at the outset of his analysis, Harry is anxious at the outset of his (in fact he is screaming). That he is screaming signifies that he is refusing 'the register of the symbol' (p.269): 'The imaginary is decipherable only if it rendered into symbols. Harry's behaviour at this moment is not; rather, he is himself drawn in by the image. Harry does not imagine the symbol; he gives reality to the image.' Harry's anxiety is more a consequence of his position in the imaginary, and of the extent to which he remains 'captured' by it. It is right to say that without some awareness of the symbolic there is no anxiety, but wrong, I think, to conclude that anxiety signifies the attainment of a symbolic position. Rather, anxiety signifies both an awareness of the symbolic and that the relation between imaginary and the symbolic is balanced, so to speak, in the imaginary's favour. And if one were to conclude from all this that social anxiety was a stage on from a kind of social apathy, and that some such apathetic condition would prevail in the absence of any symbolic at all, that conclusion might not be wrong.

an account which will also amplify the *physis* presupposed in the idea
that the spatially constricting environment has psychical effects. The
physics of the process need amplification because, while Lacan gestures
to a dialectic, he does not give us a mechanism by which the social
psychosis of the ego's era follows the same path of a psychosis studied
in microcosm. What he does do is gesture to that mechanism, by
writing that the various pressures and fears produced in the social
psychosis produce a sense of spatial constriction and a fear of loss of
territory. Since the sense of self depends on a certain spatial definition
these pressures have a persecutory feel; they jeopardize that spatial
definition. To grasp more of what is at stake here, we need to take
account of how the spatial mirror-stage, and the master–slave dialectic
it gives rise to, is also an energetic event.

Demonstrating this will involve a brief detour through ethology, for
Lacan's concern with energy in the mirror-stage is initially a concern
with ethological examples of mirroring. Roger Callois's (1935) work on
morphological mimicry was pursued by Lacan, in a series of observations about the physical effects of the mirror-stage which the commentators have neglected, just as they have neglected Lacan's historical
allusions.[26] Now what will be of particular interest to us is that Lacan's
use of morphology shows he presupposes that energy is psychically and
therefore potentially socially malleable. As I have indicated, the social
malleability of energy will be critical in unravelling the ego's era. But
enough initially to repeat what Lacan says. It is in defining the mirror-
stage that he introduces ethological evidence to support his claims.
Having explained how it is that the *gestalt* of its own image introduces
the infant to the mirror-state opposition of visual wholeness and
internal fragmentation, he writes:

> That a *gestalt* should be capable of formative effects in the organism
> is attested by a piece of biological experimentation that is itself so
> alien to the idea of psychical causality that it cannot bring itself to
> formulate its results in these terms. It nevertheless recognizes that it
> is a necessary condition for the maturation of the gonad of the
> female pigeon that it should see another member of its species, of
> either sex; so sufficient in itself is this condition that the desired
> effect may be obtained merely by placing the individual within reach

26 This discussion of Lacan and energy redeems a promissory note in Brennan (1992). The one
aspect of Callois's work that Lacan does not pursue is the former's argument that morphological mimicry entails a loss of psychic energy.

of the field of reflection of a mirror. Similarly, in the case of the migratory locust, the transition within a generation can be obtained by exposing the individual, at a certain stage, to the exclusively visual action of a similar image, provided it is animated by movements of a style sufficiently close to that characteristic of the species.

(1949 p. 2).

Lacan refers to the pigeons elsewhere and to similar mirror phenomena in the socialization of locusts (1953a). What, then, have the pigeons and locusts to do with the imaginary mirror-stage? Lacan's ethological references are recurrent. At one point he makes the ethological realm equivalent to the psychological realm in so far as psychology concerns behaviour (1981). Lacan's use of ethology can either be taken as a gratuitous grasping for empirical support or be passed over in silence. More is going on here; and the clue to what is given in the first sentence of the passage just cited. I suggest that for Lacan 'the idea of psychical causality' means the common presupposition that social events or experiences can cause changes in the psyche, but not the material body. The correlative views are that (1) that the material body is independent of social effects; (2) where the body does affect social relations, it does so only in a causally determinate way. Lacan on the other hand is describing a (literally) material process, but the genesis of this process is not genetic. It is social, in the broadest (environmental) sense. In a philosophical tradition dominated, although by no means ruled,[27] by the split between psyche and soma, mind and body, matter and mentation, the notion that social/environmental forces act on the body, as well as the other way around, is alien. Lacan says that many facts of the pigeon/locust order 'have now come to the attention of biologists, but the intellectual revolution necessary for their full understanding is still to come' (1953a, p. 14). Of course, just how socially malleable Lacan thought the formative effects of the mirror-stage *gestalt* are is another question. It would be possible to say that he saw the particular redeployment of psychical energy the *gestalt* presupposes as induced by social interaction, but structurally circumscribed and therefore precisely not malleable.

---

27  Many contemporary feminists write as if 'Western philosophy' is uniformly founded on a mind/matter split, and ignore the complexities within Western philosophy on this question. See James (1994), especially on Descartes, whose name is frequently invoked as the founder of the mind–body split, but whose own writings on the category of the emotions are ignored. Like other seventeenth-century thinkers James discusses, Descartes saw the emotions as intermediate territory, crossing between mind and body.

This is consistent with his general approach to physical energy. Like Freud, Lacan assumes that energy can only be studied in terms of a self-contained system. While he stresses that energy has to be taken into account, Lacan does not attempt to advance Freud's commitment to understanding the nature of psychical energy.

Lacan justifies the former omission by saying that we can know nothing of the nature of psychic energy. We can only hypothesize its existence. Boothby's excellent discussion of Lacan and energy draws this point out well, via an example in which Lacan ties psychic energy to the real, and compares the real with a hydro-electric dam. For Boothby 'The important point is that it is impossible to specify the energy of the river without referring to the structure of the dam that will interrupt and redirect its flow' (1991, p. 62). Lacan himself writes:

> To say that the energy was in some way already there in a virtual state in the current of the river is properly speaking to say something that has no meaning, for the energy begins to be of interest to us in this instance only beginning with the moment in which it is accumulated, and it is accumulated only beginning with the moment when machines are put to work in a certain way (Lacan Seminar IV, 28-11-56 cited Boothby 1991, p. 62).[28]

On the other hand, as I have indicated, there are indications that Lacan took the shaping of energy seriously: for instance he notes Schilder on the function of the body image (1953a, p. 13) and how it determines the

28 The problem with thinking about energy 'only beginning with the moment in which it is accumulated' is that it begs the question of how it is accumulated. This dam example is equivalent in fact to the assumption that the subject is a contained energy system. Even if one is not curious about the source of the energy contained, the mechanism of its accumulation has to be an issue for psychoanalysis, especially given that the mechanism, 'the dam' seems to be faulty in psychosis. As Freud was the first to point out, and Lacan notes this (see below), there is a similarity between Freud's libido theory and Schreber's theory of divine rays. The similarity did not bother Freud, 'since the drift of this whole exposition is to reveal a surprising approximation between Schreber's delusion and structures of inter-individual exchange and intrapsychical economy alike' (Lacan 1955–6b, p. 37). There is a key distinction here – between the inter-individual and the intrapsychical. Lacan implies that like structures are being compared, rather than that the same phenomenon is being addressed. Lacan's distinction is consistent with his belief that while psychical energy is not confined within structures, it begins to be of interest to us only when it is so confined. At the same time, he insists that the psychotic experience is of an interconnected universe, and real enough. But if the psychotic's experience is real, then to rule out the study of un-contained psychical energy is to limit the understanding of psychosis. It is also to limit the understanding of how neurosis (the more habitual or normal human condition) is distinguished from psychosis, and thus to limit the understanding of the normal as such. Needless to say, any hypothesis about the real, energy or nature might be wrong. But it is no more wrong, a priori, than any other relatively coherent proposition, subject to the same laws of criticism.

perception of space. Given that the body image is the mirror-stage _gestalt_, and given that Schilder notes massive variations in individual spatial perceptions of the same phenomena, this points to the existence of a fluctuating factor shaping both image and perception. And given the importance of the spatial dialectic in my reading of Lacan's theory of history, we can suggest that the spatial perceptions of people in given historical periods will vary along with their body images and perceptions of the other. Indeed Lacan notes, in the same article in which he refers to Schilder, that the symptoms of the ego and the machine often parallel one another, and that 'the relationship between man and machine will come to be regulated by both psychological and psychotechnical means' (1953a, p. 17).

The idea that the spatial perceptions of people will vary historically fits with the idea that the dynamics of the ego's era jeopardize the subject's special definition. But we need more information, an account of the 'fluctuating factor' shaping image and perception, and how it can affect subjective spatial definitions adversely. We need this information to understand how the subject produces more anxiety than it can release through further aggression, and thereby contain in the social psychosis dynamic. In the meantime, we can still ask: how does (or did) the subject contain that anxiety at all? Is or was this the function of the psychical fantasy of woman? In the next sections, I will argue that the aggression is contained by the psychical fantasy of woman (and this containment by definition is a social process), in so far as the fantasy identifies the woman with the losing side in the ego's master–slave rivalry, which Lacan neglects to note. I will also point to why the psychical fantasy of woman is only one representation of the foundational fantasy that produces the ego's era in the first place. But none of this is self-evident in Lacan's texts. One can infer that there must be some connection between the spiral of aggression and the fantasy of woman, if both are tied to psychosis: the former as its 'cause', the latter as an ostensible means of preventing it. The nature of the connection remains to be clarified.

## 'ONE RETURNS, COMES BACK, COMING ACROSS THE SAME PATH, ONE CROSS-CHECKS IT'

To sum up so far: Lacan argues that the imaginary ego dominates more over historical time, leading to social psychosis. The controlling objectifying knowledge that characterizes this psychosis is counterposed in Lacan's account to the process of making consistent connections, and the symbolic activity of rewriting history. Objectifying knowledge is paralleled by the territorializing dynamic of the imaginary ego's era. There is a rudimentary theory in Lacan's texts as to the mechanism of this dynamic; namely, the interlocking dynamic of psychical space, techno-spatial domination, (physical) pressure, competitive rivalry and anxiety: the spiral of aggression. This is the trend of history in so far as it is locked into a totalizing imaginary fixation. But history is saved, perhaps, from a disastrous teleology by the break the symbolic imposes. Lacan is not saying

> that our culture pursues its course in the shadowy realms beyond creative subjectivity. On the contrary, creative subjectivity has not ceased in its struggle to renew the never-exhausted power of symbols in the human exchange that brings them to the light of day.
>
> (Lacan 1953b, p. 71)

Just as the intervention of the symbolic phallus breaks up the imaginary mother/child dyad, Lacan seems to suggest that the symbolic is a cultural means for rewriting history out of the present. It is a creative, rhetorical order in human affairs that breaks up the psychotic process, the Hegelian murder to which history is otherwise committed. Lacan does not expand on this suggestion, and the gesture he makes to the hope the symbolic holds is problematic, for many reasons, not the least being that he changed his mind. In his later work, Lacan moved away from the idea that the symbolic was 'at least potentially' the 'break' on imaginary unity, and towards the idea that the symbolic was implicated in the fantasy of unity (Rose 1982, p. 46). More especially, given that the psychical fantasy of woman is constituted together with the symbolic order, this fantasy needs to be situated in relation to the psychotic process the symbolic is meant to be breaking up. If the symbolic is or was breaking up the imaginary, the woman was not faring well in the process. Moreover, as I have already indicated, an analysis of the relation between this fantasy and the symbolic break-up might help us to understand how the ego's era came into being.

By implication, although this has yet to be argued, Lacan makes sexual relations the heart of his historical process. But to say that Lacan does this *by implication* is to say no more than that. This idea only emerges when his various statements about psychical formation are cross-referenced and thought through in relation to the historical perspective sketched here. It emerges too when connections are made between some of Lacan's later observations on sexuality and knowledge and the earlier theory of the ego's era.

Yet to try to think through the logical implications of Lacan's early claims, and to find those implications reflected in some of his subsequent observations, is not to say for a moment that Lacan himself was conscious of those implications from the outset. We are told, and he is famous for this, that he writes in language like that of the unconscious; his work resembles 'free association'. On the surface free association is nothing if not elliptical. But there are underlying connections. They emerge, writes Lacan, through the process of cross-checking.

Recalling that the unconscious, despite the activities of the censorship, is trying to say something, and that it has to battle through the ego to do it, and recalling that psychoanalysts adopt free association for exactly this reason, one can read Lacan's use of this technique as the decision of a man seeking to subvert his ego. (I just do not believe that Lacan's own explanation for his style is sufficient; that he wrote as he did to stop the crude popularization of his ideas. Anyway, it did not work: the ahistorical Lacan is very popular.)

Or, as I suggested, one can take the difficulty in deciphering Lacan's texts as a symptom: of the battle between the ego (ours and/or his?) and the truth he is seeking. (I mean, perhaps I have been unjust; he is crystal clear, but the ego interferes with the flow of understanding in reading him; on the other hand, the writing difficulty is his, and embodies the scars of his battle.) But given that Lacan also locates the need for free association in the context of the ego's era, where it substitutes for the Dialogue, he can also be read as issuing an invitation to circumvent the ego by logic, rather than free association. He can be read this way if his theory of the ego's era leads to the conclusion that there is a position beyond the dominant ego, of which more soon.

In what follows, we will try to circumvent the ego, not by rewriting history on the basis of the subject's free associations in analysis, but by the path signalled at the outset: seeking an internal consistency in Lacan's texts.[29] Whether it works or not, the next sections attempt this logical route. They try to follow the path of implication.

In the first instance, the path followed concerns the relation between the ego's master–slave dialectic and the construction of sexual differ-

---

29 Lacan's own reference to cross-checking one's path is a reference to the real; it anticipates a similar discussion in (Lacan 1972–3). For more on this non-arbitrary network, see Lacan (ibid., p. 45).

ence. After this we backtrack, establishing connections between the psychical fantasy of woman, elliptical knowledge and Lacan's historical perspective on the ego's era. I can then argue why, far from being the means of preventing the social psychosis, the psychical fantasy of woman may be its trigger; it may help explain why the territorializing and totalizing imperative arose in the West.

## 'A PASSIFYING IMAGE . . .'

The grounds for cross-referencing sexual difference to Lacan's historical perspective on the ego's era are built into his theory of sexual difference: the grounds are there in that the formation of sexual difference presupposes an imaginary component. In Lacan's theory, coming to terms with sexual difference, entry to the symbolic (assuming the position of 'I') and the constitution of the sane subject go hand in hand. I repeat: his subject is always sexed. It is formed in a complicated series of differentiations, of which the paternal symbolic break-up of the imaginary mother/child dyad is only one. In addition to differentiating between the (m)other and itself, the child must differentiate between the sexes. Moreover, recognizing the differences necessary for logical differentiation is in part the response to a sexual difference based on sight.

These differentiations are tied together by the phallus, in so far as it signifies all of them; it does not only refer to the anatomical distinction between the sexes. As I have discussed elsewhere (Brennan 1989), this poses a problem: on the one hand, the difference between masculine and feminine is like that between a and b; the masculine and feminine positions are not fixed to biology. Both sexes speak and think. On the other hand, the identification of the feminine with the absence of the penis in women and of the phallus with the penis is fetishized in desire. Lacan makes it absolutely clear that such fetishization is imaginary. But imaginary or not, the foundation of identity, and, it seems, knowledge, cannot be separated from a visual, imaginary recognition. The subject's formation is marked by the convergence of the lack in the signifying chain and the lack in the drive. Both lacks are signified by the phallus, as the privileged signifier 'of that mark where the part of the logos is joined to the coming of desire' (Lacan 1958a, p. 287). The phallus, when it is tied to the advent of desire, is tied to the visually significant penis. Critically, Heath stressed exactly this (Heath 1978).

Are the historical aspects of the imaginary, in the form of the ego's era, implicated in this imaginary tie in sexual difference? An answer to this will emerge through more enquiry into what is involved in the subject's assumption of the position of 'I'. This enquiry will also return us to the relation between the social psychosis and the spatial dialectic, the spiral of aggression.

This 'I' position is not only a matter of establishing a position in relation to the phallus; or rather, that relation depends on a 'positioning' in two senses of the word. It not only involves positioning in the more familiar Lacanian terms of sexual difference and language: an appropriate identification with and relation to the positions 'I', 'she', 'he'. It also involves a literal spatial positioning of oneself. The spatial positioning of the mirror-stage not only underlies the *méconnaissances* of the ego; it forms the spatial and specular basis on which the subject is able to assume the temporal position of 'I'. To make sense of this apparently paradoxical statement, add that the initial specular positioning of the mirror-stage is lost in the drama of rivalry and aggression that follows on from it, and it is later recovered in language. In other words the mirror-stage lays down the earliest form of the 'I'. It is then objectified and lost in the aggressive master–slave dialectic of identification with the other. And then 'language restores to it, in the universal, its function as subject' (Lacan 1949, p. 2). Given that this is the process of becoming 'I', and that a mark of psychosis is the failure to become 'I', it is appropriate to enquire further into the relation between the master–slave aggressive rivalry, and the 'match' between the 'I' position in language, and that of the spatial, specular 'I' of the mirror-stage.

The problem starts when the rival is perceived as like the self. Because of this, it becomes a threat to one's separate identity; and a threat to one's 'space', a potential invader of one's territory. But the rival is only felt to be this (a) because its likeness makes it a potential equivalent for oneself, as if only uniqueness guaranteed a place in the world, and (b) because of the assumption that the rival feels similarly: believing that the space for its separate existence is threatened, it would therefore obliterate the self.

The trouble is, despite this fear of the rival, one has to identify with that rival. As indicated above, this for Lacan is the solution to the whole drama. The rivalry generated by the mirror-stage, in which the becoming-subject loses and confuses itself in myriad others, finds its resolution in the Oedipus complex, where the subject identifies with the rival parent. This identification, as much as the competitive imitations that preceded it,[30] exemplifies the process whereby one half of the ego's internal structure is projected onto another in the social world. As this projection is basic to how it is that an individual subject identifies with the dominant side of the ego's standpoint, and thus, ultimately, how an 'ego's era' could come into being, it warrants more investigation. Let us start with the obvious problem posed by the fact that the subject manages a parental identification despite its fear of, and aggressiveness towards, its rival. How does the subject overcome its fear and aggression when confronted with the prospect of *this* identification?

We might hypothesize that the identification can only be made if it is divested of its aggression. But how could this be done, when the very foundation of the aggression is the likeness, the mirror-stage captation? Much as the subject-to-be resists this captation, it also depends on it. It needs to be recognized. The master–slave struggle is precisely a struggle for recognition, and the dilemma we are encountering might be illuminated by recalling Hegel's resolution of it. For Hegel, the master wins, in so far as the slave is fixed in a position wherein that slave has to recognize the master, while the master gives no equivalent recognition to the slave. When cast in the position of recognizer, and by this casting objectified, the slave loses the recognition necessary for becoming a subject. But while free use is made of Hegel's master–slave dialectic in psychoanalytic social thought, this is on the basis of a reading of Hegel that Gillian Rose's brilliant study shows is trapped within the very structure of mirror recognition that Hegel overcomes (Rose 1981).[31] In light of her major reinterpretation, Lacan's, and therefore Kojève's, reading of Hegel has to be treated with caution. Psychoanalytic readings of Hegel's master–slave dialectic, moreover, are usually based on an *analogy* between the structure of this psyche and Hegel's staged encounter between two consciousnesses. The notion of analogy is also misplaced. Rée has argued that Hegel himself intended the master–slave dialectic as an intrapsychical moment in the development of spirit, when the self encounters its other within. In this encounter 'what was billed as 'a life and death struggle' between 'the two self-conscious individuals' was not a real confrontation at all; nor

---

30 On identification and imitation in Lacan see Slavoj Žižek (1989), who gives an account of it which is both lucid and witty. For more on identification and sexual difference, cf. Parveen Adams (1988).

31 I cannot do justice here to Gillian Rose's aruments in *Hegel Contra Sociology* (Rose 1981), but return briefly to it below.

did it involve two individuals . . . the master–slave dialectic i\
reworking of the myth of Narcissus' (1987, p. 91).[32] This woulc\
that the master's victory depends on objectifying part of hims\
order to secure his image.

But oddly, it is Kojève's interpretation of Hegel that Lacan uses. The slave's way out, and it was Kojève not Hegel who stressed it, is through the labour in which the slave can find a mirror for existence, and on which the master depends (Kojève 1933, p. 24). Ultimately the master is trapped, and has no way out of the dyad: aside from the fact of a denied dependence, the master must endlessly refer to whilst subjugating the slave.

For Kojève, the slave has a way out. The master does not. The paradox is that, despite his use of Kojève, Lacan does find a way out for the master. The slave's psychic way out has yet to be determined. The immediate question concerns how Hegel's (intrapsychical) resolution maps onto Lacan's. We have seen that Lacan's equivalent of the dialectic is generated by the ego, because the formation of the mirror-stage image, one's self-image, the nascent *moi*, involves a captation. Or, as Lacan puts it in his famous Rome report, it involves being held still, being turned into a thing and therefore objectified: it means being 'passified'. When 'the subject makes himself an object by displaying himself before the mirror' he constitutes a 'passifying image' (Lacan 1953b, p. 42). In its context, the passive/pacification pun harks back to the discussion of the ego's aggressiveness. In its master–slave struggle to the death, the ego desires to make the other into a thing; and arrogates to itself the right to form or shape it, to objectify it, to make it passive. But it also fears retribution, so wants to pacify the other (or itself). Henceforth I shall use the terms 'passifying' and 'passification' in referring to the process, drama and drives involved here.

The ego's relation to the power of the shaper is obsessively ambivalent. For the passifying image is not just a thing to be feared; it is also its self-image. The ego is not sure who has the power of the shaper. It could be itself or its mirror-image. But it is sure that there is only one shaper, and only one shaped. To safeguard against being shaped, one has to shape.

Yet because the shaper needs a shaped to confirm it, then, like Hegel's master, the shaper has no way out. Except that the master-

32 Other readings of psychoanalysis which adapt Hegel's master–slave dialectic include Anthony Wilden (1972); Frantz Fanon, especially (1952); Homi Bhabha in the preface to this edition of Fanon; and Jessica Benjamin (1988).

shaper always has had a way out, of sorts, and it was Lacan's insight to see it. By focusing on language and the symbolic break-up of the imaginary dyad, he found an exit from the closed room of the dialectic, the Hegelian 'consciousness-in-self'. Which brings us back to what I earlier and too loosely referred to as a parental identification. Too loosely, because the 'parental' identification only works as a way out of the drama of rivalry if it is a paternal identification. But staying for now with the implications of that identification: if we recast it and the symbolic break with which it coincides in terms of the master–slave dialectic, what can be said?

In effect, what Lacan has done is to resolve the dyadic dilemma, and break out of the dialectic by arguing that the master identifies with another master. But for this to work as a way out, this identification has to be based on something other than the self-image captation of the ego. And by the same token, as the ego all too strongly persists, it has to have a basis for its self-image in something other than an identification with the master. In short, the basis of the master's identification with another master has to be distinct from the means whereby the master maintains a self-image. So how is this distinction effected? One master identifies with another on the basis that they are both shapers, both official recognizers, and crucially, in Lacan's terms, both namers. This identification is possible because both are identifying with a cultural linguistic temporal tradition that extends beyond the immediate spatial dimension of the ego. It is also possible because at the same time as he identifies with another namer, the master founds a self-image on the basis of the shaped, the underacknowledged recognizer.

And what of the shaped? At this point I will use some of the argument on femininity I have developed elsewhere (Brennan 1992), but recast it in terms that fit this Lacanian, Hegelian context. We have seen that in Oedipal terms the resolution of the passification drama is *relatively* unproblematic for the boy, remembering always that the Oedipus complex is not a matter of a straight identification with the same-sexed parent. His mother, or the parent he identifies as feminine, or indeed, any object to which he attaches his passifying drive, grounds his self-image. The boy identifies with his father, the parent he perceives as masculine, as a shaper and acknowledged recognizer, a namer, into whose dominating kingdom he will one day come. The girl on the other hand is unable to resolve the mirror-stage drama by putting her father in the passified position and objectifying him, while identifying with her mother as a namer. (Although on one reading, it was exactly this reversal that the second women's movement, in its early days, tried to effect: any negative projection of an image onto a homogenized other – 'rape is the way all men keep all women in a state of fear' – releases aggression, hence energy, for the projecter.)

Depending on the unconscious desires in her familial or personal constellation, the girl is more likely to accept the feminine position from the father as a condition of securing some sort of identity. But accepting this position only cements her to the passified side of the captation fix. That is to say, in the rivalry between the shaper and the shaped, the girl, like the boy, seeks to found her self-image on an other whom she has passified. But she will find herself in the passified position if she is unable to direct her aggression towards another with whom she does not identify. She may try to direct this aggression to her mother, and try very hard not to identify with her, only to find that her mother is locked into the same *cul-de-sac*, and is as reluctant to accept the passified position on her daughter's behalf as the daughter is to take it on for her mother. The rivalry of the struggle over self-image leads to the paradox, evident especially in relations between women, that you are more likely to be anxious about the success or advantage of those who are closest to or like you than of those to whom you are indifferent.

Both mother and daughter turn to the father-namer for the release provided by an identification beyond the self-image drama, but as the man may be more interested in securing his self-image through passifying the woman, neither mother nor daughter find that release in the phallus they try to borrow. Nonetheless, they may persist for years in looking for it in the wrong place. But having hoped for a releasing recognition from the bearer of the phallus, having never got it, the woman may eventually turn against her husband in the way she did against her mother. Here we can locate Freud's observation that women begin by relating to their husbands as they did to their fathers, and end up relating to them as they did to their mothers (Freud 1933, p. 133). Moreover, when a woman does not receive the phallus from the man 'as a gift', this often leads her to abandon her quest for it in a particular man. Herein we often see the master–slave dialectic reversed. The man may find that his disappointed woman ceases to ground his image, which happens when she turns her attention elsewhere. When his image is withdrawn, his dereliction can be tragic; he has often had no life preparation to deal with it.

The woman who has abandoned her quest for a releasing identification (otherwise known as the phallus) in one man may seek it in

another man, or in her son, or even her daughter. Or she may look for it
in an identification with another woman. But she will only find it here
if both move beyond the squabble over who grounds whose self-image,
and into a situation where they are both able to turn outwards, and
perceive a reality beyond themselves. Of course this can only be done if
'both' are grounded in a social cultural linguistic tradition in which they
are recognized, and which extends beyond the two of them. (Here we
might re-situate Irigaray's arguments for a 'female symbolic', discussed
in Whitford (1990).)

Incidentally, it is because they minimize this social, symbolic aspect
in their account of the cause of patriarchy that certain Chodorovian
advocates of equal parenting, some of whom also use Hegel, found their
case on a misrecognition (the best are Benjamin 1988; also Jane Flax
1990). The word *cause* is important here. Reading Chodorow, and the
more Kleinian Dinnerstein, one is left with the impression (despite
disclaimers) that if we have equal parenting, so that the mother is not
the initial sole repository of ambivalent love (the *cause* of patriarchy)
then patriarchy 'will wither away'. But it would be perfectly possible to
have equal parents at home while the father maintains a prerogative on
social prestige and power. By any Lacanian or Lacan-influenced account,
the significance of the identification with this socially powerful father
will cancel out any positive effects of equal parenting.

Equal parenting will not solve the generation of inequality between
the sexes, let alone between races and classes, unless the equal parents
have equivalent social power. If one parent is identified with and as a
social shaper, the other as a shaped, the current sexual identities will
continue to be reconstructed. Equal parenting as such may make some
relational difference, to the empathy of boys and the effectiveness of
girls (although I doubt it), but its significance is more likely to lie in the
extent to which it frees the mother to develop her creative and social
capacities. Also, the extent to which it does make a difference to the
kind of human being we produce, whether it makes that being more
kind, and less competitive, envious, aggressive and egocentric, will
depend on a variety of factors. For instance, it will depend on whether
father or mother use the daughter (and less probably the son) as an
objectified prop for an ego flagging in the face of a world in which it
feels itself to be ineffective; and whether the mother recognizes her
daughter, as well as her son; and whether the daughter can identify
with her mother as one who names and acts. In short, the desire of the
other has a great deal to do with what we become. A mother who has an

intense unconscious desire for her daughter to go forth rather ti multiply will subvert the course of her daughter's passification. B, while exceptions to the simplistic identification of boy with father, gir, with mother occur, the dead weight of previous generations (*pace* Marx) means that in general the woman is more likely to be maintained in the passified position the man needs her in, in that maintaining her in this position is the condition of his securing his self-image, and his 'entry into the symbolic'.

The self-image of the shaped is founded on another who is seen as passified. The other is seen as passified in that it is fixed on the side where it recognizes the shaper. In this process, it becomes the locus of a negative image. The image is negative because the one who is fixed in the passifying position is seen as the repository for everything that the passifier, in order to maintain its superior position (the ego's dominant standpoint), wants to project outwards. I will argue below that these projections have a physical energetic economy; the projection into another of negativity, with the disordered death drive it contains, frees the one who projects to act. More psychical energy is available; it is less necessary for the actor to direct it inwards in maintaining an immobilizing self-image, for the image is precisely guaranteed by the shaped. For Lacan, who did not pursue the implications of his mirror-stage morphology for an intersubjective economy of energy, visual representations are used in the projective process, but they are not its cause: a fact that is reflected in the terms 'negative image', 'bad image', which are not tied to visual representations as such, but which none the less point to the mirror-stage origins of the passification process. In this process, it will be recalled, the passifier fears retaliation for the badness projected onto the other. Both the fear, and the way the other is seen are caught by bell hooks, who analyses why Blacks were not permitted, even on pain of death, to look Whites in the eye (hooks 1992). The look is caught by Bhabba, introducing Fanon. It is

> the exchange of looks between native and settler that structures this psychic relation i the paranoid fantasy of boundless possession and its familiar language of reversal: 'When their glances meet he [the settler] ascertains bitterly, always on the defensive, "They want to take our place." '
>
> (Bhabha 1986, p. xv)

The look, *le regard*, the way the other is seen, emanates from the spatially oriented aggressiveness by which the passifier seeks to fix the other in place in order to secure recognition. It is the aggressive projection of the position it does not want to occupy, and that it fears losing; a positioning founded in its image of itself. It has been argued that critics conflate Lacan's work on the mirror-stage with his later work on the gaze (Copjec 1989b, p. 68), and that the mirror-stage is not in essentials different from Sartre's 'look'.[33] Lacan's own account of the difference and the similarities between himself and Sartre is elaborated in his *Four Fundamental Concepts of Psychoanalysis*; this seminar also provides the most accessible treatment of the look, and the triangular dynamics (in which master, ego and mirror are always present) of the look. It is also the place where the sinister, negative effects of the look are plainest, for it discusses the aggressive, envious drives with which it is imbued (for example, Lacan 1964, pp. 118–19).

But as I suggested at the outset, there is more logical consistency in Lacan's *oeuvre* than he claimed. By following a speculative path, thinking through the implications of Lacan's appropriation of Hegel and aggressiveness, we have drawn out an implication in Lacan's early work on the mirror-stage which he makes explicit subsequently, and in another context. This implication is that the look is negative, and its negativity hinges on the relation to the master. The master does not feature in the dyadic relation of the imaginary mirror-stage; he belongs in the Lacanian symbolic. But he is present, by implication, in the rivalrous dynamic just discussed. The point here is that the aggression and envy, and the tie to the identification with the master's desire, are there in the more youthful Lacan's work . . . in the shadows and the ellipses, waiting to be discovered by an older man with a meaner gaze.

To continue with the main thread: the imaginary process of fixing the other is not only confined to *seeing*; it also involves naming. More accurately, naming is part of how the other is seen, as well as being part of the way out. In sum, when the master becomes the master, identified with and as a namer-shaper, released into and through a cultural linguistic tradition, the master simultaneously directs aggression towards the one who is seen to be passified. But this leaves the passified in a position where they are dependent (at the level of the ego) on the image they receive from the other. They are dependent in as much as

---

33 This is Macey's position. For both Sartre and Lacan, 'the ego is viewed as an illusory representation, as a source and focus of alienation' (1988, p. 103). For Jay, 'both authors also shared a deep distrust of the spatialized self created by the reifying look, a distrust traceable to the revaluation of temporality in Bergson and Heidegger' (1993, p. 345). None the less Lacan criticized existentialism, apparently for its optimism (1949, p. 6), and presumably the optimism is about overcoming alienation.

they accept rather than project the image, and dependent again in as much as they have no cultural linguistic tradition through which they can identify with each other. Their means to identification through naming and verbal thought is received from, and directed towards, the masters, who have a monopoly on a linguistic currency (dare I say the *lingua franca*?) and cultural tradition through which naming takes place.

It would seem here that we have happened on a version of Lacan's account of the formation of sexual difference. Or we would have done, except that this version emphasizes that any other who is representing negativity can serve the purpose of fixation, and be the locus of passification. It also reveals that sexual difference is not only informed by the visual representation of difference; it is informed by the passifying 'looks that kill' (although sexual difference need not be structured in this way; see below).

At this point, I want to argue that this account is consistent with Lacan's. First, because Lacan also emphasizes that *any* other object, separate or separable from the subject, can be fixed on in securing subjectivity. Second, because it is consistent with (and makes internally consistent) Lacan's shifting views on vision. Third, the theory of the ego's era implies that the construction of sexual difference and the psychical fantasy of woman no longer resolve the massive passification demands generated by the spiral of aggression.

The preceding points will be clarified after more discussion of sexual difference, taking account of the psychical fantasy of woman. In fact, for Lacan, the tendency to homogenize sexual difference is part of the course of the ego's era. In terms of the argument so far, however, sexual difference would only be homogenized because another form of social difference takes over. In this form, the world is broadly divided into shapers and shaped, aggressors and passified.

In other words, in the ego's era some are broadly secured on the dominant side of the ego's standpoint. However, they are not completely secured there. It is perfectly possible to occupy the dominant position in economic and institutional life, and the passified position elsewhere. But one is more likely to be secured on the dominant side if one is privileged in the white, Western, masculine culture in which the era originates – which reintroduces the notion that the spiral of aggression has a possible point of departure in the psychical fantasy of woman. More specifically, it has points of departure: (a) in the way in which the 'man' makes the 'woman' the negative, the other, both to secure his recognition and simultaneously be passified, making him the victor in the master–slave dialectic, and (b) in the way in which the ideal woman of fantasy takes over from the God or Truth that concerned him hitherto.

In order to highlight the role of the fantasy in the ego's passifying resolution, this time, I will re-approach the issues through the more familiar terms of the masculine Oedipus complex. In turn, this will lead to discussion of a connection between a block on knowledge, that Lacan relates to the psychical fantasy of woman, and the ego's blocks on knowledge.

## 'THE PATH OF LOGIC . . .'

A social linguistic tradition in which he is recognized is what the boy enters one day, provided he 'defers' his desire for the mother, which he does, for Freud, by believing he will come to possess a woman who substitutes for his mother in the future, and by divorcing his affectionate and sexual feelings for his mother (Freud 1910). In Lacan's terms, as noted, that divorce is effected via the psychical fantasy of woman; she is idealized on the one hand, denigrated on the other. In the former capacity, she is the locus of his truth, and in this occupies the position once occupied by God. On this count, Lacan and at least one Renaissance scholar agree:

> At the point at which supernatural or spiritual powers began to be attributed to a female object of desire, there was an attempt to erase all traces of active sexuality from this figure. This seems to have been motivated not just by the Christian connection of physical purity with spirituality, but also by the desire to make the sign of woman better capable of mirroring a transcendent dimension which, once contacted, could enable the male lover to forge a new and idealized identity.
>
> (Berry 1989, p. 18).

But in the capacity in which the woman is not idealized but denigrated, she is the repository for man's aggression, albeit in a form where that aggression need not be recognized as such. For one can 'passify' the other, meaning one can reduce it to a state of comparative stillness, in the most loving ways (aside from binding its foot, or putting it in a corset, or denying it the institutional and economic means where, through its creative labour, it can contribute to the formation of a cultural tradition in which it is recognized).

For Freud the denigration of women – and here the implications drawn in this discussion start to come together – is notoriously tied to a sighting. It is the sight of women's genitals, the absence of a penis, that leads the man to denigrate the different other. I argued above that this sighting is tied to another imaginary episode – it is tied to the process whereby the master (the ego) secures a self-image in the slave (the other side of the ego). It is tied to the process whereby he passifies the other. What should be clear now is that the denigration involved in the psychical fantasy of woman is also informed by the aggression triggered in the master–slave dialectic. Remembering that visual difference is not the source of denigration, it can be noted here that the 'sexual difference' serves as an excuse. It enables the man identified with the ego's dominant standpoint to take more than he gives in the ego's currency of recognition; the denigratory (and, by this account, passifying) aspect of the psychical fantasy of woman gives the man the means for securing his subjectivity in the form of his self-image, at the same time as it enables him to turn outwards.

He has secured the position from which he can think, indeed speculate. He can turn outward. He is not trapped in the absolute self-referentiality of the ego seeking affirmation of its existence, except in one respect. The condition of his outward-turning is that his image is held secure, and he thinks and speculates on the basis of the same condition. The notion that the man is only able to turn outwards on the basis of an image secured in the other is why the symbolic, the means for going beyond, is implicated in the imaginary in Lacan's early theory. And it is here that Lacan's own impulse to connect failed him. Yet while he never elaborates a specific connection between the resolution of the ego's master–slave dilemma, and the denigration in the fantasy of woman, he comes very close to it in his subsequent work.

A parallel connection is implicit in his own argument on how symbolic subjectivity always needs an imaginary anchor. At first he described this imaginary anchor as the *objet petit a*. The concept of the 'a' broadens the means whereby the subject is able to secure itself. It can be any thing that is separate, or separable, from the subject (Lacan 1977, p. 103). Bowie (1991) argues that, as with so much else in Lacan, there is an early 'a' and a later 'a'. Both are 'caught up in language . . . a relay-station that distorted all messages passing through it' (pp. 165–6). But the meaning of the first is never entirely lost. It is a separable object that is foundational to the subject, which engages the subject's desire; it is the other side of, and the condition of, the eternal Lacanian 'split-subject'.

No-one has made the nature of the split-subject, and the reasons why the split is apparently eternal, plainer than Žižek (1989). Now the idea that the Lacanian subject is always split because it is born into language, and that language is imposed upon its flesh in a manner that is always alienating, has been stressed often enough. What Žižek does is to draw out the implications of this split for all ideologies, even those dearest to us. Žižek, like Laclau and Mouffe (1985), defines the split at the core of the subject as 'an original "trauma", an impossible kernel which resists symbolization, totalization, symbolic integration. Every attempt at symbolization–totalization comes afterwards: it is an attempt to suture an original cleft – an attempt which is, in the last resort, by definition doomed to failure' (Žižek 1989, p. 6).

Aside from the comment on totalization, which I have already discussed in terms of the need to understand a totalizing imperative in reality, the issue here is the impossible kernel, which gives the split, and with it some form of *objet a*, a special status as the human condition. The split itself always involves the negativity of Freud's death drive, for language itself is felt as deathly by the body. And there is always something at the core of the subject, which in essence is the knowledge of this split, which cannot be put into words. To say that the knowledge of the split cannot be put into words is of course to begin putting this knowledge into words; to resolve the paradox, we need to stress that this knowledge is itself a residuum of psychical energy, which wants an out through words and cannot have it, because words are what trap it. This excess energy, as Žižek makes plain, is loaded onto the *objet a*, 'the leftover which embodies the fundamental, constitutive lack' (1989, p. 53).[34] The left-over embodies the lack because the 'lack' is the fact that the subject cannot express 'something more'.

Part of the difficulty with these ideas, a difficulty that gives rise to the paradoxical language in which so many Lacanian ideas are expressed, is then that the 'content' of lack and of the kernel remains

---

34 Žižek talks of drives, particularly the death drive, rather than energy. I have used the term energy because, while Freud's discussion of the drives is confused when it comes to representation, his texts overall presuppose that the drives are split from a more originary psychical energy *through* representation (Brennan 1992, Ch. 3). Hence what resists representation, while it can certainly consist of drives, is at its core a form of energy existing prior to them.

unspecified. As the argument is that the kernel cannot be specified, this seems fair enough, and at one level it cannot be gainsaid. However, there is another level at which we can know more of the 'impossible kernel'. Lacan in his later seminars refers to a 'fundamental fantasy'. It is not the same as my 'foundational fantasy', but it is also tied to the splitting of the subject. It is thus tied to the deathly residuum of the kernel. As far as Lacan exemplifies it, this fundamental fantasy is most evident in sadism and masochism. In its workings it parallels our analysis of how the other, like the self, is made into an object. For Lacan it is part of the human condition, which means the notion of the fundamental fantasy is consistent too with Žižek's argument that the kernel is part of the human condition: it and the *objets a* it fixes on underpin all attempts at idealization, and inform all ideologies of redemption. It does so in that these ideologies are unselfconscious of their impulse to project their negativity onto the other while believing that they, as the bearers of the ideology in question, embody the perfect solution (and hence some form of perfection). For Laclau and Mouffe, this analysis of a fundamental and inescapable antagonism at the root of all social life leads to the advocacy of a radical pluralism, which is in part the capacity for tolerance. I could not agree more with their advocacy of tolerance.

The problem is that less politically conscious thinkers can easily make this account of the inevitability of projection and splitting into a celebration of pluralism, which not only prescribes pluralism for the future, but which takes a falsely pluralistic view of the present (Fukuyama 1992) and the recent past: falsely pluralistic because the fact that certain projections have advantaged some groups and classes over others is tactfully downplayed.

In the same vein: Lacan's *objet a* has pluralistic potential; just about anything can be an *a*, an occasion for splitting and projection. But while Lacan's examples of *objets a* proliferate, he is absolutely clear that the *a* can be a woman (Lacan 1975, p. 167) and it is to a woman that he returns in exemplifying the *objet a*; she comes up again and again. This return tacitly recognizes that historically, a favourite form of *objet a*, namely the woman, has dominated. The idea that the *objet a* can be anything in principle does not mean it has been anything in fact. But before addressing this in detail, the issue I want to raise in connection with the *a* is that it makes explicit what was presupposed but untheorized in the early theory of the ego, and the notion of an ego's era. That is to say, the idea that the ego secures its self-image by passification, and projecting its other half into the world, is paralleled by the idea that the *a* secures subjectivity in something separate or separable. This conceptual parallel exists, I am arguing, because different levels of the same process are being described. But the questions then become: what happens, in this parallel, to the aggressiveness in securing subjectivity? Second, what happens to the symbolic tradition which afforded a releasing identification to the masculine subject? The answer to the first question is that denigration, the aggressiveness in securing subjectivity, reappears in a different guise, but it is recognized as if it were new; it is not applied to women. The answer to the second question is that it is at this point that Lacan gives an explicit account of why there is no clean break between the imaginary and the symbolic. In doing so, what he emphasizes is not denigration, but the idealization of woman. He does so via the concept of the Other.

The Other is the 'locus of speech and potentially of truth' (Lacan 1972–3, p. 129). As a concept, it is related to that of the symbolic. When the subject secures the 'I' position, and thereby enters the symbolic, it is also entering a realm of knowledge that goes beyond itself; in this it is establishing its relation to the Other, as the origin and sum of all chains of signification. However, what the subject can know is limited by the nature of its imaginary anchor, its *objet petit a*; it cannot see past it. The *a* as the point of the symptom has to be circumvented, the Other links in the chains of signification followed by free associating, in order that the subject go beyond the meaning it gave its speech from its own standpoint.

Lacan's pre-eminent interest was in how it is that the subject managed to conflate its *objet petit a* with the big A, the *Autre* or Other. For he argued that the subject did conflate them, and in this conflation, implicated the symbolic in the imaginary.

> The aim of our teaching . . . is to dissociate the *a* and the O, by reducing the former to what belongs to the imaginary and the latter to what belongs to the symbolic. That the symbolic is the support of that which was made into God, is beyond doubt . . . .
>
> (Lacan 1972–3, p. 77, pp. 153–4)

If its past tense is taken into account, the last sentence points to how it is that the subject manages this conflation. The symbolic once supported what was made into God, but it now supports what is made into woman. It seems the woman comes to represent, 'in the phallocentric dialectic, the absolute Other' (Lacan 1958b, p. 94). How she does so is evident in two ways. The first is that the nascent subject confuses the mother, a small other, with the Other as the exterior language into which it is born. The second and related way by which the woman comes to stand in for the Other has already been indicated. She becomes the locus of his truth, the thing he believes in. It is clear for Lacan that a purely formal belief in God could coincide with the woman as what the man really believes in. In fact, it is the transition to this deep belief in, this idealization of, the woman that marks the historicity of the psychical fantasy of woman. By Riley's account, it also marks the historicity of the *category* of 'woman', which comes into vogue in this transitional time (Riley 1988). But by this account, it does so not only to conceal differences, but to seal off and cover up something else as well. By believing in the *woman*, the man comes to close off the potential the endless symbolic afforded him hitherto. He does so because he has made both his *objet petit a* and his way out, his symbolic Other, into the same object. Far from being a way out, the symbolic Other is now something he believes he controls.

Control has already been referred to in the discussion of the ego's era and objectifying knowledge. It is worth adding here that in the context of his remarkable seminar on sexuality and knowledge, *Encore*, Lacan makes another implicit connection between the blocks on knowledge produced by the *objet petit a* and the knowledge blocks of the ego's era. In comments reminiscent of his condemnation of objectification in science in the ego's era, Lacan writes that one side of scientific discourse

> makes you to a much greater extent than you are aware, the subject of instruments which, from the microscope to the radio-television, become elements of your existence.
>
> (Lacan 1972–3, p. 76, p. 152)

Lacan continues by writing that this science and the conceptual knowledge that subtends it has its origin in the *objet a*, which is produced in a sexual fantasy that makes up for the fact that there is no sexual relation (between two subjects; there is only a relation between master–subject and slave–object). This compensatory *a* results in the categories passive and active, categories which are at base of the division between form (or intelligence) and matter which, for Lacan, has dominated in the West since Plato, categories which are reflected in the categories 'subject' and 'object'. But the implicit connection between the objectifying knowledge of the ego's era and the idea that a sexual fantasy supported by an *objet a*, which in turn supports the division between mind and matter, subject and object, breaks off.[35]

Had Lacan pursued the connection between objectifying knowledge and sexual fantasy, we might have had an explicit discussion of what has here, perforce, been inferred. That is to say, what we have gained by establishing these connections between Lacan's earlier and subsequent writings is more than consistency. We have also laid out the basis of an argument on how the psychical fantasy of woman fosters an ego's era. But there are two subsidiary matters that should be addressed before returning to this argument.

One is that although the *objet a* concept loses the explicitly passifying aspects of the means by which the ego maintains its self-image in the woman, it is a critical innovation. It means that the formulation of sexual difference and sexual desire are not tied to any essential whole body; desire can be born from any (separable) object. Also, if Lacan's actual references to the *a* are studied, it is clear that he tacitly recognizes an asymmetry in who or what gets to play the part of the *a*, and in this tacit recognition, the massive social disparity between the sexes inferred in the ego's era re-enters the scene. In referring to the woman as an *objet a* causing desire, Lacan also notes that the woman 'busies herself with other *objet a*, being children' (Lacan 1975, p. 167). The thing is, her *objets a* are not men. By this account, they could scarcely be men, if the woman is already occupying the passified position.

The second matter I wish to raise before returning to the ego's era concerns an 'other side' of scientific knowledge, which Lacan outlines in *Encore* in order to contrast it with the objectified science of the 'radio-television' and other technological accoutrements. This should also indicate how Lacan's earlier formulation of psychoanalysis as the 'true science' that runs counter to the ego's era comes to be developed, and its logical concerns made explicit, in opposition to knowledge blocks that are now attributed to the *objet a* and sexual fantasy. The 'other side' of scientific discourse is 'subversive'. It is the side that psychoanalysis inherits, and it was glimpsed in the Galilean revolution:

there was a moment when with some justification we were able to boast that scientific discourse had been founded on the Galilean

---

35  However, it could be pursued in the context of how the *objet a*, as the meeting point of the lack in the drive and the lack in the signifying chain, implicates the death drive. There is a relevant argument in Joan Copjec (1989b).

turning point. I have stressed this often enough to mean that some of you will have gone back to the sources, meaning to the work of Koyré.

(Lacan 1972–3, p. 76, p. 152).

Lacan does not elaborate on Koyré, a controversial philosopher of science,[36] who believed that 'it is thought, pure unadulterated thought, not experiences or sense perception, as until then, that gives the basis for the "new science" of Galileo Galilei . . .' (Koyré 1943). Koyré believed that Galileo renounced an Aristotelian 'variegated, qualitative world of sense/perception and common experience' and replaced it with a 'colourless abstract' (Platonic) world, where nature is governed by the laws and relations of numbers. Galileo's reasoning process, in which logic preceded experimentation, went against and was challenged by his Aristotelian opponents, who based their conclusions on common sense, on the senses we have in common, on what they could *see*; 'we must choose: either to think or to imagine. To think with Galileo or to imagine with common sense' (ibid.).

Apparently then, for Lacan, Plato occupies an ambiguous position in relation to good and bad knowledge: on the one hand, he held to a reason that went beyond visual common sense; on the other, he divorced form and matter. Nonetheless the distinction between thinking and imagining provides a key to Lacan's attempt to tie psychoanalysis to the 'abstract, colourless world of numbers'. I mean mathematics. Throughout his post-Rome work, Lacan tends more and more to explicate, perhaps to substantiate, his theory by algorithms and equations. Lacan's mathematical leanings are queried by some of his readers. Gallop notes that Clément wonders if Lacan's mathematical devices, 'all these equations, are not façades to hide the shabbiness of a thought at its wit's end' (Clément 1981; cited Gallop 1985, p. 161). Gallop does not feel free to dismiss these devices, and I think she is right. Lacan's mathematical explications, by this argument, are part of an attempt to formulate how psychoanalysis, as 'true science', goes beyond the blocks on knowledge produced by the ego's *seeing* the other in order to fix it in place, or by the symptomatic *objet a*. Consider this observation of Lacan's on the real.

The real can only inscribe itself out of an impasse in formalisation. It

36 Koyré's hypothesis is seriously questioned by English-speaking philosophers of science: I use him less to endorse his interpretation of Galileo's reception as a battle between Aristotelians and Platonists than as a palimpsest for interpreting Lacan.

is for this reason that I have believed it possible to draw the model of
it [the real] starting from the mathematical formulation, inasmuch
as this is the most developed elaboration of the process of meaning
[*signifiance*] that we have been able to produce. This mathematical
formalisation of the process of meaning runs contrary to sense
[*sens*].

(Lacan 1972–3, p. 85)

What Lacan is doing here (I think) is distinguishing between the
process of producing meaning (*signifiance*) which of itself means
nothing fixed, and the attachment to a fixed sense (*sens*). This
distinction is not one between meaning and non-meaning. The distinction is precisely between producing meaning, and settling on it. It is a
distinction that echoes the earlier insistence on rewriting history, and
making connections, as a means for going beyond the present
standpoint. Almost immediately after the passage just quoted, Lacan
compares mathematics, which finds its coherence in the written
formula, with Hegel's historical theory, which coheres in spite of the
contrasts in the Hegelian dialectic, and with whatever we do, or is done,
in analysis (ibid., p. 86). These last cannot be right in any final sense,
but they move. There is another hint that Lacan throws out at this
point: he notes Spinoza's amazement on the extent to which the
structure of writing parallels that of the natural order (1972–3, p. 36).
Of course Lacan says no more, but this allusion in itself is a far cry from
thinking limited to a language based on binary oppositions. It is also a
way to begin thinking about logic in something other than subject–
object terms: in one respect, it is consistent with any argument that
(the prototype of) logic could be the generative chain of sensory natural
connections, with their own impeccable order, which writing and
reasoning, at their best, attempt to approximate. On Gillian Rose's
reinterpretation, Hegel is as relevant here as Spinoza. Rose draws out
how Hegel's speculative logic goes beyond any form of matching or
oppositional category in a kind of generative growth process, in a logic
which also goes beyond the subject. The subject–object distinction, as I
indicated earlier, cuts up connections and tries to re-establish them
from the subject's own standpoint.

Lacan himself did not propose a logic based in the natural order, and
his attitude to Spinoza is in fact ambivalent. In *Les Psychoses*, Lacan
compares Spinoza's thought with that of Daniel Paul Schreber, whose
memoirs of his psychosis prompted Freud to write an analysis of them

(Freud 1911). In reading Schreber, 'we are not far from the Spinozan universe, to the extent that it is founded on the coexistence of the attribute of thought and the attribute of extension. Very interesting dimension for situating the imaginary quality of certain stages of philosophical thought' (Lacan 1955–6b, p. 79). Aside from the implication that the social psychosis hit Spinoza full on ahead of time, the comparison of Spinoza and Schreber makes the perception of conative energy that transcends individual boundaries psychotic. (Perceiving it is not the same thing as theorizing it; although Schreber did both, Spinoza to our knowledge only theorized.) So on the one hand, Lacan compares Spinoza's theory with Schreber's world-view. On the other, Lacan seems to endorse the parallel between writing and the natural order, which presupposes that both are underpinned by logical connection. We will try to disentangle these orders, which compare with the two orders in the real, in Part II.

To sum up: I have argued that there is a parallel between the *objet a* and the means by which the ego maintains its self-image, and argued that the passification involved here informs the denigration that marks the recognition of sexual difference. As sexual difference is also the point where logic meets desire, which Lacan elsewhere ties to the *objet a*, it is evidently the block past which reason does not venture. But it is this block not because of the difference involved (differentiating is the core of logic) but because the man makes the woman into an object that confirms his identity. He compounds this block by trying to identify the woman with the Other (making her his Truth and the locus of the word) which means that he tries to make the Other, which could have taken him beyond himself, into something he controls. In the denigration that parallels the ego's aggressiveness, in the objectification and control that limit knowledge, the fantasy of woman is the prototype for the massive passification and knowledge-reversal of the ego's era.

Currently, for Lacan, the limits on logic lie in the *objet petit a*, the kernel of ideology, and the fantasy of woman. This leaves the woman in a rather odd position. She is writing in a time where logic is meant to be tied to phallocentrism, as indeed it is for the 'man'; he purchases his ability to turn outwards, to think beyond himself, by grounding his image in her. Yet, many writers, having realized that this egocentric grounding is there, have made the exercise of logic one with a phallic identity, and condemn all logic as phallogocentrism (cf. Harding 1986). Before summing up and returning to the Western historical course, in which the *objet a* of the woman held the ego's era in check, let us note that logic, in the commonly understood sense of that term, has had a bad press because of its association with phallic identity and the ego and, by extension, an objectifying reasoning.[37] Given the tie between objectification and the subject–object distinction, and the significance of the latter in this argument overall, a note on the difference between logic and objectifying reason seems appropriate.

Perhaps the most appropriate way to differentiate them in this context is to capture the negative aggressive emotions that imbue objectifying reason. To do this, I suggest the term 'sadodispassionate' for the objectifying reason which is other than logic. The term 'sadodispassionate' is meant to indicate that the dispassionate attitude, even when it is manifest in what could otherwise be described as 'fair', 'just' and so on, has an edge in common with sadism when it is directed towards another. When the dispassionate attitude is directed inwards, it is the means for detaching or distancing oneself, for evaluating, endorsing or refusing anything from one's passions in the seventeenth century (cf. James 1994) to the unconscious or bad faith in this one. It is the vehicle for self-criticism of desires and feelings which otherwise strive to legitimate themselves simply because they are *our* feelings' (*our* feelings matter, and the other can go hang). When directed towards another, the dispassionate merges readily with sadism in that it denies or cuts off empathy or identification with the other.

The sadodispassionate has concealed its presence under the cloak of the opposition between reason and emotion. Another way of putting this is to say that while 'being reasonable' and 'being emotional' refer to apparently opposed states, both these states are emotional ones. The opposition between them consists in the nature of the emotions involved. The refusal of empathy in a dry attitude can also be an aggressive act towards the one who is refused. When the one asks the other to 'be reasonable', the request could well be sadodispassionate. The opposition between reason and emotion permits the sadodispassionate to masquerade as reason or logic on the binary grounds that it is simply, apparently not emotional. That this non-emotionality is only apparent has also been commented on by Fox Keller (1985), who describes the objective attitude as 'affectively imbued'. From the foregoing, it is clear that the affects imbuing this attitude are aggressive, sadistic and narcissistic.

37 A similar point is made by Longino and Doell (1983) in their excellent critique (see also Fausto-Sterling 1985, Tuana 1989 and Haraway 1989).

Lacan's own position is similar precisely in that he sees the barrier on logic as an objectifying fantasy. His way beyond the limitation on logic lay in analysis. Yet this chapter implies that there are other means for circumventing that limitation. If the grounding of an image sets the limits on logic, if it is a barrier to logic rather than coeval with it, then by implication the shaped, those whose identities are not founded on the aggressive passification of others, are more likely to see and think past that barrier.

They can do this much, but they can only express what they see if they have an anchor that enables them to express it – or rather, two anchors, one being a means for identification in a cultural tradition, and the second being a grounding for self-image. Finding the first anchor is complicated by the fact that they are to some inevitable degree identified with the dominant culture. Finding the second anchor in a non-exploitative way would entail exploring the complicated concept of co-operation. And yes, these other anchors will in turn constitute new points of closure or blind spots, new ellipses whose filling in would call differently anchored identities into question.[38] But to seek other anchors is also to gain some understanding of the present standpoint.

## 'THE SYMPTOM, AS DEFINED BY MARX IN THE SOCIAL. . .'

So far, I have indicated that the psychical fantasy of woman and the ego's era have a common source, in so far as both have their origin in the process of passification: the means whereby the ego maintains its self-image. The difference between them is one of magnitude. This shift in magnitude is somewhat similar to the shift Heidegger identifies from the (post-Socratic) Greek way of seeing and knowing embodied in *techne* to actual technological expansion on the grand scale (Heidegger 1949, p. 13). Heidegger describes a kind of 'mindset': an attitude in which the seeing of the other is simultaneously a shaping of it; to some degree, Lacan follows suit.

This attitude, this objectifying potentiality, is always present, but only makes itself fully actual and dominant in the modern age. It is vital to remember this in analysing the ego's spiral of aggression. Lacan

---

38 Laclau and Mouffe discuss identity in terms of Lacan's *points de caption*, the fixed points of signification where the signifier stops sliding, because they are embedded in the subject's psyche precisely in order to secure some unmoving reference points, whatever the cost in terms of knowledge.

describes a variety of effects which apparently begin with changing patterns in spatialization: colonization, urban and territorial expansion; he also refers to changing language use. But the passification process pre-dates the seventeenth century. It is the means by which the ego always has secured its self-image in the West. Here, we should encounter the objection that it has also secured its self-image in this manner elsewhere. In addition, while I noted the ethnocentrism of the psychical fantasy of woman at the outset, there are some other cultures where women are split into two types. But what seems to make the psychical fantasy of woman specific to the West is that its other side, its ideal side, is reputed to substitute for Truth or God. In making the woman both the repository of his truth and substitute for God (as Lacan argues he does, at a certain 'historical moment') the man is directing his urge to control and his belief in something beyond himself to the same object. He has no reference point for his 'I' that is distinct from his ego, in that he has no grounds for separating that to which he defers (the woman as truth) from that which he seeks to shape. This factor may be critical in the knowledge 'reversal' of the ego's era, in which the subject refers everything to itself, rather than finding itself in the other.

In the context of the notion that the psychical fantasy of woman is probably Western, it is worth recording another of Lacan's remarks on the ego's era. 'What we are faced with, to employ the jargon that corresponds to man's subjective needs, is the increasing absence of all those saturations of the superego and ego-ideal that are realized in all kinds of organic forms in traditional societies. . .' (Lacan 1948, p. 26). If and as the woman becomes the ideal, so do other projections of that ideal, exemplified in God in particular, decline.

The idea that the passification of women pre-dates the ego's era needs to be stressed in case this argument is read as nostalgia. If the psychical potential for the ego's era was and always is present in a passification process by which the ego secures its image at the other's expense, then the ego's era (Lacan), the modern age (Heidegger), the Classical age . . . and its discontinuous aftermath (Foucault), or simply capitalism (Marx), has merely built on an already established process of passification. To go back, to yearn for 'the (patriarchal, feudal) world we have lost' is to wish not only to re-build a dam that broke, but to re-establish the conditions of its overflow. If the denigration in the psychical fantasy of woman did constitute a dam for the ego's aggressiveness, it is also one of the means whereby the ego gets out of hand. That is to say, fixing the woman in the place whereby she afforded recognition whilst embodying the negative image may have contained aggression, but it is also a condition of aggression. For the process of passifying the other generates the fear of retaliation, hence anxiety, and hence more aggressiveness.

If the psychical fantasy of woman is a means for the man to control that to which he hitherto deferred (God becomes the woman as Truth), and if he has no reference point for his identity beyond what he controls, then this too would feed his anxiety. If he defers to something he acknowledges to be beyond him, then he is not only reliant for his identity on the self-image he founds in the passified other. There is a 'break', in the sense of an alternative, to the process by which he generates more anxiety and fear of retaliation, at the same time as he founds his self-image. Without that his only option is to *do it again*. He has to find further outlets for anxiety, which means extending his arena of aggression and control. 'He', in the sense of one identified with the dominant ego, has been endlessly ingenious in his quest for new peoples, territories, and natural resources to make over in his own image. In this quest lies the social trend to totalization in reality. In Part II we turn to how that totalizing trend realizes itself materially, in terms of an interactive (energetic and monetary) economy that makes the ego a global force. If the psychical fantasy of woman has covered over this material force, it is time to get beneath it.

# Part II

'(T)he commodity.' That is what I analyse, and I analyse it initially in the form in which it appears.

Karl Marx, *Marginal Notes on Wagner*

# Chapter 3

# The foundational fantasy

Summing up the 'doctrine of antiquity' in a sentence, Benjamin writes: 'They alone shall possess the earth who live from the powers of the cosmos'. He continues:

> the exclusive emphasis on an optical connection to the universe, to which astronomy very quickly led, contained a portent of what was to come. The ancients' intercourse with the cosmos had been very different: the ecstatic trance. . . . It is the dangerous error of modern man to regard this experience as unimportant and unavoidable, and to consign it to the individual as the poetic experience of starry nights. It is not; its hour strikes again and again, and then neither nations nor generations can escape it, as was made terribly clear by the last war . . . . Human multitudes, gases, electrical forces were hurled into the open country, high-frequency currents coursed through the landscape, new constellations rose in the sky, aerial space and ocean depths thundered with propellers, and everywhere sacrificial shafts were dug in Mother Earth. This immense wooing of the cosmos was enacted for the first time on a planetary scale, that is, in the spirit of technology. But because the lust for profit sought satisfaction through it, technology betrayed man and turned the bridal bed into a bloodbath. The mastery of nature, so the imperialists teach, is the purpose of all technology. . . . [But] technology is not the mastery of nature but of the relation between nature and man. . . . In technology a *physis* is being organized through which mankind's contact with the cosmos takes a new and different form from that which it had in nations and families. One need recall only the velocities by virtue of which mankind is now preparing to embark on incalculable journeys into the interior of time. . . .
>
> (Benjamin 1925–6, pp. 103–4)

Benjamin wrote the above passage in 1925–6, a year before Martin Heidegger published the treatise that was to become *Being and Time*. Like Heidegger, Benjamin thinks about the relation between technology and the mastery of nature, and between physics and metaphysics. Like Heidegger, he appeals to the ancients, the pre-Socratics, for a world-view in which intercourse with the cosmos contrasts with the discrete thinking that begins with *technē*. Yet Benjamin makes the *physis* involved more literally physical than does Heidegger. He differs in another way in that he ties technological mastery to capitalism and imperialism. Benjamin is also politically optimistic about the possible outcome of this energetic unleashing, seeing it as the source of the proletarian revolts that followed and accompanied the First World War.

Nonetheless, the 'cosmic power' that runs beyond and through individuals (poetic or otherwise) is a two-edged sword. Tied to technological mastery, it is destructive. It can also unleash energy for the good. Benjamin says little more, which is a pity, but the idea of connecting forces as two-edged will be fundamental in what follows. So will the idea that energy can be unleashed; this points to why the notion that humans are closed or contained entities is now under suspicion in popular culture, and under a little nervous scrutiny in the academy. It points to it because it suggests that the historically shaped technological shifts have energetic effects on human beings. If they do, we need to conceive energetic interaction in ways which allow for a natural and technological interactive economy. This means a new slant on the notion of 'cosmic connection', one which introduces the dynamics of social and historical construction as forces which shape energies.

To write of a social psychosis contingent on an escalating ego, to assume that symptoms can manifest themselves on a broader spatial scale, is to assume that madness has an end-point if not a starting-point that lies beyond individual vicissitudes. This assumption involves more than the obvious. It is not only the case that their social milieu can make individuals psychotic: a well-attested claim. What is at stake here is the idea that the agency of madness has a locus that is not subject-centred, or more accurately not only dependent on individuals. When agency is defined as directed, motivated will, an intelligence with fears, loves and ideas, together with the means for actualizing them, the implications of this idea become more apparent. It means that the founts of fear, love and ideas, together with the agency that runs in fear or love, or attacks in anticipation of attack, are founts that spring up not only inside but around the individuals through which they course.

But it is exactly this implication of his claim that Lacan does not pursue. Yet if his theory of the ego's era is to be more than an interesting parable, if it is to be a convincing argument which explains key dynamics of the times, it needs to account in more detail for the mechanism by which a process that occurs in individuals can occur globally over longer time and larger space. As I said in the introduction, for that, some notion of an interactive economy of energy is necessary. It is necessary to explain how the environment literally gets inside the subjects who in turn act in similar ways in reproducing it, in a spatial, technological dialectic of literal physical pressure and aggression.

Now the notion that there is a conative, energetic force coursing through and activating individual subjects and their living environment is not new. It was with us before, and is appearing now. In its naturalistic form, it enjoyed a certain popularity in the guise of pantheism, Romanticism, *Naturphilosophie*. It attained some intellectual respectability in Spinoza's name. Today it is prominent in the cosmic consciousness theories that inform the New Age culture, and which spill over into the theories of the German greens (Bahro 1984; Kelly 1984).[1] In New Age culture especially, the idea of a connecting force survives, but it survives on miserable arguments, and is always assumed to be good. The idea also survives in popular culture, where notions of energetic connections between beings are seen as both beneficient and malign. The idea has returned in a series of blockbuster films ('May the force be with you') and in writers ranging from Arthur C. Clarke to Toni Morrison. Morrison's *Beloved* was revolutionary, ahead of academic time, in writing of psychical feelings and forces which were not self-contained but crossed between individuals. But these works are a long way from those of Jacques Lacan.

One of the tasks of this chapter is to explore the economy of energy Lacan's theory requires. Another is to establish grounds for tying energy to an account of how time is made over in favour of space, as Lacan following Heidegger thinks it is. But the main purpose of this chapter is to show how we come to conceive of ourselves as individually contained, and thus come to resist thinking about energy in interactive

---

1 But the German green movement is diverse. In addition to the dominant wing which stresses the cosmic interconnectedness and common sensibility of nature and humans (*à la* Lovelock's Gaia hypothesis), there is also a socialist wing which puts capital's exploitation before cosmic consciousness (Boggs 1986). The following argument is relevant to both tendencies.

terms. This needs to be shown in a way that ties the illusion of containment to the formation of the ego and the fantasy of woman. For this tie is the condition of a consistent development of the argument that concluded Part I: namely, that the fantasy of woman fosters the ego's era, in so far as the subject thenceforth believes that his Other, his reference point beyond himself, is something he controls. But to tie this together is to ask rather a lot. I try to do it by detailing the foundational fantasy which I argue founds the subject and the ego's era. As I said in the introduction, some of the fantasy's dynamics have been discerned by Klein, others by Freud, as well as Lacan. A synthesis of these dynamics does lead to an understanding of how it is that we conceive of ourselves as contained, without psychical energetic connections to others; it also shows that the ego's construction of the boundaries that seal off knowledge of these connections objectifies the mother (or other) as it constitutes a nascent subject, and thus that a form of subject–object thinking is intertwined with conceiving of oneself as contained.

But this analysis does not of itself establish that the characteristics of the historical ego's era match those of the psychical ego. It only lays the theoretical grounds for it, by showing how psyche and social order are connected. To *establish* the match would require a detailed investigation of the historicity of the psychical position of women, which carried Part I's discussion of the psychical fantasy of woman and demise of God further, and also showed that we are more inclined to think of ourselves as contained, and in subject–object terms, than we were before modernity. Such an investigation requires a history of ideas which is beyond the scope of this book. This is a one-sided theory of history, one-sided in that it analyses the dynamics of a totalizing trend, and neglects that trend's intersection with specific historical contexts. But I will gesture to some historical shifts in contained and subject–object thinking, before turning to a detailed analysis of the foundational fantasy.


A little investigation suggests that the notion opposed to psychical energetic connection, the notion of psychical containment, may be historically and culturally specific to the modern West. Michèle le Doeuff has argued that the late Renaissance introduces a

> philosophical revolution which gives to the 'I' a discretionary omnipotence over the concrete self. . . . In the Avicennean tradition

*my* imagination is not really *my* imagination, because it is moved and affected by images which I receive, by the other's charm, by his or her wishes, beliefs and fears.

Le Doeuff goes on to argue that this tradition is replaced by one which seals the subject off from the influences of others. She suggests that, for instance, Hobbes and Shakespeare 'agree in what they deny: that fancy can pass from one person to another. Each individual becomes a closed space in relation to their fantasmagoria: their desires and dreams are their business' (1986, p. 86).

Certainly we find notions of psychical connections and energetic transmission in Montaigne, whose sixteenth-century essay on the imagination begins with the information that the author is 'one of those who are very much affected by the imagination. Everyone feels its impact, and some are knocked over by it' (1580, p. 36). Montaigne makes it clear that the imagination works energetically between beings, for better or worse, in sickness and in health. He records how an ill, rich old man asked a physician for advice on how he could be cured. The physician replied that it would be by infecting Montaigne with a wish for the old man's company.

Then if he were to fix his gaze on the freshness of my complexion, and his thoughts on the youthful gaiety and vigour with which I overflowed, and if he were to feast his senses on my flourishing state of health, his own condition might well improve. What he forgot to say was that mine might at the same time deteriorate (1580, p. 37).

This resonates with the theory I advanced in relation to Freud and femininity, but more of that in a moment. It also resonates with Elias's argument that Western pre-moderns did not have an 'invisible wall' dividing them one from another (Elias 1939, p. 249). But let us step outside the West, for if we put the above gestures together with the cross-cultural argument of Strathern (1988),[2] there is more support for the idea that the 'ego's era', as a Western event, coincides with the advent of the contained individual. Strathern argues that the notion of indivisibility, which underpins the etymology of the word 'individual',

2 Strathern's originality here is to have formulated a systematic critique of the concept of the individual, and to have elaborated on it brilliantly. The concept of the self-contained individual, terminated by death, has been put in question by Bloch (1988), who focuses on the idea that in some cultures parts of the body survive after death, and remain in a meaningful unity with the same parts in other (living) bodies. See also the classic Dumont (1966) on the absence of a concept of individuals in 'holistic' societies.

is culturally specific, and that other cultures conceive of people as potentially divisible (unbounded or uncontained). Moreover, these other cultures also eschew subject–object thought, if one takes the subject–object distinction to be a split between mind and body.[3]

As I noted at the end of Part I, my argument that the ego's era enacts a psychical fantasy, in which contained subjects counterpose a world of objects, is similar to Heidegger's notion of a metaphysical mindset that modern technology makes dominant. Given this, it is worth noting that the idea of the individual as contained is also foreign in the pre-Socratic times[4] that Heidegger invokes as the period before the metaphysical stance, and subject–object thought, is born. This period is also (very broadly) one where there is 'no unified concept of what we call "soul" or "personality" ' (Dodds 1951, p. 15). Dodds has connected this with the belief in psychic intervention, by which the gods planted 'monitions' (notions, energetic gifts or depletions) in humans which made them act in ways which they felt came to them from without, and for which they could disclaim responsibility whilst retaining credibility. Heidegger himself comes very close to this line of thought. Pre-Socratic thinking for him fitted an age when

> in Greece, the arts soared to the supreme height of the revealing granted them. They illuminated the presence [Gegenwart] of the gods and the dialogue of divine and human destiny. And art was simply called *technē*. It was a single, manifold revealing. It was pious, *promos*, i.e. yielding to the holding sway and the safe-keeping of truth.
>
> (1936, pp. 315–16)

In this revealing, the fluid source of all possibilities (Being?), was not

3  Cf. Read (1955) and La Fontaine (1985). La Fontaine's study is also a critique of Read, for an 'ethnocentric' treatment of the Gahuku–Gama subject-object distinction. But Read (1955) is also interesting on this question. Read argues that different constituent parts of a human personality are considered to reside in different parts of the body and bodily excretions, and that injury to certain parts of the body leads to that aspect of the personality also being injured (p. 265). I am indebted in this research to Sarah Green (1993).

4  A great deal is currently being accomplished in the name of a firm divide between the pre- and post-Socratics. The pre-Socratics for Heidegger had it all; the post-Socratics lost it. Lacan, as discussed in Part I, attributes the distinction between form and matter to Plato. Irigaray has also followed Heidegger in seeing the pre-Socratics as the paradisiacal thinkers, from whom Plato and his successors Fell into a world where matter and form were split, and the subject reigned over the world without regard for its Being. For the classicist scholar, the idea of an abrupt division is simply not accurate. Nussbaum (1986) has traced the pre-Socratic lineage in Aristotle's thought, and argued that it would be a mistake to take the Platonic system as one which ruled out all or most pre-Socratic ideas.

confined to fixed forms, perceived in objective terms or as objects from a subject-centred standpoint. After Plato, for Heidegger, the world is conceived in terms of immutable forms and their imitation, which leads to the process whereby thought becomes *technē* in the restricted sense, which Heidegger locates as the beginning of the dominance of technical thinking and technology. It is vital that we 'free ourselves from the technical interpretation of thinking: The beginnings of that interpretation reach back to Plato and Aristotle '[who thus reduced thought to . . . ] a process of reflection in service to doing and making' (1949, p. 194).

However, while subject–object thinking (and possibly the notion of containment) have been with us since the pre-Socratics, the point is that these ideas have hardened. Le Doeuff has given us an account of the hardening of the notion of individual containment, which ties it to Renaissance thought. My argument that this notion goes together with object-oriented thought also has tacit support from Charles Taylor (1989) whose remarkable synthesis shows how interiority or inwardness, a condition of being an 'individual' with an 'inside' is born in this period.

> Thought and feeling – the psychological – are now confined to minds. . . . As long as the order of things embodies an ontic logos, then ideas and valuations are also seen as located in the world, and not just in subjects.
>
> (Taylor 1989, p. 186; and Cf. Greenblatt 1980)

For Taylor, to become a subject is to become a 'punctual self', a being imbued with the mechanistic laws of time and space. It is 'to identify oneself with the power to objectify and remake' (ibid, p. 171). There is also support from Bordo (1987), who gives us a brief history of the hardening of the subject–object distinction, which she also ties to the Renaissance, although for the main part she concentrates on Descartes. Bordo draws on Rorty's brilliant analysis of how the mind, as the 'inner arena' of ideas, the 'inner Eye' (Rorty 1979, p. 62) is born in Descartes' context. For Rorty, this inner arena remakes the distinction between subject and world. Bordo locates Rorty's analysis in what she sees as 'a profound cultural development . . . the construction of experience as occurring deeply *within* and bounded by a self' (1987, p. 49). This self is also aware of distance, Bordo argues, in a way that pre-modern people were not; this modern self no longer thinks of itself as connected with the cosmos, but as dislocated (*passim*). While Bordo does not discuss energy and the sense of bounded containment as such, her study supports the idea that this sense is born of the ego's era. She also ties 'the flight to thinking in subject–object terms' to shifts in the attitudes to women and nature (cf. Merchant 1980 and Thomas 1983).

In sum, there is support for the idea that the force of the subject–object distinction changes over time, as with the notion of individual containment. It may be that the idea of the contained individual, who thinks in subject–object terms, based on an 'interiorized' consciousness who is the agent of and responsible for its feelings, fancies and thoughts, is the modern Western exception, rather than the rule. But we still need a theory of energetic connection which enables us to account for changing historical inflections in the experience of it. In contemporary writing, the idea that there are energetic connections between beings and environment has two main exponents in the academy: Deleuze and Guattari. Deleuze especially expressly connects himself to Spinoza, and more or less to Spinoza's ideas of *conatus*, or striving, *potentia* or power, and the indivisibility of thought and matter, as well as the idea that all things are energetically connected.[5] Like Spinoza, Deleuze and Guattari do not conceive of these connections in terms that are historically modulated. I will come back to this; first, the distinctiveness of Deleuze's theory warrants attention.

The difference between Spinoza and Deleuze is that Deleuze wants to replace Spinoza's emphasis on the logic of God as Nature (*Deus Natura*), as the One Substance which is thoughtful as well as substantial, with a dice-throwing, desiring chaos which has no logic. Logic, for Deleuze and Guattari, is inseparable from a subject–object distinction (in language and in perception), in which the subject has a rule of signification and related forms of oppression imposed on it, which it in turn imposes on an object. Both logic and the subject–object distinction are inseparable from a bound, contained subject. My disagreement with this position is not the equation of containment with a particular subject–object distinction, but the further equation of both with logic, and the assimilation of all subject–object distinctions under the same structural rubric. One can have an inherent order of connection which is not linear; this is the order found in nature's logic which perpetuates the living, a logic of multitudinous paths that intersect, which works through living things rather than imposes itself upon them from outside and above.

5  Cf. Howie (1992) and Bogue (1989) on Deleuze and Guattari's intellectual lineage.

The equation of logic with an oppressive subject–object distinction is based on a common confusion, between any order of connection as such and an imposed and limiting rule. While oppressive political regimes exploit the confusion mercilessly in appeals for law and order, order is not the same as imposed rule, any more than logic is the sadodispassionate. That aside: the great merit of Deleuze and Guattari is to have put the Spinozan world-view on the poststructuralist agenda and, with it, consideration of a mindful connected physicalism.[6] Their major disadvantage, apart from their treatment of logic, is that they make it impossible to think historically whilst using the framework they advocate. History is styled a metanarrative, and histories which try to account for change partake of a totalizing imposition (etc.). Deleuze and Guattari's rejection of history and of logic also go together: history as a metanarrative is, like logic, an emanation from the subject. But this means that the state advocated by Deleuze – a state of being without or before a subject–object distinction, a state of panting pulsing flows connecting bodies ungoverned by the rigid law of Oedipus, in a world of discontinuous energetic throws of dice, where subjects are not contained and therefore not subject – it means this state is in some way the natural state. Historically, the best Deleuze and Guattari can do is to argue that capitalism reinforces that state, through its trend to fragmentation. Their insight about subjective containment as an illusion is constrained by the inability to account for the production of that illusion; by the above brief survey, it has not been uniform in its strength, nor necessarily always with us.

Spinoza's concept of logic makes it possible to think historically, but only because the historical process can be contrasted with it. By noting the contrast, we come closer to a theory of how it is that the sense of self-containment is historically produced, and currently in question.

In Part I, I suggested that logic functioned in a manner similar to nature. I am now proposing explicitly that this similarity is in fact an identity, as Spinoza argues, and that logic as the process of connection is the same as the process of connection in nature.

As I have indicated, Spinoza gives us an account of logic which is not transcendental, not the province of the masterful subject, not split from

6  The affinity between Spinoza and Deleuze is undernoted; there is a tendency to write as if the idea of 'a new materialism' began with Deleuze alone.

the body, any more than mind is split from the body. God as nature is One substance with dual attributes, thought and extension, which cannot be separated although they have to be separately conceived. Because Spinoza sees logic as existing independently of and prior to the human subject, because he does not split thought and matter, Spinoza's philosophy is in fact not guilty of most of the charges levelled against 'the metaphysical systems of the transcendental subject of reason' (supply your favourite reference). He expressly dispossesses the subject of exclusive claims to the logos, in a magnificent dispossession which Freud, who acknowledged his indebtedness to 'the great philosopher', could well have added to his list of the great blows against man's narcissism.[7]

Yet even though Spinoza's idea of logic is extremely radical, in that it is not subject-centred, it has been neglected in the critique of foundationalism. Derrida, the founder of anti-foundationalism, linked logic and truth to the narcissism of the 'self-identified subject', whose narcissism requires that he take possession of, and lay claim to truth, while excluding others from the right to any such claim (Derrida 1966, p. 419; 1980, p. 212). But while Derrida himself has moved beyond this position, many of the anti-foundational advocates who follow him have refused to speculate about an origin before the foundation Derrida takes apart for the narcissistic charade it is.

Of course the person who has thought about this origin (although not in these terms) is Luce Irigaray. She has argued that all Western philosophy has been built on the suppression of maternal origin, whose denial makes the subject present and central. Derrida's more recent position, 'I call myself my mother who calls herself (in) me', is close to this. As Cornell notes, 'Derrida is emphasising the precedence of the Other to the subject. The subject only becomes himself by recalling

7  Spinoza also has a contrast in his thought that parallels that between the life drive and the imaginary, between activity and passive fantasy. The contrast is drawn in terms of *conatus* and the passive imagination. The former is a striving for expansion, which Hampshire compares with Freud's concept of the libido, the precursor of the life drive. Ideas of the passive imagination are associated by proximity, rather than the striving logical process which marks real thought, a striving which at its highest would lead to an identity with Nature (Hampshire 1951). The relation between Freud and Spinoza is discussed in Yovel (1989, p. 136ff.). Yovel quotes Freud as writing to an old Spinozist, who called Freud to account for not acknowledging his similarities with Spinoza: '*I readily admit my dependence on Spinoza's doctrine*' (p. 139). The three blows to man's narcissism were: (1) the discovery that the earth was not the centre of the universe; (2) Darwin's theory of the descent of species; (3) the discovery of the unconscious, which showed that the idea of conscious control of one's actions was an illusion.

Her' (Cornell 1988, p. 1607; Derrida 1986). Irigaray also recognizes a 'sensible transcendental' – a Spinoza-like postulate. Where I differ from her is in reclaiming logic for the origin before the foundation, and in extending the argument on suppression to nature. Irigaray, in all other things so brilliant, thinks, like Deleuze, that the way to oppose a subject-centred masculine logic is to do away with logic. Yet if we think in terms of reclaiming logic, we begin sundering an old misalliance between logic and the phallus, rather than remaining within a mirror reversal of its terms.

I do not want to do away with Spinoza's radical non-subjective logic in favour of a desiring dicey chaos. In the next sections, it should be plain that my difference from Spinoza lies in stressing how far 'the imagination' actively rivals the original logic, how it constructs an alternative to it, and how this construction introduces the historical contrast and sense of change that is absent in Spinoza, an absence reflected (for instance) in his belief that all forms of government that might exist have already been tried.[8] As well as giving us an historical tension otherwise absent in Spinoza, this will also give us a way of concretely specifying how the fantasy is reinforced, and how 'time-space' is compressed, in a manner that goes beyond a vague invocation of 'technology'.

By the same argument, we will be able to see how technological shifts have energetic effects on us and this might help explain why we theorize energy and boundaries in different ways at different times. If, as I am arguing, the sense of internal containment is historically inflected, it is inevitable that our theories are similarly affected. The odd thing about psychoanalysis is that while it is limited in this way, its implications and its inconsistencies point to a different, an interconnected theory of psychical energy. Freud himself missed the implications of his reasoning in this respect, as he set out from the assumption that psychical energy is internally contained. He had not the context of a Montaigne; in Freud's self-contained assumption, he embodied his times.

Enough for now that our ideas about energy, our own psychical boundaries, reflect, or to use a more accurate term, literally embody the specific energetic continuums we inhabit. If we are beginning to

---

8 In addition, we might consider that, in part, logic exercises its attraction because it is experienced in its pure form, as substance and thought, *in utero*; the memory of this experience serves as an incentive to find it again. This helps account for the teleology Spinoza assumes.

question the notion of containment now, that may be because it is currently subject to an energetic shift, resulting, as Deleuze and Guattari argue, in the sense of self-containment breaking down (Deleuze and Guattari 1972). But our immediate concern is with how the sense of containment is produced, and tied to a form of subject–object distinction, conceived in terms of energetic objectification. Enter the foundational fantasy.

## THE FOUNDATIONAL FANTASY

Of what then does the foundational fantasy consist? The difficulty with describing it is that it is perceived necessarily from a present standpoint, although I am assuming that it is a kind of mindset or psychical fantasy which is reinforced historically and acted out technologically. In the present, I have suggested, the subjective psyche is shaped and thoroughly overdetermined by the technological acting out of this fantasy, as the totalizing trend eliminates difference. If I am right, we are reaching a point where the fantasy can have no clear locus in either the psyche or the social order, so we need to focus on a point midway between both.

Such a point is provided by the commodity (in the narrow sense of a 'consumer good'), a thing that is socially produced for exchange and psychically desired. A second reason for focusing on the commodity is that we know ourselves best by what we do. Or what we make. In this world, we make commodities. To the extent that commodities are shaped by our desires, they indicate what those desires are. There are of course problems with beginning with the commodity, which I come to in a moment. But a psychoanalysis of the desires encapsulated in commodities will eventually yield the rudiments of the fantasy that founds us. As time must be central in this fantasy, let us start with the desire for instant gratification, described by Freud, and realized in a proliferation of commodities.

The vending machine that provides instantly upon the insertion of a coin, the fast-food establishment that promises no delay, the bank card that advertises itself as the one that does away with the need to stand in a queue, all promise the abolition of *waiting time*. Yet a little reflection shows that commodities cater to more than a desire for instant gratification. They are also marked by an attitude of appealing availability: the 'I'm here for you' message signified by the trolley at the airport that asks you to 'rent me', or the advertisement that once asked you to 'fly me'. These appealing items are akin to those that promise service, such as the credit card that delivers the object of desire to your door. 'Pick up the phone; we come to you.' More than the abolition of waiting time is offered here; one will also be *waited upon*. And if the promise of service appeals to a desire for domination and control, it has to be noted that the illusion of control is also provided by vending machines and their ilk. The consumer makes it happen; or rather, the consumer is catered to via the fantasy of making it happen with minimal effort, even none at all. In this connection, the car is an exemplary commodity. It provides mobility without much activity to a passive director. At the same time it pollutes the surrounding environment.

In proposing that the desires encapsulated in commodities embody a foundational fantasy, I am proposing that we treat the commodity as an expression of it. But immediately, this proposition raises three problems. The first is that the desires encapsulated in commodities do not tally exactly with any existing account of a psychical fantasy. The second problem of course is demonstrating that the fantasy expressed in commodities is in fact foundational. This problem is exacerbated by a third, which figured in the last chapter, particularly in that Lacan neglects the technological dimension when it relates to the economics of profit. This is the problem of why it is that a fundamental psychical fantasy is expressed in a form which is on the socio-historical increase. For commodities, whether in the form of consumer goods or in the form of the technologies that underlie their production, are evidently increasing.

We are not entirely in a void when it comes to considering these problems. As noted at the outset, while there is no extant account which tallies precisely with the psychical fantasy I am assuming commodities encapsulate, a synthetic reading of certain psychoanalytic theories will provide one. In addition, that synthetic reading coheres because it makes central the psychical fantasies Klein describes about the mother's body. This focus on Klein also reveals just what objectification, and with it the subject–object distinction, entails. The focus is appropriate in another way, given that it is a feminist reading of Klein, as well as Lacan, that raised the question of the relation between fundamental or

even transhistorical psychical fantasies and socio-historical circumstances.[9] But Freud comes first.

Persistently, consumer goods appeal through visual media. This,
together with the desire for the instant gratification these commodities
encapsulate, directs us to Freud's pleasure principle. Freud's pleasure
principle, more strictly his principle of *Unlust* or unpleasure as he first
defined it, is about an hallucinatory visual world where instant
gratification is paramount. It is also about how psychical reality as
distinct from 'material reality' comes into being.[10] When the longed-
for object (initially the breast or mother) is not present it is hallucinated in its absence. This hallucination founds psychical reality; the
breast is present in the imagination, but not present in the material
here and now. The act of hallucination provides instant gratification,
but the satisfaction it affords is only short term. For the breast is longed
for because the infant is hungry, and the hallucination cannot appease
the unpleasure of the need for food. In other words, unpleasure is due to
the tension of need. Any need (to eat, urinate, defecate, ejaculate)
increases quantitatively, and pleasure is felt when the need is relieved.
An hallucinated breast does not of itself relieve the need. Indeed it
ultimately leads to more unpleasure, in that it generates motor
excitations it cannot dispel; the expected satisfaction that accompanies
the hallucination gears the body up, but the energy amassed through
this excitement cannot be relieved, any more than the original need
itself.[11]

It should be clear that Freud's (un)pleasure principle is an economic
or quantitative principle: it is about the quantitative build-up of tension
or need. In Freud's own terms, it is a matter of psychical economy,
loosely based in Fechner's psycho-physics.[12] The economic or
quantitative physical aspects of Freud's theory of the pleasure principle
are frequently criticized. Its descriptive aspects are more generally
accepted; few commentators have problems with the notion of instant
gratification, or with that of visual hallucination. Yet, as I said in the
Introduction, it is the fact that Freud had a reference point in physics,

9  This idea is elaborated in Brennan (1988) and (1989). While the word transhistorical is used in
   the psychoanalytic, feminist writing the point is simply that a psychical fantasy *can* exist
   independently of and across a variety of historical circumstances, not that it must always do so.
10 The distinction between psychical and material reality is Freud's. It has been criticized by
   Laplanche and Pontalis (1968).
11 See in particular the well-known seventh chapter of *The Interpretation of Dreams* (Freud
   1900).
12 For the most thorough discussion on Freud's relation to Fechner, see H. F. Ellenberger (1970).
   As with most of my references to Freud, this is discussed in more detail in Brennan (1992).

even if it was the wrong reference point, that will be of most use in long run.

Moreover, if one reconsiders the desires implicit in commodities, it will be plain that while the pleasure principle accords with the desire for instant gratification that they express, and with their visual presentation in various media, it does not account for the other desires revealed in their design, namely: the desire to be waited upon; the desire to believe one is the source of agency who makes it happen; the desire to dominate and control the other who is active in providing, but whose activity is controlled by a relatively passive director, and the aggressive desire towards the other, if we take pollution as evidence of aggression.

The last-named desire returns us to Klein. In her theory, the infant desires to spoil and poison the breast (and the mother) with its excrement. In discussing the infant's desires in Klein's theory, I should repeat the brief caveat on the notion that 'the infant' is the sole culprit when it comes to pinpointing the origin of the aggressive desires under discussion. 'The infant' is always that origin for Klein, although we will see later that the question of culpability is more complicated, as is the idea that the target of all this aggression is simply 'the mother'. But for the time being, I shall continue to write in terms of monstrous infants and mauled mothers. As well as desiring to poison, the infant also desires to devour and fragment the mother's body. 'Cutting up' the mother's body is a recurrent theme in Klein's analyses of small children. She ties this cutting impulse to the drive for knowledge: the urge to get inside, grasp and in this sense understand what is hidden, and in the process destroy it.[13]

For Klein, the desires to poison, devour, dismember and to know through dismembering are prompted by two interrelated forces. The first is the strength of the death drive working within. The second is the envy of the creativeness embodied in the mother and mother's breast. While the death drive and envy motivate these fantasmatic attacks on the breast, they also lead to a fear of retaliation. The fear is that the aggressed breast will respond in kind; this fear results in what Klein terms the paranoid–schizoid position. It is paranoid because the infant projects its own aggressive desires onto the other, and the retaliation it fears (being cut up, poisoned, devoured) mirrors its own

13 For representative illustrations of these and many of the following Kleinian ideas from different periods of Klein's work, see Melanie Klein, 'Early stages of the Oedipus conflict', (1928) and 'Envy and gratitude' (1957).

desires. It is schizoid because this paranoid projection involves a splitting both of the ego and of the other. For to deal with its dependence on the breast as the source of life, and its simultaneous fantasy that the breast is out to get it, the infant splits: there is a 'good' breast, and a 'bad' one. Yet because the badness the infant fears originates within itself, the splitting of the other presupposes and perpetuates a splitting of the ego. The ego, by depositing its own aggressive desires in the other, impoverishes itself by the splitting, and the repression or 'denial' that this entails.

The ego can only recover its full potential by reclaiming that which has been cast out. This reclamation, when it occurs, can lead to depression: the recognition that the erstwhile projected badness lies within. It may also lead to reparation: the attempt to repair the damage done in fantasy;[14] this reparation is manifest in creativeness or, I think, creative labour, both means to integrating a psyche felt to be in pieces. Lacan too thinks the infant feels itself to be in pieces, due to its premature (relative to other mammals) birth, and consequent lack of muscular co-ordination. The mirror-stage, in part, is founded on the appeal of an erect posture; the infant idealizes not only its whole image, but an image in which it is standing up (1949, p. 7).[15] But while these accounts have a certain phenomenological similarity, Klein injects an ethics into the realization of wholeness, and a pathway to it other than that of erection.

Leaving that hopeful note aside: it is important to add that the extent of the splitting, and of the poisoning, devouring, dismembering fantasies that accompany splitting, is mediated by anxiety. For Klein, anxiety derives from the death drive working within. In the last analysis, she posits that the strength of the death drive, and envy, are innate. Moreover, Klein's account of the splitting process presupposes a psychical fantasy which has no direct correspondence with reality (the breast is not really cut up, etc.). It is a psychical fantasy, and clearly not a consequence of the infant's actual social environment or social events. It is also important to note that the splitting of the good and bad breast is remarkably similar to the splitting of women into two types, mother and whore, which suggests that the Oedipal, symbolic split embodies an

14 The most representative if difficult account of the views summarized in this paragraph is 'Notes on some schizoid mechanisms' (Klein 1946).
15 Standing up is actually a recurrent preoccupation of Lacan's, and he finds a similar interest in it in Heidegger's use of the term *Dasein*. 'The idea of standing erect, of life, of evolving is what comes of an etymological analysis of [the verb 'to be'] completed by a grammatical one' (1955-6b, p. 339).

earlier one. The psychical fantasy of woman, for all it is meant to be a bulwark against the ego's era, only comes into being at a 'certain historical moment'. Klein's account of the splitting into good and bad has more claims to generality, as we shall see, and will help explain why the expression of this split in the fantasy of woman contributes to the ego's era.

Thus far, we have a theory that accounts for the desire to poison or, in commodity terms, the desire to pollute. We also have some elements of a theory that accounts for the desire to dominate and control (insofar as the desire to get inside, cut up, devour and so on involve control and domination). It remains to tie this theory to the instant hallucinatory gratification embodied in the pleasure principle, and the desire to be waited upon from a passive though authoritative position. Here Klein's analysis of envy provides an indirect clue.

> Though superficially [envy] may manifest itself as a coveting of the prestige, wealth and power which others have attained, its actual aim is creativeness. The capacity to give and preserve life is felt as the greatest gift, and therefore creativeness becomes the deepest cause for envy. The spoiling of creativity implied in envy is illustrated in Milton's *Paradise Lost*, where Satan, envious of God, decides to become the usurper of Heaven. Fallen, he and his other fallen angels build Hell as a rival to Heaven, and becomes the destructive force which attempts to destroy what God creates. This theological idea seems to come down from St. Augustine, who describes Life as a creative force opposed to Envy, a destructive force.
>
> (Klein 1957, pp. 201–2).

This passage is interesting because it points out, although it does so obliquely, that envy superficially focuses on attributes or possessions, rather than the creative force which may (or may not) result in them. The quotation from Klein also points out that envy will attempt to rival that which it envies, and that it will do so by constructing an alternative. More generally, Klein's analysis of envy in the essay from which the above quotation comes shows that while envious motivations are readily recognizable in destructiveness or calumny, they are less recognizable, although present, in denial. This is the form of denial which simply ignores or forgets that which is displeasing to the ego. It is present in the denial of the labour involved in creativity. I add that we recognize it where creativity is seen as accidental, or where it is attributed to a lucky circumstance or an unearned possession.

Let us add to these observations a notion that is best elaborated by Freud. This is that the infant, or small child, imagines the reversal of the actual state of affairs, and imagines that the mother is a dependent infant (Freud 1931, p. 236). In reversing the passive experiences of childhood into active ones in his play with a cotton-reel, Freud's grandson not only masters the mother's absence and introduces himself to deathly repetition (Freud 1920); nor does he only, if simultaneously, enter the world of language through the mother's absence that forces him to call. He also makes the mother into a fantasized small child which he controls, a child which is also an inanimate *thing*.

If the notion of the reversal of the original state of affairs is made central, rather than the incidental aside it is for Freud, it has the advantage that it reconciles otherwise diverse findings. When realities are seen in terms of their opposites, the fact of nurturance and the means to grow becomes a threat to narcissism; it establishes the reality of dependence. From this perspective, the envy of the mother's breast is the resentment of that dependence, and the reason why nurturance, or love, or protection, or assistance, are interpreted as assertions of superiority and power. 'Only saints are sufficiently detached from the deepest of the common passions to avoid the aggressive reactions to charity' (Lacan 1948, p. 13). There is a related, if less relevant, offshoot of the reversal of the original state of affairs into its opposite, an offshoot which we might usefully term 'imitating the original', in which rivalry with the original is clearly apparent. The child imitates the mother; the commodity, harking back to this chapter's point of departure, is often an imitation of the original.[16] Writing this, I went to the corner store for orange juice, and found only artificial orange drink in an orange shaped container, with green leaves. (It is not a good store.) I also took in late night television, worst amongst it *The Stepford Wives*, which is all about constructing a reliable and completely controllable imitation of the original wife and mother, and *Star Trek II*, where 'Project Genesis' shows us humans reinventing the entire process of creation.

The idea that we live in a culture of simulacra is developed by Baudrillard (1981 and 1986), whose study of *America* (1986) shows how much of its culture is a copy of a copy, and sometimes of yet

16 The imitation of the original is an often implicit and sometimes explicit theme in discussions of women and technology, particularly reproductive technology. For a general representative collection on this theme, see Stanworth (1987). For a discussion which bears more closely on the issues discussed here, see Haraway (1985).

another copy. In Baudrillard's world of hyper-real, more real than real copies, the disappearance of the distinction between the original and the imitation is due to the inability to locate an origin or referent for meaning.[17] Yet in the *Zeitgeist* what is lost, in fact explicitly rejected, is any notion of an original; an original is a notion of a foundation, hence suspect. I am challenging this suspicion by focusing on the mother's body, an origin before the foundation, of which more in a moment.

But keeping to the main thread: the tendency to look at realities in terms of their opposites is manifest at another level, which will explain the desire to be waited upon. Originally, the infant is perforce passive, and dependent on the mother's activity for survival. Yet it would be consistent with a fantasmatic reversal of the original state of affairs if the infant were to correlate its actual dependent reality with the fantasy of control through imagining that the mother's activity takes place at its behest. The infant does not wait upon the mother; the mother waits upon it. It is precisely this fantasy that is catered to by the commodities with which we began. But a little of reality lingers on, in the association between passivity and luxury, which recognizes that it is not the passive controller, or 'the infant', who labours. At the same time, the labour or activity involved in fulfilling the wish is denied in so far as its intelligence is denied. In fantasy, the mental direction and design of what labour effects is appropriated, only the manual activity is left out. Thus the mental whim and control is the infant's. The work goes elsewhere.

The split occasioned by this fantasy prefigures a deeper dualism between mind and body, in which direction or agency is seen as mental and mindful, while activity, paradoxically, is viewed as something that lacks intelligence. By an ineluctable logic, the activity of women as mothers is presented as passive. In fantasy, it lacks a will of its own; it is directed. And because direction is too readily confused with a will of one's own, this denial can readily be extended to living nature overall. In this connection, it is worth noting that the oft-repeated association of women and nature can be explained not by what women and nature have in common, but by the similar fantasmatic denial imposed upon both of them. In the case of women, it is one's will that is denied. In the case of living nature, its own inherent direction is disregarded. The

17 Baudrillard also identifies the loss of the sense of history in America as a fact, not a theoretical lapse.

denial of will also holds for people of colour, in terms of 'a belief structure rooted in a concept of black (or brown or red) antiwill, the antithetical embodiment of pure will. We live in a society where the closest equivalent of nobility is the display of unremittingly controlled wilfulness. To be perceived as unremittingly without will is to be imbued with an almost lethal trait' (Williams 1991, p. 219).

That creativeness is not viewed as intelligent or directed activity is consistent with envy's predilection to focus on creativity as the possession of certain attributes, rather than as a force in itself. Creativeness is seen less as what one does, than what one has. Or, to say a similar thing differently, the dialectics of envy conduct themselves at the level of images. It is appropriate that the word envy is derived from the Latin verb *videre*: the derivation signals the tie between the concept of envy and visualization.[18] What matters is the appearance of the thing, rather than the process of which it is part.

To say that what is envied is the mother's possession of the breast is to work already within the terms of envy, which are those of possessions, things, appearances, discrete entities, separable and separate from an ongoing process. Which brings us to the crux of the matter. While a fantasy of controlling the breast cannot survive at the level of feeling (pain or pleasure), it can survive at the literally imaginary level of hallucination. In fact, the controlling fantasy can be perpetuated through hallucinations, and this ability to perpetuate it must contribute to the addiction to the pleasure in hallucination, despite its unpleasure at other levels. In other words, by this account, the fantasy of controlling the breast and the act of hallucination are one and the same, which means that the amazing visual power of hallucination is tied to a desire for omnipotence from the outset.[19]

Of course feelings of omnipotence, for Freud, are infantile in origin, and tied to narcissism. But while there has been some discussion of how it is that narcissism can only come into being through fantasy or hallucination, the other side of this issue, which is how it is that hallucination is by nature an omnipotent or narcissistic act, has not

18  Conceptual ties such as this are fascinating pointers to the notion that Benjamin's 'prelapserian state', in which the expressive value of a word was tied to the signifier, may have something to it. Cf. the discussion of Freud's 'common source' below.

19  A qualification. While omnipotence is tied to the act of hallucination, most non-Western cultures do not regard an hallucination as deceptive necessarily. What is likely in this culture to be dubbed hallucinatory could as well be styled a vision, or spirit-possession. It is only in the psychoanalytic vision that hallucination is tied in its origin to infancy. I have followed this vision, but its cultural specificity, and the phenomenology it presupposes, is questioned in the book's conclusion.

been discussed.[20] It is one thing to concentrate on how it is that the subject's sense of itself as a separate being is inextricably linked to narcissism; that is to say, that it is only by the narcissistic act of fantasizing about its own body or circumference that it establishes its separate self. It is another to think about how the narcissism involved is also, and simultaneously, an omnipotent fantasy about controlling the other. For to establish itself as separate, the subject has to have something to be separate from. This much is foreshadowed by Lacan's *objet petit a*.

But by this account, the thing the subject is separate from is the breast or mother it imagines as available to it, subject to it, and towards whom it feels the aggressive desires that lead in turn to paranoia. Moreover, in the omnipotent act of hallucinating a breast it controls, the nascent subject separates and gives priority to its own visual capacity for imagination over its other senses. It is this visual capacity that allows one to imagine that things are other than as they are; it is this capacity that enables one to focus on the distinctiveness of entities other than oneself, rather than the senses or feelings that connect one with those others; it is this capacity that enables the subject to believe in (and even achieve) a situation where mental design and direction can be divorced from bodily action.

By this account, hallucination should be the mechanism by which Lacan's split subject, which is the human condition for him, comes into being. But at the same time, the tie between hallucination and envy means that the very act of hallucination can never be neutral. In St Augustine's imagery, if the fallen angel of light (Lucifer: *lux* = light, *ferre* = bring) fell because of envy there is no reason for supposing that he lost his power of light altogether; rather, in the act of hallucination, light becomes actively distorted and re-directed as an imaginary and necessarily envious vision. Lacan, like Klein,[21] also refers to Augustine, who, of course, is writing long before the ego's era began. In this quotation, Lacan is discussing the individual ego as such, and the death drive.

20 Although Borch-Jacobsen comes close when he pinpoints the core of megalomania in many of the dreams Freud analysed (Borch-Jacobsen 1989). Borch-Jacobsen's analysis of why narcissism is necessary, in fact the key, to the constitution of the subject is the outstanding discussion of this theme. Also important are Laplanche and Pontalis (1968) and Laplanche (1970).
21 In addition to those aspects of Lacan's indebtedness to Klein discussed above, it is worth adding that he also writes of art and its relation to aggression against the mother's body, citing Klein. See Lacan (1959–60, p. 126).

The signs of the lasting damage this negative libido causes can be read in the face of a small child torn by the pangs of jealousy, where St. Augustine recognized original evil. 'Myself have seen and known even a baby envious; it could not speak, yet it turned pale and looked bitterly on its foster brother' . . .

(Lacan 1953a, p. 16)[22]

It is after quoting Augustine that Lacan moves swiftly on to Hegel's master–slave dialectic, and the attempted destruction of the other consciousness, or other within, that the dialectic foretells. While Lacan makes it plain that that dialectic is the key to the 'most formidable social hell' (1949, p. 7) of the ego's paranoid era, the nature of the destructive objectification involved in the master–slave dialectic needed elucidation, and requires still more.

By this argument, the desires to poison, fragment and destroy the mother's body constitute the process of objectification, a process which has a physical reality. We have seen that turning the other into an object also means fragmenting it (in order partly to know it) or poisoning or in other ways attacking it, as well as making it a controllable thing. A very similar point is made by Kristeva, who, in an argument which echoes that of Mary Douglas, makes 'abjection' the foundation of objectification. Abjection is the feeling that one has revolting (including excremental) substances within; objectification comes from the need to exclude these substances by depositing them in the other, which brings the other, as object, into being.[23]

Some of the resonances between Klein's theory of the infant and Lacan's theory of the ego's era should now be evident. I will assume that the links between their arguments on the role of anxiety in 'objectification' can be taken for granted. Also, Klein's account ties the objectifying desires to the drive for knowledge. While she does not stress visualization in this connection herself, the fact that Foucault ties objectifying

22 Lacan does not give a reference for the quotation from St Augustine. It comes from the *Confessions*. The context is an argument that sin is present in infancy. When considering various possibilities, St Augustine asks whether as infant he sinned by endeavouring to harm 'as much as possible' those larger beings, including his parents, who were not subject to him, 'whenever they did not punctually obey [his] will'. ('*Non ad nutum voluntatis obtemperantibus feriendo nocere niti quantum potest. . . .*' One sentence later comes the observation that Lacan also quotes: '*vidi ego et expertus sum zelantem parvulum: nondum loquebatur et intuebatur pallidus amaro aspectu conlactaneum suum.*' S. Aureli Augustini (c. 400, p. 8). For my purposes, it is the failure to *punctually* obey, in connection with envy, that is interesting.

23 Kristeva (1980, pp. 17–32); Douglas (1966). Douglas's cross-cultural enquiry lends further weight to the notion that what we are dealing with here is a foundational fantasy with a very wide application in some of its aspects.

power/knowledge to visual mechanisms of control fits the theses I am elaborating.

The objectification of knowledge, for Lacan, is paranoid precisely because it is knowledge based on a need for control. It is knowledge tied to a 'positivist' world-view in which what is seen, or what can be tested or proved to exist, especially on the basis that it can be seen, is privileged. The objectification of knowledge helps construct a world in which only objects (or discrete entities?) are recognized, and they can only be recognized by subjects. In turn these subjects are affected, if not driven, by the objects they construct,[24] objects whose energetic process of construction will be discussed below, in an account that builds on Lacan's assumption that the subject–object distinction is tied to sexual fantasy, and his ethologically based belief that the impact of an image was both social and physical, and critical in the nature of the objectification that founds the ego.

Thus far it seems we have an account of a psychical fantasy which tallies with the desires encapsulated in commodities. It is this psychical fantasy I am positing as a foundational psychical fantasy. That is to say, I am positing that the desire for instant gratification, the preference for visual and 'object'-oriented thinking this entails, the desire to be waited upon, the envious desire to imitate the original, the desire to control the mother, and to devour, poison and dismember her, and to obtain knowledge by this process, constitute a foundational psychical fantasy.

It is a fantasy which accords certain attributes to the subject, and dispossesses the other of them as and by the process that makes the other into an object, a surrounds (as Heidegger might say), an absent background against which it is present. It is a fantasy that relies on a divorce between mental design and bodily action to sustain its omnipotent denial. In this fantasy, the subject must also deny its history, in so far as that history reveals its dependence on a maternal origin. There is no 'before' before this very present subject. We have also seen how the subject denies time, how it must do this to sustain its fantasy, by imagining that there is no delay between what it desires and its presence.

It remains to see of course how far what I have called a foundational

24 Although at one point Lacan indicates that objectification means turning the other into a controllable thing, he does not pursue this point, as we saw in Part I. Lacan is more concerned with the objectification of knowledge as such; in this concern, he is again at one with Heidegger, although Heidegger centralizes the objectification of nature as 'standing reserve', and the technocratic drive for mastery over nature, in a way that Lacan does not. Cf. Heidegger (1938).

fantasy is in fact foundational, how it connects to its macrocosmic enactment, and how, precisely, it connects to instantly gratifying commodities. In detailing this, more understanding of the role of delay will be essential.

## THE SUBJECT'S INERTIA

Delay is something I theorized at length (and slowly) in *The Interpretation of the Flesh*,[25] in an argument that hallucination was the key stone in a psychical constructed inertia, the first fixed point that enabled the subject to experience itself as contained. I now want to recapitulate elements of that theory, both in order to show how it holds for the environment, as well as the psyche, and to expand on the time factor in the foundational fantasy.

So far, we have the subject counterposed to an object founded by the act of hallucination. What prompts the hallucination is the desire that the longed-for object be present here and now. Yet if we examine Freud's account of hallucination, we find hallucination not only introduces instant gratification (in theory); in practice, it also introduces delay. In Freud's terms, the secondary process comes into being through an inhibition (*hemmung*) of the primary process (Freud 1900, p. 601). In the primary process, almost all things are possible; it is governed by the pleasure principle, and marked by hallucinatory wish-fulfilment, a lack of contradiction, the much-discussed mechanisms of condensation and displacement, and timelessness, amongst other things. The secondary process is governed by the reality principle. It is the locus of rational thought, directed motility, and planned action or agency. When it inhibits the primary process, it checks out or 'reality-tests' whether the image before it is a real perception or an imagined hallucination. In other words, it makes the psyche pause before it responds to the image it is offered. So, on the one hand, hallucination inaugurates a delay; on the other hand, I think that hallucination is a response to a delay, on the grounds that the wish for instant gratification must be prompted by the experience of a gap between the perception of a need and its fulfilment.[26]

25 *The Interpretation of the Flesh*, especially Chapter 3. Basically, apart from the discussion of the life drive and the death drive as a matter of direction, which are new, the next section summarizes that argument, so I have not given extensive references to Freud; the interested reader can find them there.
26 Of course this has consequences for real perception as well as imagined hallucination. One cannot respond immediately to the former. It has to be evaluated. Nothing visual can be taken for granted. What is more, it only becomes taken for granted at the price of establishing

The nature of the primary process is one of the most taken-for-granted yet confused areas of Freud's theory. In addition to the characteristics already noted, the primary process consists of freely mobile energy, and there are reasons for thinking Freud identified it with the 'movement of life' as such.[27] At the same time, the primary process consists of the pathways in which energy is bound in familiar patterns, a bondage which leads to repetition, and repetition, in turn, is the hallmark of the death drive. The bound and repetitive pathways of the primary process come into being via repression. They do this because repression is the way the subject copes with the fact that hallucinations do not satisfy the needs that prompt them. It has to banish the hallucination in order to respond more appropriately to the need, and avoid not only the unpleasure of the continuing need but the unpleasure of the excitations amassed with the hallucination.

But this banishment does not dispose of the hallucination; like all banishments, it only puts the hallucination in another place, which is why Freud writes of its repression. The hallucination stays, and in its repressed form does double duty. It is the foundation of the subject's memory for Freud; and, as I have argued, at the same time as it founds the subject's memory, it founds the unconscious. The subject-to-be has to remember that the hallucination was ineffective, and to use its excitations more productively. 'Memory is evidently one of the powers which determine and direct [an excitation's] pathway' (Freud 1895b, p. 300). Memory is also one of the powers influencing judgement, which the ego employs in the delay during which it decides whether an hallucination was real or imagined.

But this memory and that judgement are built on the retention of a lie, of a foundational fantasy that cannot be exposed: this is the fantasy that the subject controls the breast, the source of all bounty, that the buck starts here. As Lacan says of the fundamental fantasy, this lie is destined never to be recalled. The repression of the hallucination brings the repressed unconscious into being, together not only with memory but, as we shall see in a moment, direction from a subject-centred

familiar pathways for psychical energy to follow. The more certain the pathway, the less energy is involved; the less the pathways are disrupted, the less the stress. Yet the more the pathways are fixed, the more energy, in Freud's terms, is bound: rigidity and anxiety, in the face of unfamiliar pathways, are the consequences. Two points are critical here. The first is Freud's notion that energy comes to exist in a bound, rather than freely mobile, state through checking out hallucinations. The second is that, as we have seen, Lacan ties anxiety to spatial constriction. The argument on bound and freely mobile energy is one that Freud attributes to Breuer, and Breuer attributes to Freud (Freud and Breuer 1895a, p. 194).

27 See the concluding chapter.

standpoint. Indeed this memory and that direction require an unconscious. What we regard as properly unconscious is conscious in psychotics (1955-6b, p. 1ff.). And psychotic symptoms include conscious hallucinations, absence of memory, or the experience of past events as present, and of course confusion over 'subject-centredness', location and direction, especially the location and direction of ideas, energy, images: these are often conceived as coming from without rather than within, as rays, probes and pronouncements, rather than thoughts and impulses. In turn, this experience signifies a confusion over boundaries. So the repressed hallucination must contribute in some way to the success of the boundaries, the sense of self-containment the subject enjoys.[28]

None of this makes real sense unless it is located in an economy of energy. Freud is insistent that the repression of an hallucination requires a persistent expenditure of energy. But aside from theories of sexual repression (Reich, Marcuse), Freud's belief that psychical energy was the key to and means of unravelling psychical knots has received little attention. We need to give it that attention, both for the sake of the interactive economy and for theorizing how the subject-centred standpoint, and the self-contained subject, are born. Both depend on the repressed hallucination, as this constitutes a fixed point from which the nascent subject garners its bearings. But uncovering this means dealing with a level of repression that comes before sexuality and sexual repression.

Freud terms the force that represses hallucinations primal repression, which he distinguished from repression proper, or secondary repression. Sexuality is tied to repression proper. This repression is connected to primal repression (of some idea or ideational event), in that this establishes a nucleus which attracts subsequent 'proper repressions' towards it. But what I want to suggest now is that the act of repressing a hallucination is basic to establishing a sense of space–time in that it establishes a fixed point of reference from which the nascent ego can get its bearings. Literally, its spatio-temporal bearings. This means that the sense of perspective is a construction, as may be the sense of passing time.

The idea that the sense of perspective is a construction is attested to

28 I suspect that sound is critical in constructing these boundaries and giving the subject its distinctive 'self'. Freud talks of how the superego begins through internalizing the parents' voice-residues, and perhaps this should be taken literally. This would mean that the subject's boundary is a spatio-temporal construction which is also based in some sense on soundings.

by, for example, the fact that when sight is recovered after blindness, the sense of perspective (distance and size) does not necessarily accord with the perception of others. It is often completely out of proportion with what we know as reality. The idea that the sense of passing time is also constructed is demanded by the theory that space–time is a continuum; time is measured in terms of space, and the interval between one event and another depends on the speed it takes to cover the distance between them, and speed, in turn, depends on the potential motion or energy of the body involved.[29] But if one looks more closely at what the initial repression of hallucination involves (the process by which the hallucination becomes unconscious), it is evident that something is happening to energy in the process, and also that 'time' is measured relative to something other than the constructed space–time of which it is also part.

I suggested that an hallucination is prompted by the delay between the perception of a need and its fulfilment, and noted that Freud (although he does not postulate an initial delay) argues that the secondary process comes into being through an inhibition of the primary process, which in turn amounts to a further delay. Postulating an initial delay between the perception of a need and its fulfilment as the condition of hallucination means postulating a prior state in which perception and need coincide, or in which the delay between the need and its fulfilment was shorter. The fact that there is an intra-uterine state which is experienced before birth meets the requirements for this prior state. That is to say, if we suppose that *in utero*, there is no experience of a delay between perception and need, or that any delay is shorter, the intra-uterine state should constitute another pole against which the construction of space–time could be measured.

This supposition will have more substance if one considers what happens to psychical energy when it is bound. Freud's argument on this (elaborated in his *Project for a Scientific Psychology* (Freud 1895)) has led to a debate amongst psychoanalysts as to whether the bound pathways that come into being through distinguishing between hallucination and real perception are on the side of the life or the death drive. The key opposed positions here, which I shall only sketch briefly, are represented by Laplanche and Lacan respectively.

Laplanche disputes Lacan's location of the ego on the side of the

29  There are several excellent histories of physics and the story of the shift from one dominant paradigm to another, but see in particular Jennifer Trusted (1990). For reasons of space, I cannot give an exposition of the relevant paradigm shifts here.

death drive (Laplanche 1970). He does so on the basis of an interpretation of Freud's assumptions about inertia. (For Laplanche, these were
'outdated even at the close of the nineteenth-century'; from my
investigation, they were not outdated. Freud invented an idea of inertia
which had some justification precisely in nineteenth-century interpretations of Newton's first and second laws, not before.) The essence of
Laplanche's argument is that, first, the ego is a kind of giant fantasy in
itself. This much he has in common with Lacan. Laplanche bases his
view of the ego as a fantasy in itself on the *Project*, where Freud posits
the ego as a mass of cathected neurone-pathways. Or, if we put this in
terms of Freud's subsequent, less physiological vocabulary, the ego is a
mass of pathways in which psychical energy is bound. I think that this
bound mass tallies with Lacan's mirror-image, which is critical for him
in establishing the spatial sense, but making this tally will require an
additional argument.

Laplanche also argues that Freud confused the principle of inertia
with the principle of constancy. The former is a state in which there is
no motion, nothing. It is the desire to restore an earlier state of things
in which the governing principle is rest. In Freud's 1920 formulation on
the death drive, he termed it the Nirvana principle (Freud 1920, p. 56).
The principle of constancy is the desire to keep energy constant. For
Freud, freely mobile energy will follow the path of least resistance,
which is the path towards Nirvana. For Laplanche, while the ego is a
giant fantasy, it is none the less a vital one, in that its bound pathways
are the essential means for action against or towards what is necessary
for sustaining life. There is no essential contradiction between its
actions towards or away from life and the principle of constancy.

Where things get more complicated is that, as we have seen, the
bound pathways are also tied to the death drive. This is because energy
will flow along the paths that are familiar to it, and these paths might
be completely inappropriate for dealing with a novel situation. The
repression that brings both the pathways and the ego into being figures
here; bound energy flows along pathways that are unconscious. In
addition, there are two complications which reinforce the notion that
the bound is on the side of the deathly. The first is that the ego is less
likely to adapt and follow new pathways in a situation which arouses
anxiety (which should be borne in mind in relation to Lacan's spatial
dialectic: this connection also yields the link between Freud and
Heidegger, in that Heidegger sees the subject as becoming more rigid
(cf. Hodge 1994)). Furthermore, it is precisely the protracted attach-

ment to any fantasy (which must necessitate a bound pathway) that characterizes neurosis. Such attachments make it harder to act upon the world; they are similar in their effects to anxiety, in that they counter 'the movement of life' (Freud 1926, p. 148). The movement of life here is equivalent to freely mobile energy; in turn, the same as the life drive. Hence Lacan's position.

Now it would be easy enough to take a liberal approach here and say that, on the one hand, the ego and bound pathways are necessary: one has to deal with life's exigencies (Laplanche). On the other, if too much psychical energy is bound, if the pathways are too rigid, if anxiety is greater, then vaulting ambition overleaps itself and the result is deathly (Lacan). But this balanced solution allows one supposition to escape unchallenged. This is the notion that as freely mobile energy follows the path of least resistance, it *therefore* tends towards inertia. There is a related supposition, which is that for Freud an inert state is a restful one, and that any body seeking rest will seek to be inert or motionless. It is in supposing this that Freud to an extent invents an idea of inertia, in that he equates a commonsense understanding of the term with its meaning for physics. In physics, inertia does not mean lack of motion. It is the tendency to restore the state of motion existing before a disturbance in equilibrium. But Freud's interpretation is a potentially productive mistake. The fact that an hallucination has to stay repressed involves a persistent expenditure of energy. It means that freely mobile energy is permanently bound in the repression. The repression of the first hallucination thus constitutes a fixed point in relation to freely mobile energy, and we can call this fixed point and the bound pathways which spring from it constructed inertia. Freud, in other words, was theorizing how inertia is constructed relative to the freely mobile energy in which the subject-to-be is conceived. The fixed point of the repressed hallucination founds the subject as a potentially discrete entity in psycho-energetic terms, not only because it founds its memory, not only because it is the point of reference for future decisions about true and false, real and imagined, but because it founds an energetic system which gives the subject boundaries. A few more words are in order to make this plainer.

First we need to return to the idea that freely mobile energy follows the path of least resistance, and therefore tends towards inertia. Our postulate of the natural state (experienced *in utero*) means that 'the path of least resistance' needs to be reformulated. As the state *in utero* could well be one of more rapid motion (freely mobile energy is not

impeded in calling or responding), this living state could be restful in
that it appears to be without the conflict contingent on delay, and
therefore it appears 'timeless'. In other words, what leads freely mobile
energy on its quest for the path of least resistance is not the notion of
constructed inertia, as Freud understood it, but the principle of
constancy embodied in the memory of a state of timeless (yet, relative
to the subsequent sense of time, more rapid) motion.

Of course the spatio-temporal notion of rapidity only comes into
being after the fact, that is to say after birth, and the experience of
delay. The point is that after the fact, the resultant slow plight of the
ego is measured retroactively, in spatio-temporal terms, against the
prior intra-uterine state. In addition, the very thing that leads freely
mobile energy into conflict with the exigencies of life is the fact that it
encounters a point of resistance. If there were no resistance, nothing
would ordain it to follow paths set up from the subject's standpoint, and
there is no *a priori* reason why freely mobile energy could not regain its
prior rapid motion. Naturally, this means external as well as internal
points of resistance, for it would be a travesty of what logic underlies
Freud's reasoning on the ego to reduce the points of resistance the ego
encounters to its own self-sustaining fantasies. The ego evidently
encounters other points of resistance that would harm its chances of
living (very bad weather, aggressive others, etc.), and to these it has to
respond. Nonetheless, as the pathways for coping with these exigencies
multiply, and as, or if, they become the only pathways we follow in
relation to life's exigencies, we become more rigid. This I think is why
we age. There are too many familiar pathways riding freely mobile
energy.

What I want to suggest now is that the pathways which direct energy
make the quest for Nirvana deathly, not the quest in itself. In other
words, the subject-centred pathways are the problem, not the energy
which flows through them. On the other hand, without this energy,
there would be no movement towards a deathly end. There is no energy
outside the life drive. The differentiation between the life and death
drives lies not in the energy they in fact share, but in the pathways
anchored in fixed points formed through repression. The life drive *is*
the death drive, but what makes it deathly is the fact that it seeks to
regain its prior state on the basis of pathways, and in spite of the
pathways, which fix the subject in place. The only way it can regain the
prior state is to do away with the pathways, and this means the death of

the subject. In one sense, then, the idea that life tends towards death is based on a mistake about direction.

But let us keep to the subject. If there is no resistance, there is no death drive, but there is also no subject. This is because, without a fixed point, there is nothing that marks the subject out as separate, with an individual history and a personal memory. A poor thing, but its own. But the fact that the subject has to expend energy in maintaining this repressed fixed point and the pathways that follow from it leads to a further paradox, which by my argument can only be resolved in terms of an intersubjective economy of energy. In fact this economy is already implicit in the idea that in the state *in utero* there is less delay between the perception of a need and the response to it. To suppose that there is less delay is to suppose that there is a system of fleshly communication between two parties; it is the maternal organism that responds to embryonic messages.[30] This both establishes and embodies what I term the original logic of the flesh, a system of connection and communication that may contribute to the generative grammar of language.

In this fleshly logic there is no separation between thought and substance: the message and the response are communicated in bio-chemical codes which are meaningful precisely because they are interactive; they involve two parties. Another name for this fleshly logic is found in Freud, who writes of a 'common source' (*gemeinsame Quelle*) at base of language and affect alike. Freud was not speculating on the intra-uterine state, but on the connection between hysterical symptoms and the words they reflect. Thus 'a stab in the heart' referred

30 It means that the mother is not, as Aristotle had it, a passive garden in which a tiny, active, fully formed homunculus is planted and grows of its own accord (Aristotle c. 335 BCE). The tendency to regard the mother's role in gestation as passive persists past the discovery of ovulation. It is evident, however, that the mother's role is only passive if things go right. That the mother's body can actively upset the development of the embryo is acknowledged and stressed when things go wrong. Thus the injunctions not to smoke, drink and so on during pregnancy are an oblique recognition of the mother's agency. Needless to say, I am not arguing for feckless pregnancies, merely for an extension of the logic that underlies strictures against them to a recognition of a positive agency, which just might lead to some interesting biological research. Kristeva has also argued that the fact of maternity and existence *in utero* influences all later psychical development. She has done so partly on the basis that there is no effective division between mother and embryo, and that their merging abolishes a subject–object distinction. Irigaray makes a similar point about the placenta. I suppose the difference between the argument I am putting and Kristeva's is in fact a difference of degree, and a difference in elaborating the premise and following through on its consequences. To say that pregnancy reveals a state where there is no subject–object distinction is to point to a remarkable fact. But what do we do with this fact? How is the subject–object distinction abolished? I have argued that it is abolished by a rapidity of communication which is only possible where this rapidity is not impeded by the fixed points at base of subjectivity, which leads us into the various implications for nature and technology, as well as the psyche, discussed in the text.

to an affective response located originally in the heart, a location recalled in words. The implication of this for Freud is that language and affect were originally one, but become split. How they become split is another question, which we come to after discussing how the intersubjective economy enables the subject-to-be to move, to direct energy to other ends while it maintains itself.

After birth, an intersubjective economy makes itself felt in terms of energetic *attention*, and in the transmission of affects and emotions from one party to another. This transmission is presupposed by Kleinians and Lacanians alike in the clinic. For Lacan, the child is always the symptom of the parents, meaning it carries the unconscious desire of the other. This desire, transmitted in infancy, actually gets into the child, but the energetic implications of this idea are untheorized. Similarly, Kleinians work with the idea that the 'feelings' the analyst has are actually a communication from the analysand about the analysand's feelings, but how they are transmitted from one party to another is not discussed. This lack of discussion is surprising, as the notion of migrating affects questions the subject already 'in question' in a most radical way. It questions something that has been unchallenged. Structuralism and poststructuralism have argued for the construction and deconstruction of the subject at linguistic and social levels, while the idea that our 'feelings' are socialized has a much longer-standing theoretical currency. But the idea that these feelings are nonetheless ours (even if they are socialized) and not someone else's is retained.

Yet despite a lack of curiosity about the mechanism of transmission, the Kleinian corpus does include a theory that one person can contain the emotions of another, and in some way give the other unconscious as well as conscious attention. It does not say how, but it says that it is done. The theory is Wilfred Bion's (1962). Bion argues that the mother's containing the projected aggressive, sadistic impulses of the infant is the condition of the infant's learning to think. He also argues that the attention the mother gives the infant is a condition of its thriving and thinking; by attention, Bion evidently means something stronger than interest. The mother more or less lends her intelligence, and this loan or (let's be realistic) gift is evidently capable of crossing from one apparently discrete body to another, which means that it has to have a material existence itself. The material or physical existence of energetic attention is the cornerstone of my theory of an intersubjective economy of energy. It is the means for resolving the paradox of how it is that the subject keeps going, while it simultaneously 'resists', meaning expends energy on itself. The attention or attentive energy received from another means that the subject-to-be is able to deal with a problem that would be difficult for it to resolve if it existed in an individually contained energetic system.

But this facilitating attention is not perceived for what it is. In part, this is because attention comes hand-in-hand with the desire of the other, with the image the other gives (I term the conjunction of attention and image an imprint). In larger part, it is because the infant confuses the imprint of the other with its own hallucination. The two form an interlock, which is the first boundary or border for constructed identity. As the infant has no means for formally differentiating itself from the other, it has no means for differentiating the restrictive fixity of hallucination and image from the facilitating attention that comes with the latter. It can imagine that it is the source of the attention it receives, just as it imagines it is or controls the breast. Indeed, this very imagining could be occasioned by the lack of differentiation, and would explain the *ressentiment* that is always a part of envy: the sense that the thing envied has been unfairly removed, that it really belongs to oneself. And the subject-to-be most surely resents the fixity it needs, but fears. That is to say, the fixity of repressed hallucination is felt as a restriction on motion, which it is, but because it interlocks with the imprint of the other it is felt as a fixity imposed from without. As fixity in turn intensifies anxiety, and as anxiety intensifies the impulse to project, the result is an increase in projected aggression onto the other.

Herein we see Lacan's master–slave, spatial dialectic recapitulated, or rather prefigured: the dialectic of fixity, aggression, anxiety and projection is once more played out, but it is played out in the expressly energetic, intersubjective terms that Lacan's mirror-stage morphology demands. But unlike Lacan's account, the one I have outlined here is also replayed in the constitution of sexual difference. By my argument, the second border or boundary for identity is founded when the subject projects its own imprint onto the other, in a way that fixes the other in place, while enabling the subject to move, free of the fixity that constrains it. The one who projects this fixity is styled masculine, the one who receives it feminine. But the exchange does not end here. The feminine party also receives an identity through this exchange, but it is an identity that reinforces constructed inertia rather than alleviates it (hence the rigidity Freud noted but could not explain in femininity). The feminine party moreover directs living attention to the masculine one, which means he can sustain his self-image without diverting too much attention to this fixed end himself. This is where the foundational fantasy is translated into the fantasy of woman. The difference between this sexual difference replay and the hallucinatory level that precedes it is that the replay establishes spatial distinctness, and it is effected through the splitting of the 'common source' into words and affects.

Spatial distinctness and language go together. To go from a world ruled by hallucination to one which thinks in terms of past and future, near and far, is to be able to locate events. This depends on recognizing the difference and distinctness of the other. For Freud, it meant giving up the instant gratification of hallucination for the deferred gratification of achieving the desired end in reality at a later point, whilst maintaining an attachment to the wished-for object in fantasy. In my terms the substitution of fantasy for hallucination is in itself an acknowledgement of space and time. If I close my eyes to daydream, the images I have are literally smaller, located elsewhere in space and time, than the immediate, here-and-now-seeming perceptions I have if I hallucinate. But to have a fantasy of a distinct object, to know it as separate and outside the self, one has to be able to name it.

In the theory I am summarizing, language is not only critical in establishing the sense of space; it is also a means to miming the original logic of the flesh, but it does so at a slower pace than that experienced *in utero*. It attempts to make similar connections, but it can only do so from a subject-centred standpoint, from a fixed standpoint, if it makes them across space and time, by difference and deferral. This is the Derridean point. Also, the subject can only make these connections if it excludes the things that would otherwise interfere with the path it wants to track. And given that it was the repression of a fixed point that founded the subject's memory, the location of a further fixed point in another also has a role in maintaining the subject's memory and sense of continuity. In our terms, the things it excludes are the affects that otherwise interfere with the reasoning process, an exclusion which also facilitates its movement and its memory. We have seen that the affect that does this most is anxiety. The subject is more free of anxiety and able to think when anxiety is projected into the other, together with the fixity that accompanies it. But all affects for Freud are in some way tied to fixity. One of his great unappreciated points is the idea that an affect *is* an hysterical symptom. In other words, an affect is a frozen or fixed memory of a previous response. Affects are carried by the feminine other who, because she becomes more fixed (relative to the subject) precisely because she carries them, becomes an object.

This leads to a less attractive slant on 'feelings' than that found in much contemporary feminism, but it needs to be remembered that the subject who projects out his anxiety and aggression is also imbued with affects. I have styled them sadodispassionate affects. While the sadodispassionate subject appears to be without emotion, he is in fact riddled with the castrating aggression that is the vehicle for projecting the affects he would otherwise have to contain. There is a world of difference between the sadodispassionate and genuine detachment; both appear cool, but only one is cold.

The displacement of the first level of constructed inertia onto masculinity and femininity secures a workable if inequitable distribution of movement and fixity, thought and affect. The replay at the secondary level of masculinity and femininity works by splitting the common source in which thought and affect, mind and substance are one, but it attempts to recapture the original connections it mimes. This replay erects a contained masculine subject, who is sealed off from any knowledge of the energetic connections between beings, connections on which he none the less depends. The feminine object may be more likely to have knowledge of these connections, but less likely to be able to express it. This is what Lacan may have meant when he said that the woman 'as *mystérique*' knows the Real, but is unable to say anything about it (or so he assumed).

## FROM THE COMMON SOURCE TO THE ONE SUBSTANCE

The critical point about sexual difference as a replay is this: it implies, as I argued at the end of my study on Freud, that masculinity and femininity are merely the terms in which an underlying war of inertia, hostility and anxiety is played out. In Part I, I reached the same conclusion in an analysis of Lacan's concept of the *objet a*. The underlying war could well be played out in another force field altogether, which would affect the constitution of sexual difference, and a great deal else. This book's concern is with that other field, which is now an open field to the extent that the fantasy of woman no longer contains the action within it. This is the world in which commodities proliferate, providing the instant gratification which had hitherto been deferred. In the next chapter, we trace the path of proliferating commodities, showing how energy is bound in them in the same way that freely mobile energy is bound in the repression of an hallucination.

On this basis we will be able to see how the ego's era tries to make itself total, or global, and how it reinforces the psychical power of the foundational fantasy in the process. But in the open field it seems that, in theory at least, the idea of the subject as a contained entity is being re-examined, and we need to see why this is so. This is a matter I return to in the book's conclusion, where I will suggest that we are dealing with something like a three-stage process: first, a period before, or 'another place', where the idea that human beings are contained (and therefore subjects) is not axiomatic; second, the era of the contained subject, which coincides with the ego's era; and third, the present period in the West, where containment is breaking down in an hallucinatory culture. But this three-stage idea is only suggestive; as I noted at the beginning of this chapter, the history of the concept of the contained subject is one which would require far more detailed investigation. That investigation is the condition of working out whether my theses are useful, and how specific genealogies intersect with the totalizing trend of the ego's era. In the remainder of this book, what I try to do for the most part is outline a general theory of one side of the history of modernity: the totalizing side. Accordingly I concentrate on the manner in which the production of commodities for exchange acts out the fantasy and makes totalization an actuality.

But first I need to reiterate that while the foregoing theory parallels Lacan's in so many ways, the parallels emerge through stressing an interactive economy of energy, and a theory of constructed inertia based upon it. It is only by this stress that we reach the origin beneath the foundational fantasy, and perhaps the way beyond it.


On the basis of my hypothesis about an intra-uterine state, and an intersubjective economy of energy, I have argued that hallucination makes us self-contained because it divorces mindful agency from the matter that executes it, that it makes passive in fantasy, *and* because it situates the subject in a fixed place, from which it functions at a slower pace, in energetic terms. These points are related. We think in terms of thought divorced from matter because the divorce sustains the omnipotent illusion at base of a subject-centred standpoint. Yet the hallucination is not immaterial in its effects, however fantasmatic it is. It does, through its repression, effect a divorce between freely mobile and fixed energy, and this division functions henceforth as a seal which closes the subject off from the knowledge and experience of its interconnection. It gives it a boundary; this boundary also cements the imagined separation of thought and energetic substance, precisely because it does effect the beginnings of a material split between them. Energetic substance is manifest in anything from motion to the intermediate experience of 'feelings': feelings are especially important as a category in which some of the original indissolubility of thought and substance are retained; they keep the tie to matter, as emotions are indubitably corporeal, at the same time as they reflect ideational responses; we can regard them as the slower-motion residues of the original connection between thought and substance.

Unlike psychosis, neurosis defrays omnipotence because it recognizes the other, or at least agrees to a social contract in which omnipotence is shared with other subjects. In psychosis, hallucination defaults on its double duty, and only performs one task. The hallucinatory omnipotence, the self-referential standpoint, in which actions and ideas are meant to be aimed at the self is retained. What is lost is the closure, the boundary that seals the subject off from knowledge of connection. It is lost because the hallucination is not repressed; it is not unconscious. The result is that interconnectedness is still experienced, but the 'connections' the psychotic experiences are conceived from its own hallucinatory, omnipotent standpoint: Schreber believes that he is the special beneficiary of the 'rays of God', just as a psychotic suffering from a different delusion believes he is the persecuted (but therefore privileged) object of, say, Communist Plots. In other words, the psychotic experience is a mixture: of the subject-centred standpoint, and knowledge of a world in which all things are connected, energetically and conatively. Because it is a mixture, the psychotic understanding of energetic connection is distorted. But it is informative precisely because it tells us that there is a mixture, and we can seek to understand intersubjective and interactive economies of energy in terms of that mixture.

So far, I have discussed this psychical mixture in terms of a contrast between the original fleshly logic and the attempt to remake the connections of that logic from a subject-centred standpoint. This attempt, this remaking, rests on a foundational fantasy which in turn rests on the repression of the hallucination with which the fantasy begins. The expression of the fantasy in commodities indicates that the miming and remaking from the subject's standpoint goes well beyond a parody of linguistic logic and into other hallmarks of the original fleshly connection: in particular, this miming seeks to abolish time in favour of instant gratification.

Yet while the subject's fixity does in fact make it distinct relative to a state of more rapid and interconnected motion, fixity can only make the subject distinct, after birth, if the state of more rapid motion is not confined to the womb. This means there has to be a field of contrast which has the same effects and the same benefits as the flesh, but which is lived in after birth. The obvious candidate for this field of contrast is the unbound primary process, the life drive. But what is that, other than nature? To nature overall I have attributed the same process of connection and inherent logic, the same inseparability of thought and substance experienced *in utero*. This attribution will make more sense if we note that the split between mind and matter, as it has been described here, is also the split between the individual and the environment. This has to be so by the implications of this argument so far. We can only be self-contained in relation to an environment with which we are potentially connected. The boundary the subject erects is a boundary against freely mobile energy and excitations in general. The contrast with the intra-uterine state explains the omnipotent aim of the pathways that redirect the life drive on the basis of fixed points, but the experience of the intra-uterine contrast is not the end of the experience of more rapid motion.[31]

However, the idea that nature also provides a more rapid energetic field of contrast will have yet more substance when we see how the technological production of commodities plays out the same dynamics, in relation to nature, as the foundational fantasy does in relation to the maternal body. In other words, the relation between commodities and nature enacts the same dynamics of fixity, inertia and the abolition of time, dynamics which require the diversion of the energy of the life drive. Evidently, this means that the life drive not only works between people in an intersubjective economy, but between nature, including people, and technology, in what for convenience I have called an interactive economy. The reader will recall that this term is used to stress that energetic connection is not only naturalistic. The importance of this idea is that it counters the uncritical holism that characterizes thinking about 'cosmic connection'. We can be historically constructed, we can construct history, but these constructions have physical effects

31   The experience of energetic connection after birth is discussed in relation to Freud's concept of excitations and a 'protective shield' against them in Brennan (1992, Ch. 5).

on the interactive economy we inhabit.[32] In turn, these effects rebound on us.

The idea of the interactive economy means that, in the microcosm of the psyche, the effects of the foundational fantasy are felt more strongly as the fantasy is acted out technologically. Thus, for instance, Klein's belief that the infant wants to poison the mother with its excrements, to cut her up and fragment her, becomes more plausible. It becomes more plausible because the infant psyche, as yet unbound, becomes a catch-all through which historically constructed energies flow. Amongst these are impulses directed toward poisoning and cutting up nature. In the contained psyche, the psyche that retroactively claims the impulses it experiences as its own, the impulse to poison and fragment is expressed on a smaller scale. It is expressed in terms of the tiny concepts to hand, where 'poisons' are something expelled by the body, and the world is the mother.

Who knows which came first here? The impulses as they are recorded in the psychoanalytic case study, or as they are manifest on the larger scale? The mindset or fantasy predates its technological enactment, but it was socially enacted in more limited ways long before this present. Still, the discovery, in these psychoanalytic times, of the ingredients of the fantasy in each and all suggests the impulses are stronger. We will come back to the question of priority, but the probability is that our contribution has to be restricted to understanding how the fantasy gains in strength, in an interactive economy ruled by commodities.

32 By this I mean not just that we interfere with the biosphere; we may also be creating physical energetic effects which function on the broad scale like 'feelings' – mixtures of natural and technological forms of energy, atmospheres that feel like hell.

# Chapter 4

# From the reserve army of labour to the standing reserve of nature

In this chapter I will suppose that the construction of a commodity binds energy in the same way that it is bound in the repression of a hallucination. The energy bound in this way is that of living nature; it correlates with Freud's 'freely mobile energy'. I have suggested that the paths of freely mobile energy and those of the life drive are the same, once we analyse the idea that freely mobile energy follows the path of least resistance. Freely mobile energy only follows this path because something exists that resists. Like the hallucination, the commodity provides a point of resistance, in that it encapsulates living nature in forms which remove them from the flow of life. It functions analogously with hallucinations in that it binds living substances in forms which are inert, relative to the energetic movement of life. We can assume that the more of these relatively inert points there are, the slower the movement of life becomes. This slow movement underpins a different sense of time, which presents itself to consciousness, via a paradox, as the rapid time of modernity.

Time, as a glance through the various chapter headings of *Capital*[1] makes plain,[2] occupied Marx as well as Heidegger. But the temporal

---

1 Most of this discussion is based on *Capital*, given that this is the text where Marx's political economy is presented in its most developed form. However, I also draw extensively on the *Grundrisse*. For convenience, I have referred to the main works cited by name: thus *Capital*, and the *Grundrisse*.

2 In addition to the temporal dimension which is integral to the labour theory of value advanced in Volume 1 of *Capital* (see the appendix), Marx was also interested in time in a way that paralleled the interests of the 'bourgeois economists'. This is reflected in Volume 2 of *Capital*. It is generally regarded as the least original of the three volumes of *Capital*, and this may be because 'time' was so much the preoccupation of the bourgeois economists Marx was writing against, and of mainstream economists since. Marxists assume that time is important, or appears to be important, only at the level of the fantasmatic or 'mystical' appearance of capital's movements. Marx distinguished between this fantasmatic level and the level of real exploitation of surplus-value. The distinction between these levels is of particular importance in the following argument, precisely because the fantasmatic level is material in its effects, as Marx

dimension in Marx's value theory has been downplayed, obscured by Marx's own emphasis on subjective human labour-power as the key factor in profit. In this chapter I will try to use Marx's value theory without this subjective emphasis. I will argue that used this way, it becomes a theory of time and speed, in which time is compressed in favour of distance by the binding of nature in the fixed points of commodities. Read without its subjective emphasis, Marx's value theory also shows that profit depends on the fixed points of commodities proliferating at nature's expense.

But why the labour theory of value? It is the least used and possibly the most criticized aspect of Marx's *oeuvre*, yet it remains unique in its stress on the 'two-fold' nature of a commodity.[3] In a market system, a commodity is always produced for exchange, and has exchange-value. But it also and always has use-value, and there can be no use-value without nature, or natural substance. Because of Marx's emphasis on the two-fold nature of a commodity, the labour theory of value can become a theory whose essential contradiction is between natural energy and the time or speed of exchange. Marx, however, saw this basic contradiction in terms of labour-power and technology, where labour-power alone adds value, but where value will necessarily be diminished as more is spent on technology. Technology adds no value in itself, but more has to be spent on it, in order for capital to produce in the fastest time possible, and thus compete.

Understanding of this contradiction has been limited because of Marx's subject-centred perspective which singled out labour for special treatment: labour was the subject, nature was relegated to the realm of object.[4] But if nature or certain natural forces are shown to have an

was the first to acknowledge in writing on the fetishism of commodities. But in the light of the 'reality' of the fantasmatic, time once more comes into its own.

3  Amongst other things, sympathetic critiques focus on the neglect of supply and demand, gender and the environment. The 1970s generation of feminists tried (and failed) to deploy Marxist political economy in analysing patriarchy. We have yet to see the results of recent attempts to wrestle with the environment from a Marxist stand-point. Roughly speaking, the rich work on the environment that is indebted to Marxism assumes (a) that Marx had overlooked the finite limitations on nature (which he had); and (b) that capital would exploit nature in order to make a profit (which it does). But it tends to assume that the key dynamic here is profit above all. This limits the analysis of environmental factors in state socialism. For a survey on the literature on Marxism and the environment, see Ryle (1988). Two seminal works in the field of socialism and ecology are Gorz (1980) and Williams (1973). Probably the leading radical non-Marxist exponent of environmental thinking is Bookchin (1982). There are excellent articles by Benton (1989); also Goldman and O'Connor (1988) and other contributors to the journal *Capitalism, Nature, Socialism,* which I discovered whilst this book was in press.

4  The odd thing is that with the partial exceptions of Deleuze and Guattari, and Spivak, the attention to the subject/object distinction in general, and binary oppositions in particular, has stopped short at criticizing these oppositions and their effects on Marx. See the discussion of

energetic property in common with labour-power, the 'essential contradiction' has more explanatory power. Nature is the source of all value, and ultimately of all energy, but it is my thesis that the inherent dynamic of capital is to diminish this value and this energy in favour of time and technology.

For those who are unfamiliar with the labour theory of value, I have included an appendix on it, which draws out how much value theory is a theory of time. This appendix also analyses in detail Marx's reliance on subject–object thinking, and shows how it is connected to his abstraction from natural conditions. In addition, the next section of this chapter is expository. It also draws out aspects of time in value theory, and bears on the contradiction between nature and technology. (The trouble with including an exposition at this point is that it breaks up the flow of this book's argument somewhat. Readers who want to get back to the foundational fantasy, and the question of how capital plays out its dynamics in relation to nature, may wish to skip this section.)

This chapter's third and subsequent sections suggest how Marx's value theory would work without his subject–object distinction. They do so with very broad brush strokes: these sections follow a speculative path, whereby the conclusions I reach are entailed by the internal logic of the narrative. The advantage of this procedure is that it results in an argument which, if it is right, has implications not only for the environment, but for how the approach to many standard problems in Marxist thought might be reformulated: it bears on the reproduction of labour, hence on women, race and different dimensions of class; it also bears on the state. While these bearings are speculative, while they are not based on an empirical overview of the extensive literature in these fields, they could readily be measured against it.

## THE TIME–ENERGY AXIS

In the context of nineteenth-century political economy, it was Marx's great discovery that profit originated in production, not distribution. For Marx, profit originated in the difference between what labour added in production within a given time, and the time taken to reproduce labour-power. The distinction here between labour, which is

Deleuze in Chapter 3. Spivak analyses the use of oppositions, and the subject-position, in Marx's value theory, but insists on a 'materialist predication', in express distinction from Deleuze and Guattari (Spivak 1987, pp. 154–5 and *passim*). In another context, Gallagher (1987) has argued that the category of labour was especially and unduly priveleged in the nineteenth century.

what is done at work, and 'labour-power', which is the 'capacity to work', available for sale, is crucial. Marx regarded this distinction as his most important contribution to political economy, his most significant move beyond Ricardo.[5] It was crucial for Marx because it pinpointed the source of profit, or surplus-value. It did so because it recognized that under capital, and only under capital, the capacity for labour, as labour-power, could be bought and sold like any other commodity in the free exchange of the market. In all other modes of production, the buying and selling of labour was in some way restricted. A profit is made because what labour adds in production, *during a given time*, is worth more than what it costs to maintain and reproduce labour-power, *at a given time*. This is labour-power's socially necessary labour-time.

In fact socially necessary labour-time sets the value of any commodity, although how far labour-time as such *is* 'socially necessary' is determined by technology. Labour-power working with primitive technology adds no more value than labour-power working with technology that is advanced. Thus labour-time, as a concept, runs technological time and labour together.

The exchange-value of a commodity is measured by its labour-time. This exchange-value is 'no substantial thing', Marx insists. It is immaterial. Yet Marx also says that labour-power, like labour, is always 'energy'. Indeed he says this repeatedly: the 'living quality' of labour-power, its ability to embody its own energy in the product, is something that capital needs. Despite this, time, and not energy, is the factor that figures in exchange-value. At least, energy does not figure as long as the quantitative calculations of exchange-value are made in an environment that is nothing more than a fantasy. It is a material fantasy, to be sure, but it is still a fantasy.

This will become plainer after more details of Marx's theory have been laid out, beginning with the means of production. These include both the inanimate tools or technology used to work on nature, and

5  Like John Locke and others in a line of political theorists and political economists before Marx, Ricardo adhered to a labour theory of value. But for Ricardo, the value of a particular commodity reflected the particular labour embodied in it, and wages in turn were meant to reflect this value; surplus-value arose through an unfair exchange between labour and capital. The particularity of this definition meant that individual commodities were meant to reflect the value labour added to them, but this meant that it was difficult to see how labour ruled their value, in an overall system dominated by apparently free exchange. Marx overcame this problem with the labour/labour-power distinction: (a) this enabled him to look at profit in overall terms, and move from the particular to the general; (b) the distinction also meant Marx could conclude that capital was not 'unfair': it paid for labour-power at its value. It was just that labour added something more.

nature itself. These are the 'instruments' and material for labour. For Marx, they are the 'object'. They represent or embody that part of capital Marx calls 'constant capital', or the 'objective factor' in production. Constant capital is the capital used to purchase buildings, raw materials, energy and machinery. Marx further divided this constant capital into two forms: fixed and circulating capital. Fixed capital was literally embodied in fixtures: buildings, machinery and so on. Circulating capital includes forms of energy and raw materials.[6] The value of the capital deployed in the mode of production is constant in that it is not of itself capable of producing more value. Labour is 'variable capital' because it can add more or less value. Just as labour is the subject counterposed to the object, so variable capital is the 'subjective factor' in production.

The means of production are also critical in another key Marxist concept: the productive forces or forces of production. The productive forces, however, consist of more than the means of production. They consist of the infrastructure of the production process; thus assembly-line production, which speeds things up, belongs to the productive forces. The productive forces are counterposed to the relations of production, to the social division of labour and control of the means of production, which in turn determine class relations.

We need to note two more of Marx's premises. The first is about how capital, because it is governed by competition, must expend more on constant capital in centralized production sites. The second is about the political effects of this centralization. On the first point: to be governed by competition is also, for Marx, to be governed by time. When Marx predicted that more and more wealth would be embodied in constant capital and expenditure on the means of production, he did so because 'our capitalist', or 'moneybags', as Marx also called the agent involved in the profitable enterprise, had to ensure that more and more commodities were produced and put into circulation in a shorter and shorter *space of time*, in order to capture a share of the market. Our capitalist can only do this by expending capital on technologies which produce faster, or at any rate no less rapidly, than other comparable enterprises and by reducing unit production costs. The greater the outlay on constant capital, the more capital-intensive production is, the lower the

6 To complicate this a little, circulating capital also includes the variable capital needed to purchase labour-power. There is here a tacit indication of what we will argue explicitly later in this chapter, which is that all forms of energy, including labour-power, should be treated both as variable *and* as circulating capital.

unit production costs (in general). They are lower because more fixed capital expenditure per unit output is the means to economies of scale. Our capitalist compensates to some extent for what he loses in real profit (surplus-value contingent on variable capital) by capturing a larger share of the market. But he can only do this if he moves fast.

Precisely because they involve honing the time of production through detail labour (cf. Braverman 1974), the expanding technologies necessary for economies of scale require centralized production sites, embodied in ever-larger spatial conglomerates. Now as I just mentioned, but wish to stress, this is a necessary but not a sufficient condition of successful competition for our capitalist. He can only capture his share of the market by putting his commodities into circulation no less rapidly than his competitors. In order both to produce and distribute as (or more) rapidly than his competitors he has to acquire the means of production and labour-power within a time-scale appropriate to his production and distribution. In Marx's schema acquisition belongs to the sphere of exchange. Marx himself insisted on the *interdependence* of what he designated the four spheres of capital: production, reproduction, distribution and exchange, but production was always the privileged sphere. Yet once value theory is read without the subject-object distinction, and as its emphasis shifts to time, the speed of distribution and exchange becomes cardinal. Distribution and exchange, while they are answerable to speed, obviously involve space and the regulation of space.

But keeping to the exposition. For Marx, the very expenditure on more rapid means of technological production contains the seeds of capital's demise in that constant capital, of itself, can add no surplus-value. The ability to do so remains the property of labour or variable capital alone. Yet because technology is the means by which the production of profit is speeded up, and given that it can offset a fall in profit in the short term, capital will tend towards the situation where it relies more on technology than it does on living labour; thus a machine capable of producing $X$ amount of cloth may require only one labourer to work it, while many labourers would be required to produce the same amount of cloth without the machine. At this point the dual aspects of 'labour-time' stand opposed once again. Labour is the only thing that adds 'more', but unless it adds it within the prevailing socially necessary labour-time capital will not make a profit.

We have shown here how time figures in the bare essentials of the labour theory of value. Its key measurements are (a) the rate of value added in the time of production compared with the time of reproduction; (b) the speed (another way of saying time) of production in relation to competitors. Both measurements converge in the concept of socially necessary labour-time, which determines the prevailing speed, and the cost of, reproduction. In the next section, we will ask if the 'socially necessary' measurement of value was ever in fact a *necessary* consideration. Or was it not, rather, an assumption (however sensible and rational) that could be sustained only as long as natural sources apart from human labour were discounted in estimations of value? They were discounted as long as the level of energetic substance, one side of the commodity's 'two-fold' nature, was taken for granted.

## FROM THE RESERVE ARMY OF LABOUR TO THE STANDING RESERVE OF NATURE

One cannot begin to grasp the importance of the material, energetic dimension in value-theory without taking account of how natural energy works on and in a continuum of natural substances overall. This is why terms such as 'biosphere' and 'ecology' have their current currency: they embody the recognition that the natural continuum is precisely that; you cannot inflate or diminish one part of it without having effects on another, hence the whole.

The notion of the transfer of matter into energy, more exactly, the idea that matter *is* energy, it also part of contemporary currency, and in one sense it belongs in Marx's. Labour-power, as Marx said quite precisely, is energy transferred to 'a human organism by means of nourishing matter' (1867 *Capital* 1, p. 207 *n*.1); nourishing matter, in turn, is produced by other natural sources and the socially directed energy of humans (usually women).

Just as nourishing matter feeds labour-power, so is nourishing matter fed by other natural substances. Just as the reproduction of labour-power cannot take place without or outside the cycles of natural reproduction, neither can the reproduction of other natural sources and forces. So on the one hand, all these forces and sources are connected. On the other, they are not equal from the temporal perspective of capital. But for the time being, I will continue to refer to natural sources and forces without qualification, whilst bearing in mind the obvious point that not all of them add energy, or useful energy, to the same extent. Some of them add more energy than others, including labour-power. Some add less.

For Marx himself, energy can only be added by living labour ('the subject'); all other constituents of production are supposedly lifeless ('the object'). As far as the behaviour of capital is concerned, their livingness is irrelevant. But this does not mean that it is irrelevant to the inner workings of production. It is important to remember that Marx, in discovering what he thought was the source of capitalist profit, also showed how capital loses consciousness of that source; it spends more on constant capital, less on the variable capital that adds value. This source was so obscured that part of it remained hidden even from Marx.

Endlessly, Marx stresses that labour is the only living factor in production, and this is entirely consistent with the foundational fantasy. He not only identifies the 'living factor' with subjective human agency. In the characteristic fantasmatic gesture of reversal, he endows the subject alone with the capacity to give life. The gesture is only possible where it is assumed that nature gives nothing of itself; and that is only possible in a mode of production in which living nature is marginalized. Yet it is exactly this marginalization, a concomitant of industrialization, that Marx generalizes to all epochs, regardless of its evident historical specificity. But the gesture of itself is not enough to make labour-power alone the source of value, to the extent that this source is that which lives.

As labour-power is precisely energy, even 'tension' (1867 *Capital* 1, p. 583), it has everything in common with other natural forces, capable of realizing energy as humans can. For that matter, it has a potential affinity with natural substances which are inanimate as well as animate, in so far as these can be made into sources of energy. Of course they still have to be *made* into these sources, and on the face of it, it would seem that only labour has this power of making. But our immediate concern is with their energetic dimension.

Like labour-power, natural sources and forces are commodities capable of releasing and adding energy. Like labour-power, they have a certain time of natural reproduction, which means that potentially, the value they add in production can be greater than their reproduction time. Like labour-power, they can add more or less energy in the production process. Of course, we have to distinguish between these natural sources and forces in terms of (a) what kind of and how much energy they generate, and (b) the cost of acquiring them, in relation to one another and to labour-power. Both these points will be addressed at length below.

The point here is that because Marx begins from a subject–object world in which all things, artefacts and natural substances, are already commodities, objects for the consumption of a subject, he may suppose that the only new substantial value added in the (industrial) production process is the *energy* newly materialized by labour in the product.

But once labour-power is treated as a source of energy, one form of all natural sources of energy, once the opposition between subjective and objective factors is replaced by one between living nature and the commodified dead, then value-theory's logic can be extended. We can keep the logic that led Marx to break capital down into two components: constant and variable capital. We can even say that variable capital is the source of surplus-value, while constant capital is not. We can deduce too that the greater the outlay on constant as opposed to variable capital in production, the less the surplus-value extracted. We can deduce further that the imperative to produce more in the shortest possible time will lead to a greater outlay on constant capital.

But the change we will make, on the basis of my argument that, *at the level of substance, productive* living labour-power should not be distinguished from other natural sources and forces that materialize energy, is that we will assume that *all natural sources of energy entering production should be treated as variable capital and sources of surplus-value*, and some can be replaced by others. The logic of this replacement will encompass labour-power. If another natural substance can supply what labour supplies, it, too, counts as variable capital. Moreover, this series of assumptions entails that *there is no real check on the speed with which variable capital can be used up, apart from whether or not a particular form of variable capital can be replaced*, meaning its reproduction has to be guaranteed.

If all energetic sources entering production add value, the tendency of the rate of profit to fall will be offset.[7] It will only fall where constant capital is really 'fixed' in relation to labour-power, in that no other natural force figures in production, disguised as constant capital. It is readily disguised by Marx's original conceptual armoury. Just as his definition of the 'objective factors' elided nature and technology, so too does the definition of 'circulating capital' elide technological and natural

7  In the literature on Marxism and the environment thus far, it has been supposed that if capital has to make provision for environmental safeguards, this will increase the expenditure on constant capital and therefore exacerbate the tendency of the rate of profit to fall. Gorz's (1980) argument to this effect has been influential. There may be a minor increase, but the additional natural energy sources massively offsets it.

forms of energy. Our redefinition of variable capital encompasses the natural sources of energy, which have been conceptually locked-up in the concept of circulating capital.

The significance of circulating capital in this epoch is recognized by Marxist political economy. For Mandel, it is probably the most important factor within it, because of its increasing range and speed.[8] My re-reading of value-theory will explain this phenomenon as one that is basic rather than incidental: the range and speed of circulation is one key to how surplus-value is extracted and profit made. However, by making speed basic, we will be able to explain capital's behaviour in relation to agricultural commodities: including animals, whose reproduction is speeded up when possible. We will even be able to re-situate labour-power in a privileged and crucial place in surplus-value extraction, a place which depends on its voluntary portability (which does after all mark it out from other sources of energy: see the Appendix). But these things can best be done after we have discussed the idea that one energy source can be replaced by another in industrial production in more detail. I will enter a brief note on this, before outlining the overall argument of this chapter's remainder.

## THE LAW OF SUBSTITUTION

We can formulate the process by which one energy source will be replaced by another in terms of a law of substitution. According to this law, capital, all other things being equal, will take the cheapest form of energy adequate to sustaining production of a particular commodity at the prevailing level of competition. Many of these energy forms will be refined; they will be – from one to many times – removed from their natural state. But this does not mean they cease to be valuable. They only cease to be this when their capacity for adding energy is exhausted. Up to this point, their value may be increased as other forms of energy (including labour-power) are mixed into them, although this mixing can also diminish energy sources overall, especially when their

8 See Mandel's classic and comprehensive *Late Capitalism*. Incidentally, referring back to Chapter 3's discussion of the commodity, it is worth noting Mandel's difficulties with the service industry. Having shown in effect in Chapter 12 (Mandel 1972) that not only circulation in general but the service industry in particular gets completely out of line with any logic of profit, he concludes in Chapter 15 (pp. 454–5) that this is only one instance of the more general disequilibria that mark late capitalism. He insists on the general disequilibria analysis in order to distinguish himself from Friedman's and Rueff's conventional quantity theory (p.431) although he concedes a 'certain similarity' (p. 435).

reproduction is ignored. It will be discounted whenever possible; forms of energy are likely to be cheaper when reproduction is discounted.

From this standpoint, I can now qualify 'natural sources and forces'. Some substances are more ready forms of energy, or are more readily converted to and add more energy than others. In everyday thinking, the extent of the energy they have or add is precisely what makes them valuable. And this cuts both ways. If labour can stand in for another energy source more cheaply and more effectively, it will be the source chosen. The points are that at the level of substance, the material energetic level, the common denominator is energy, not labour-power, and that all energy sources, including labour-power, vary in what they cost compared with what they add.

Do we have any warrant other than the direction of my argument for assuming that capital will operate by a law of substitution? In fact a similar assumption about substitution was made by Marx, when he discussed the various permutations of labour-power as a commodity. Capital, he claimed, would not hesitate to force down the wage as much as possible (keeping 'socially necessary labour-time' to the minimum) or import (that is, replace) labour-power from another source. This is why Marx assumed that the need to extract surplus-value could lead to the immiseration of the working class. He assumed that as the organic composition of capital changed, and a greater expenditure on constant capital meant less outlay on variable capital, it could be that the only way to make a profit or increase surplus-value was to keep wages down, to the extent that the level of subsistence became the level of near survival. Thus also the advantage to capital of a reserve army of labour (the unemployed, and the famous *lumpenproletariat*), whose existence in itself is a way of keeping the price of labour-power down: it weakens the bargaining power of the working class.

Now if certain natural forces capable of adding value within the sphere of industrial production are interchangeable, then capital's range of cheap options is greatly extended. It has in its back pocket not only Marx's 'reserve army' but Heidegger's 'standing reserve' of nature. In line with the logic of substitution that governs capital's selection of labour-power, where it will always, all other things being equal, take the cheapest option, it should be the case that capital operates by a general law of substitution where living forces overall are concerned. If one energy source can stand in for labour, and stand in more cheaply, it will be the source chosen. Such energy sources can offset any trend towards the immiseration of the working class, to the extent that they can stand in for labour.

The effects of the law of substitution here are similar to those wrought by imperialism, and the creation of a labour aristocracy. When Lenin, following Marx and Engels, argued that a labour aristocracy, a richer segment of the working class, could be created through the exploitation of other sections of that class, nationally and inter-nationally, he was drawing attention to how the rate of surplus-value extraction of one portion of the labour market could be less in one place if it were higher elsewhere.[9] We can now see how a similar 'benefit' to portions of the labour market can be effected through increasing the rate of surplus-value extraction of other natural entities and things. Thus, to pick up on Marx's nineteenth-century cloth example at the tail-end of the twentieth century: natural fabrics cost more than synthetic ones, whose raw materials can be 'reproduced' at a faster rate, unless the natural raw materials as well as the fabrics are reproduced and produced in 'cost-effective' labour-intensive centres, where the cost of labour-power is so low that the fabrics can compete internationally (*100% Cotton: Made in India*).[10]

In certain circumstances, and from its utterly ruthless perspective, capital might be concerned for the reproduction of natural forces, and the substances on which they depend, but it will only be concerned in so far as these sources (i) if replaced, provide a continual cheaper option and (ii) are irreplaceable. While capital has to be concerned about labour-power's capacity to wage resistance, it only has to be concerned about resistance in relation to natural forces when they are spoken for. Needless to say, natural forces, substances and non-human beings, are un-unionized, unrepresented and therefore frequently not spoken for. It is ironic that the avant-garde at this point discourages speaking on behalf of the other.[11]

## PRODUCTION AND REAL VALUE

I will summarize the main issues facing us in the light of my redefinition of variable capital and the related law of substitution. On

9 The concept of a labour aristocracy belonged more to the previous century than this one (Hobsbawm 1964) but the logic remains the same. The labour aristocracy was more likely to perceive itself as middle class.
10 On the relation between the exploitation of nature and that of people in the non-metropolitan countries, see Redclift (1984, 1987). On development as such see Lehmann (1990).
11 This is a distortion of Foucault and Derrida, but it has some currency.

the one hand, this new value-theory seems not to be a value-theory at all, but a theory headed towards the standard economic measure of supply and demand, or availability. It takes us towards that measure as there is no reason for assuming that capital is the least concerned about the reproduction of any natural force, unless it is irreplaceable. And if capital is not intrinsically interested in reproduction then for 'reproduction' we should read 'availability'. That is to say, reproduction is only of interest to capital in so far as it guarantees a continued supply of a commodity necessary for production to continue. If production can continue through the availability of other natural forces and entities whose reproduction can be disregarded, this availability is what matters.

On the other hand, we now have another way of looking at value-theory, which sees, as Marx saw, the relation between value added in production and the cost of reproduction as the real measure of value. But it sees it in terms of substance. This is not to say that capital adheres to this substantial measure of reproduction; not for a minute. It is just that this measure will make its effects felt: both in terms of forces that have to be reproduced in the relatively short term, and in the last instance. Both for some natural forces in the short term and for all in the very long *durée*, the relation between production and reproduction *is* a question of supply and demand: the logical if generally long-term compatibility of these two measures of cost has been obscured by the subject-centred perspective which meant that labour-power alone figured in calculations of value measurement. The idea that 'supply and demand' has a measure beyond itself is critical:

> Supply and demand regulate nothing but the temporary *fluctuations* of market prices. They will explain to you why the market price of a commodity rises above or sinks below its value, but they can never account for that *value* itself . . . . At the moment when supply and demand equilibrate each other, and therefore cease to act, the market price of a commodity coincides with its real value . . . .
> (Marx 1865, p. 45)

The measure of value now becomes, or rather is extended to, the substantial level: energy in production and its reproduction. But the short-term incompatability of this measure, and that of supply and demand, or acquisition, is another issue, the crucial issue in fact. And it is the issue which shows that value-theory, once its measure of reproduction is generalized from humans to other forms of nature overall, has a long life yet.

The measures of availability and reproduction have to be incompatible in the short term in that capital is also and always governed by time. To get more on to the market in the shortest possible time, capital has to acquire more raw materials at commensurable speed. Just as there are two levels in value-theory, one concerned with time and exchange, the other with energy, so we find these levels recapitulated in relation to labour and nature. One is the real level of substance and energy, which determines the time of reproduction. The second, which governs the workings of capital in its day-to-day competitive workings, is the fantasmatic level of time.

Reproduction time, as the real measure of value, intersects with the speed of acquisition to the extent that capital has to take account of the reproduction of raw labour-power, and by my argument, of the reproduction of other natural forces. But if capital can avoid this reckoning, if it can cheat, it will do so. It cheats by substituting one natural force, whose reproduction time it can ignore, for another which it cannot, where the former will do the job and can be acquired at greater speed.

Accordingly the reproduction of labour-power compared with the value it adds in production must cease to be the measure of profit, although it remains the sticking-point, the most obvious reminder of real or substantial value presented by the natural order, as distinct from the order of speed. I will argue below that the conflict between these orders is manifest in an increasing distance between real value, measured by the time of natural reproduction, and price, measured by speed (another, socially produced, measure of time). But while it figures, the fantasmatic level of speed has the overriding power in the short term.

But to argue this, we need a measure of short-term profit, which is not based directly on the relation between production and reproduction, but which can be tied to this relation in the long run. We need, in fact, to distinguish between short- and medium-term, and long-term profit. For short- and medium-term profit I am proposing the speed of acquisition as such a measure; it will sometimes reflect reproduction time, but it is also overridden whenever reproduction can be made a non-issue from capital's perspective.

Acquisition is a term that resonates with the name of Ricardo. In Ricardo's value-theory, exchange-value embodies the quantity of labour expended in the acquisition of goods, as well as their relative scarcity. These two determinants of value work together; the more scarce a good is, the more trouble or labour it will take to acquire it. But of course, acquisition can demand more or less labour for other reasons (Ricardo 1817). As with so much classical political economy, as well as its neo-classical successors, this is descriptively accurate up to a point. The point is its intersection with the exploitation of substance, and its measurement in terms that reflect that exploitation.

The speed of acquisition, while a slippery variable, is measurable in this way. In itself a measure of time, it is tied to another measure of time: the prevailing or socially necessary time of production. It is the difference between the cost of acquiring raw materials or commodities for production at a certain speed, and the energy they add in production that gives rise to surplus-value. In this connection we can note that labour-power can be exploited in two ways. One is in terms of the energy it adds in production. The other is the fact that it carries the costs of its own speed of acquisition. This two-sided capacity for exploitation makes it hard to replace labour-power as a particular source of energy, aside from its relatively singular capacity for taking direction, and unique capacity for portability. Labour-power can speed itself up.

In proposing the speed of acquisition as the measure of short- and medium-term profit, I am retaining the temporal measure of the original value-theory, the socially necessary time in which a given commodity can be produced and put into circulation, but generalizing it. Socially necessary time is not only 'labour-time'; it is the time within which all natural forces and substances add 'something more' in production, in terms of the technology governing the particular production process in question. Comparable qualifications to all the qualifications that Marx put on labour-time hold here. A hole formed by dripping water is as valuable as one made by water-based electric power, although the former takes a millennium and the latter a minute.

The speed of acquisition will sometimes embody the cost of reproduction, and sometimes, more usually, not. It will do so because the general law of substitution is constrained by the fact that the reproduction time of certain natural forces (chief amongst them, but not only, labour-power) forces itself into account. Were it not for this, we could say that the production of exchange-value is the consumption of use-value via the imposition of portability. But the constraint means that, from the stand-point of reproduction time as a general measure, there are two ways of speeding up the rate of surplus-value extraction.

1 The first holds for labour-power, and agricultural production. It is to allow the natural substance in question to keep its form, but speed up its rate of reproduction (for how this applies to labour-power, see below). However, even when many of these substances and products keep their form, this does not make them exempt from the imperative to speed things up.

2 The other way to speed up surplus-value extraction is to speed up the means by which one form of natural energy is converted into another. Now increasing the speed of this second form of conversion leads to ever more rapid means of releasing energy, at the same time as it, of necessity, diminishes nature overall. The full implications of this for profit will be apparent after we show why the quantitative dimension of use-value has to be taken into account.

Here this enquiry branches off into two directions. The first concerns the fate of real value, meaning nature overall as the source of all value. The second is about the cost and therefore the speed of acquisition as the measure of profit (short- and long-term).[12] I will pursue these two strands to the argument in the next sections, turning first to the overall quantity of use-value, and then to how the speed of acquisition intersects with reproduction. We will see that government by the speed of acquisition must work progressively to diminish use-value and eventually real or surplus-value overall.

We can then see how this results in a process where space progressively takes the place of time, and radiates some of its effects on nations, race and gender. But throughout this discussion, it should be remembered that these two strands, speed and substance, represent two competing dynamics in any order dominated by capital. Capital will live or die according to the speed of acquisition, but to live by the speed of acquisition is to live under a fantasmatic law. Natural entities and substances will live or die depending on how far their reproduction is permitted, and it is permitted less and less under the law of speed.

12 One of the problems with any discussion of profit in relation to Marxist political economy is the elision of profit with productivity. Sraffa (1960) drew out the different bearing of both concepts and was thus able to give a working solution to the transformation problem (cf. Shaikh 1977).

## THE OVERALL QUANTITY OF USE- AND
## SURPLUS-VALUE

As we have shown, Marx insisted that no commodity could have
surplus-value or exchange-value without use-value; he also insisted that
nature was the source of all use-value, and, with Lucretius, that 'out of
nothing, nothing could be created'.

> Use-values are perishable by nature. Hence, if they are not pro-
> ductively or individually consumed within a certain time . . . in other
> words, if they are not sold within a certain period, they spoil and lose
> with their use-value the property of being vehicles of
> exchange-value. . . . The use-values do not remain the carriers of
> perennial self-expanding capital-value unless they are constantly
> renewed and reproduced, are replaced by new use-values of the same
> or of some other order.
>
> (1885 *Capital* 2, pp. 130–131).

On the other hand, as we discussed, Marx consigned all natural forces
and sources outside labour-power to the dominion of death-sleep. But
once they are regarded as variable capital, their consignment to that
dead unreproductive place becomes not an *a priori* condition, but a
consequence of the dynamics of production, with quantitative implications for use-value in the determination of surplus-value. Use-value is
only meant to be a qualitative matter. But this qualitative emphasis is
also due to the same subject-centred perspective that led Marx to group
nature and things together. He considered the living substances at the
base of use-value in terms of quality not quantity, because he considered
them solely in terms of the ease with which they may be directly
consumed by a human. But use-value has a quantitative dimension, to
which we have already alluded in terms of a continuum of substance and
energy. It is quantifiable to the extent that nature overall is quantifiable.[13]

A convenient way to draw out the quantitative dimension of use-
value is to compare agricultural and industrial production. In this
comparison we will pretend that agriculture is exempt from the speedy
dynamics of capital. In fact agriculture is not exempt at all, but this
pretence will help initially to make the point. The point is that
subjective agency can either increase or decrease the overall quantity of

13 Effectively, this means that the overall quantity of nature is equivalent to the technological
   ability to conquer and exploit the space of the infinite; and of course, we keep pushing at the
   limit implied. Cf. Lacan on pyrotechnics and space-flights.

use-value, the 'small sum necessary for the young man's fortune'. In other words, the capacity for will and design, a capacity that is exercised (at the fullest) by non-productive labour under capital, can, depending on how it is directed, either increase or decrease the sum of nature. In other modes of production, the human subject is not automatically opposed to nature as one of its own forces. As directed energy, it can either be quantitatively opposed to nature, in that it diminishes its substance, or it can increase the substances in question.

It it not difficult to see how the will enhances or diminishes. For instance, a living tree is capable of producing more trees, and will and design can direct labour in the act of cultivation in such a way that it can transform the conditions of tree production to enable trees to produce still more trees. In this way, it can quantitatively expand natural substances. In the case of the production of commodities in a form in which they can no longer reproduce themselves, the mixing in of labour quantitatively diminishes that substance: a dead tree cannot produce, nor can it be assisted to produce, more trees. One table is usually quantitatively less than a tree.

In other words, whether labour-power quantitatively expands or contracts natural substances will vary according to the subject of labour-power and the provision made for reproduction. When trees are the subject of labour, they can be cultivated so that they can be harvested for the production of more trees. When timber intended for tables is the subject of labour, the quantity of trees is expanded by labour in order that it may be diminished by it. Similarly, the production of tomatoes quantitatively expands tomatoes in order that they may be harvested, and hence consumed in production. By contrast, the production of tinned tomato soup consumes the tomatoes in the production process as such, in order that they may be directly consumed by the producer.

We have established that the assumption underpinning the theory that profit depends on the socially necessary labour-time required to produce a commodity is that the labourer has raised the use-value of the raw materials to a higher level. The product, through the mixing in of labour-power, is now something more than it was before. In turn, the assumption that underpins this is that the product is expanded rather than contracted or, to put it differently, that the product is enriched by its transformation through labour-power rather than diminished by it.

Yet from a reproductive, quantitative perspective, transformation can just as well entail that the product's basis is cut back and made poorer (cf. Benton 1989). In this case, I think we should borrow from, in fact run with, Marx's use of the term 'objectification', which he employed to describe what labour *does* in production. We should use it to describe that type of transformation which diminishes, by rendering natural substances into a form in which they are no longer able to reproduce themselves. This gives us a useful definition of the 'dead' as distinct from the living. The 'dead' is either that which cannot reproduce itself in its original form, or inanimate natural substances which have been produced over the very long *durée* in circumstances impossible to replicate, and whose longevity capital will ignore. Many, though by no means all, natural substances entering production are in this sense 'dead'.

Thus we can distinguish two types of 'transformation': that which diminishes and objectifies, and that which does not. This takes us directly to the overall quantitative dimension of use-value and substance. Because, within value-theory as it stands, the energy materialized by labour is only measured qualitatively, because for Marx, this energy was apparent in use-values only, the quantitative aspect to use-values was excluded from the labour theory of value: no common denominator could be found for them outside of labour-time itself. This means that, from the outset, any consideration of the quantitative matter of the energy materialized in production is precluded, and so, accordingly, is the question of the effects of the increase or diminution of the overall quantity of natural energy or substance capable of releasing energy.

Yet if we suspend for a moment the world in which everything is already a commodity, or destined, as Heidegger would have it, to become such a commodity, if we cease to assume the world of large-scale industrial production, *then surplus-value overall could only increase if the value realized by all the natural substances entering into production was greater than the costs of their reproduction.*

While Marx did not have a concept of the overall quantity of use-value, he did have a concept of overall surplus-value. The concept was demanded by his understanding of total profit. For Marx, overall surplus-value was equivalent to total profit. The justification for this equation rested on the notion of a *total* surplus-value. Surplus-value had to be considered in total terms because determining the price of particular commodities through the labour-time (in terms of the value) embodied in them is unworkable. Capital will move profits around from one sector to another, so that the price of a particular commodity may be more or less than its real value. But these discrepancies will iron out, in that overall profit will equal overall surplus-value extraction. Thus Marx made value equivalent to price in the last (overall or total) instance. We shall return to this uneasy equivalence, the problem of transforming value into price, in the next section. The point here is that if there is no surplus-value without use-value, if use-value overall is being diminished, and if overall surplus-value equals total profit, then total profit in the long run must diminish as the source of use-value overall diminishes. It could only increase if the literal substance of use-value (the source of all wealth) could realize more use-value, hence surplus-value; that is, it could only realize long-term profit via a substantial increase.

But a substantial increase is precisely what capital militates against. It tends to use natural raw materials more rapidly than they can reproduce themselves. While natural substances, as raw materials, are in fact used to produce a new use-value, they are 'in truth consumed'. From an overall quantitative perspective, it is inevitable that this form of consumption must in the long run diminish the amount of given raw materials available, in that it diminishes the living natural substances they contain. Unlike feudalism, in capitalism, Marx is clear that the amount of natural materials that new productive forces will have to consume must also increase.

> An increase in the productive force . . . corresponds to the increase in the instrument, [*Arbeitsinstruments*] since the surplus-value of the instrument does not keep pace [*entspricht . . . in keinen Verhältnis*] as in the previous mode of production, with its use-value . . . . The increase in the productive forces, which has to express itself in an enlargement of the value of the instrument – the space it takes up in capital expenditure – necessarily brings with it an increase in the material, since more material has to be worked in order to produce more product.
>
> (1857–8 *Grundrisse*, p. 380)

The immediate manifest limits imposed by feudal or other forms of pre-capitalist production are less immediate and far less manifest. The 'object' no longer imposes direct limits on the 'subject', although its indirect limits are making themselves felt environmentally. But this indirect return of the repressed has been relatively slow in coming to consciousness,[14] and economic formulations of its significance have been even slower in reckoning with the implications of finite quantity for capital overall.

And indeed, capital can defer its reckoning with nature, if not endlessly, then for as long as it can find energy sources that substitute for one another. Of course, capital has a very long way to go before it exhausts living nature, and would probably have destroyed the conditions of human survival before reaching that point.

The point here is simply that in order to satisfy the demands of large-scale production, more and more of nature has to be destroyed. In this sense production under capitalism is consumption, not production; it gobbles that which is already there, and gives nothing back but waste. Its form of transforming labour is not the same as that which marks other modes of the production process, in that capital is only concerned about reproducing the natural substances that are the irreplaceable conditions of its own existence, and where these conditions are an immediate condition of its survival. Because so many of the commodities it produces cannot be recycled (in general) or because, if they are agricultural, they tend to exhaust the conditions of their own production (see below), then, given that nature is the source of value, capital can only profit by continuing to exploit every available natural source.

But in this exploitation (nature is given less than nature gives out) we can see that production is not production, but consumption. For transforming production is creation, it is increase in growth, it is the *substantial* increase, the increase in substance. Consumption on the other hand is diminutive, unless it is geared to reproduction. If labour, as energy generated by nourishing matter, in turn assists the growth of nourishing matter, then consumption is directly related not only to production but to the reproduction of the conditions of consumption. But under capitalism, consumption bears no relation to production, except in its own terms, and these must diminish the quantity of use-value overall to the extent that speed is capital's imperative. The embodiment of energy in the fixed forms of constant capital not only reflects a process whereby the organic composition of capital changes, with more spent on constant, less on variable, capital. It also reflects a diminution in the overall quantity of use-value: the energetic substances

14 Although not as slow as popular writings have it. Environmental consciousness has been present to some degree since the seventeenth century (Cf. Grove 1990a).

bound in fixed capital are no longer able to reproduce themselves. The world of subjects and objects expands at the expense of the logic of natural substance.

But what needs to be stressed now is that surplus-value does assume a material embodiment. In fact, this was clear at the micro level the minute we drew attention to the incidental energy that capital acquires in its contract with labour-power. The concept of surplus-value draws on both use-value and exchange-value; we signalled this by making the two-fold nature of the commodity our point of departure. But this two-fold nature also means that surplus-value, conceptually, mixes up use-value and exchange value. The confusion over surplus-value is compounded, and may have arisen in the first place, because the quantitative implications of consumptive production were neglected. This much is now clear: as far as the long term is concerned, as the overall quantity of substance or use-value is diminished, so must the overall quantity of potential surplus-value, and hence profit, be diminished. What remains to be discussed is shorter term profit, which returns us to the speed of acquisition.

## THE SPEED OF ACQUISITION

By this analysis, for production to continue to stay in the race, it has to speed up the materialization of energy, the value added by natural substances in production, and so speed up the rate of surplus-value extraction. While this speeding-up diminishes overall surplus-value in the long term, it obviously works compellingly in the short term. We need to see *how* it works. Let us return to the two ways of speeding up. One is allowing a natural force or source to keep its form, but speed up its rate of reproduction; the other is to speed up its conversion into energy by changing its form. In detail:

(i) If we treat all natural forces capable of materializing energy or commodities produced naturally (agriculture) as variable capital, the problem with the idea of nature's expanding use-values, and therefore expanding the potential basis of exchange-value, would appear to be not that natural substances lack the 'specific' quality of labour (for materializing energy, thereby increasing value), but that they cannot be measured according to the socially necessary labour-time for, say, a plant to produce a tomato. This, as noted, is a problem for agricultural capital in particular, in that agricultural commodities are more obliged to keep their form. Yet it is not an insurmountable problem.

It will be recalled that the concept of socially necessary labour-time is based on the average amount of time required to produce a given object at a given level of technology. Now the average amount of time a tomato plant takes to produce a tomato can in fact be calculated with some precision. The real point is that the plant's technology *appears or appeared* to be fixed. Marx obviously lived in the era before genetic engineering. Accordingly, he assumed that basically the reproductive time of natural substances cannot be speeded up; that is, the tomato plant's inner workings cannot be regulated or controlled. It is historically plain that this is not so, and that capital has indeed found a variety of ways of speeding up various forms of natural reproduction.[15]

The speeding up of the natural products which need to keep their forms in order to serve as agricultural commodities takes place by regulating their conditions of production. These commodities generally are animals, animal products, trees, plants and their produce. We have succeeded in breeding pigs without trotters that cannot walk. They lie on shelves to speed up the fattening that takes them to pork; cows are next in line for the same treatment, and wingless chickens are on the way in.[16] 'Modern turkeys have been bred with breasts so large that it is impossible for them to mate . . .' (Raines 1991, p. 341).

There is no doubt about the motive, not even a coating of palaver about science for science's sake. Simply: 'a wise farmer is not going to buy a patented animal, or any other item, unless it will increase profits. That is just what transgenic breeds are being engineered to do' (Raines 1991, p. 342). The chickens already lay eggs at several times the natural rate under battery lamps; the lactation of cows is artificially increased; and the tomatoes, like a great deal else, are planted in soil which has been artificially fertilized to mean its fallow time is bypassed. For that matter the plants themselves are subject to genetic recombination guaranteed to increase their rate of reproduction.

By the processes that speed up the commodification of animals and

15  While in this section we are talking of substances which need to keep their original form, and probably their ability to reproduce themselves, in order to serve as commodities, it should be remembered that the same process applies to some natural substances capable of materializing energy as such (e.g. oil seed).

16  This information is culled from animal rights bulletins and the newsletter on connections between animal rights movements *(Lynx!)*. For more information on this topic, see Spallone (1992) especially; also Motulsky (1983), Pursel, Pinkert and Miller (1989) on livestock, and Straughan (1989). I hear *Lynx* has already adopted the slogan of the early American unionist, Joe Hill: 'Don't miaow: Organize!'

plants (amongst other things), surplus-value will be increased, but the longer-term effect may well be an impoverishment of surplus-value based on use-value, to the extent that surplus-value must embody use-value. I say 'may well be' because it is always possible to take account of the conditions of use-value production (for example replenishing soil fertility by natural or artificial means). However, if we keep our focus on the overall quantity of use-value, then this account taking must either diminish the overall quantity, or run counter to it if it is done naturally. If it is done naturally, it will be at odds with the speed imperative. If it is done artificially, and is being done at a profitable speed, it must be overdrawing somewhere else.

The price paid for speeding things up is a price paid by overall productivity, and hence overall long-term profit. There should be a decline in long-term profit to the extent that commodities embody less real substance, and this they must do as they become degraded of substance. Take the giant, airy American strawberry. Genetically recombined for improved size, and grown from degraded soil, it looks great and tastes . . . like nothing. In the medium term, even its comparative price has fallen. It is a symptomatic postmodern commodity: seeming wonderful, yet is has literally less substance, and hence less value. None the less, its price increased in the short term with the speed of its deceptively luscious production.

(ii) Short-term gain and a decline in long-term productivity and profit is also evident in the second way of speeding things up, characteristic of industrial production: changing the form of natural forces and sources beyond recovery. But it is evident at an even more accelerated pace. Changing the form of a natural force or source can involve violent conversions whereby, for instance, coal is converted into electrical power, or naturally occurring organic compounds are reproduced in artificial conditions, or recombined in chemical conversions to make anything ranging from plastic to CFCs.

Noting these forms of speeding up surplus-value extraction may help us unravel the Marxist conundrum of transformation, of how value is transformed into price. In doing so, it may also reconcile some of the insights of mainstream economics with Marx's alternative.

Within industrial production, the necessary natural forces have to add more at a faster speed, within less time, than the time in which they are acquired. This puts a fantastic temporal pressure on all aspects of capital's circulation and production.[17] To hold its own, a particular capital has to acquire its energy sources (along with everything else) at or better than the prevailing speed.

The fact that this fantastic temporal pressure affects all aspects of capital's circulation and production means that the speed of acquisition, as a measure of profit, involves distribution and exchange as much as production. This runs counter, of course, to the classical account, precisely because that account downplays circulation. Which is not to say that the *interdependence* of the four spheres of classical Marxism (production, reproduction, distribution and exchange) has been downplayed. It is rather, as I indicated above, that the roles of distribution and exchange as direct actors in the production of surplus-value have been downplayed. But they become direct actors once the focus is on the speed of acquisition as a key to surplus-value. Moreover, and this will become increasingly significant, they are direct actors who show that the state, as the entity which provides 'the general conditions of production' (1857–8 *Grundrisse*, p. 533), is or at least has been inextricably intertwined with capital. What is more, they draw attention to the importance of space and distance as capital speeds up.

The role of space and distance is evident once we consider the variables affecting the speed of acquisition. In discussing this, I will use the more neutral term 'cost' in the first instance. The cost of acquisition depends on (i) how far capital pays for the stages of transformation a living entity or substance has to go through before it acquires the form desired for consumptive production; (ii) the distance of the entity or substance from the place of production, and thus on (iii) the means of

17 It is a pressure consistent with capital's behaviour, as we shall see below. As noted at the outset, time, in general, is more likely to be central in most non-Marxist economic theories. But these theories discuss time without reference to an overriding source of value. Marx explicitly notes that 'A capital's time of circulation . . . limits, generally speaking, its time of production and hence its process of generating surplus-value. And it limits this process in proportion to its own duration . . . . But Political Economy sees only what is *apparent*, namely the effect of the time of circulation on capital's process of the creation of surplus-value in general. . . . Various phenomena . . . give colour to this semblance: 1) The capitalist method of calculating profit, in which the negative cause figures as a positive one, since with capital's indifferent spheres of investment, where only the types of circulation are different, a longer time of circulation tends to bring about *an increase of prices*. . . .' (*Capital* 2, pp. 128–9, emphasis added). Marx regarded this increase as equivalent to the process of equalizing profits extracted through exploitation for surplus-value. And there is a sense in which I am saying the same thing, in arguing that value has to be consumed as distance is covered in any form of circulation. However, value has been generalized to the exploitation of nature overall, and the suggestion is that the 'increase of prices' is tied directly to the consumption of use-value where no allowance is made for the time of reproduction. On the transformation problem generally, and attempts to rework it, see Sraffa 1960, Shaikh (1977) and Harcourt (1982 and 1993).

transportation, whether they exist or have to be constructed (an additional cost), and (iv) whether the cost of means of transportation or of utilizing them, where they exist, is stood by capital. In all cases, all measures of the cost of acquisition are spatially as much as temporally relative measures; this is where the cost of acquisition becomes equivalent to the speed of acquisition, however distant from the real value inherent in the time of reproduction that cost may be.[18] Finally, and most significantly, the cost of acquisition also depends on (vi) whether the reproduction cost can be discounted by capital.

The burden of this argument is that the reproduction time, or real value, will be and is discounted the more industrial production is centralized. Discounting the cost of reproduction, in fact, is the other side of centralization.[19] It is not only quantitatively, in terms of use-value, that centralization demands more of nature than it can return, to support a political, juridical and distributive apparatus additional to those essential for local production. It is also that the pathways of centralization are simultaneously the pathways of any extended acquisition. In one respect, this was anticipated by Marx:

> The *smaller* the direct fruits borne by *fixed capital*, the less it intervenes in the *direct production process*, the greater must be this relative *surplus population and surplus production*; thus, more to build railways, canals, aqueducts, telegraphs etc. than to build the machinery directly active in the immediate production process.
>
> (1957–8 *Grundrisse*, pp. 707–8 trans. mod.)

I return to spatiality, centralization and the state below. What I want to suggest now is that the costs of distance, in the speed of acquisition, are what set the 'price' as distinct from the value of a particular commodity. While Marx noted that the price of a particular commodity need not embody its labour-time, he did not identify any particular factor which had an overriding power in the determination of price. I do not dispute that many things can remove market prices from value. But I am suggesting that distance has a special role, sufficiently special to mean that we need some way of calculating its effects on profit. Thus,

18 At the same time, if one of production's elements can be had more cheaply, this may have the same effect as speeding-up: the end result will be a lower cost, although the benefits here may be offset if there is a time-lag in the speed of production, thence distribution. The relativity of cheapness, in other words, is relative to the absolute of the prevailing speed of production and distribution.

19 It is its logical concomitant as much as the division into town and country is that of industrialization.

tentatively, I am suggesting that the effect of distance on the spread of acquisition is the major, constant factor in the determination of price.[20]

The considerable advantage of reading value-theory in terms of interchangeable energy sources is that it means we can account for distance as a factor determining price in a way that ties it to reproduction; it ties it to reproduction in so far as distance can substitute for reproduction. In more detail, I am proposing that distance figures in this way: the speed with which all commodities are acquired in production (Marx called this Department 1) and distributed to consumers in Department 2 (Marx's name for necessary goods) and Department 3 (luxury goods) consumes energy. Precisely because the surplus-value released in this consumption is not measured against the time of reproduction, but against the speed of acquisition, then price becomes further removed from value, literally removed. And price becomes higher the less the time allowed for reproduction. Paradoxically, the less the time allowed, the higher the price, because allowing for less time means that more surplus-value is released. In other words, the price is higher the greater the extent of centralization, the more distance has to be covered at a higher speed, the more energy consumed, and the less the return to nature.

But if price is set by the speed of acquisition, value remains tied to the time of reproduction: the time of the natural and social reproduction of natural substances. In many instances and for some capitals, depending on their location and their ability to outlay, the measure of value will figure more markedly, and accordingly be closer to price. It will figure necessarily in agricultural production, especially those forms of it which rely relatively little on inputs from afar. Speed ramifies here, as we have seen. But it does so mainly through speeding up production. And of course, reproduction as a source of value matters more to the extent that production relies on labour-power. This will explain why the labour theory of value appears to work by some accounts, particularly those based on case studies of neo-colonialist countries. It is when and only when the cost of reproduction can be discounted that the value added in production is to be compared, not with the cost of reproduction, but with the cost of acquisition.

The 'when and only when' is crucial. It keeps the basis of value-

---

20 Up to a point, this coincides with the 'primitive' definition of value, which defined the value of commodities in terms of their distance. See Sahlins (1972), especially Chapter 5: 'On the sociology of primitive exchange'. Cf., too, Gregory (1980), and Douglas and Isherwood (1979).

theory, in recognizing nature as the source of all use-value, and hence of value; therefore, it does not partake of capital's crazed capacity to lose track of value's source. At the same time, this 'when and only when' embraces the fantasmatic escapism of production based only on the cost of acquisition, which is the main basis that capital, and the economic theories which best describe it empirically, acknowledge.

Of course, energy cut off from its natural source of origin cannot continue to regenerate the natural energy that enabled it to come into being. However, as more and more natural substances assume this form, and as more and more natural substances are bound in fixed capital, they require more and more supplies of external energy to enable them to keep producing, owing to the obvious facts that they are diminishing the overall quantitative supply of nature, and that they have no regenerative energy of their own. However, as capital cuts back the supply of natural substances, it not only diminishes nourishing matter – one source of energy – it also diminishes the conditions for other natural sources of energy to regenerate as well. So it has to speed up agricultural production. Speeding up agriculture in turn feeds into the speed of acquisition through consumption, which depends on wide networks of distribution, as does industrial production.

In fact, this is where the two forms of speeding things up are tied together. To acquire more at a faster speed for production means distributing more, and consuming more. This puts a pressure on agriculture to produce at a rate comparable with other aspects of production and distribution. As available sources of energy in either agriculture or industrial production are diminished, capital has to create routes for the old sources of energy to come from farther away, or create new sources of energy altogether, ranging from electricity to chemicals to 'nuclear power'. But if the logic of consumption for production holds here, then 'nuclear power' should also be exhausting something. (What?)

Leaving that aside: the reproduction of natural substances and sources of energy goes according to a natural cycle taking a certain amount of time. The hyperactive rhythm of capitalism, on the other hand, means that the conversion of substances into energy leads to the further conversion of already converted substances into other energetic forms, which are more and more coming to be the basis of energy overall, with lunatic environmental consequences. As by now should be abundantly plain, the reality of what we should relabel the consumptive mode of production (CMP), or 'capital' as we will continue to call it for the time being, is this: short-term profitability depends on an increasing debt to nature, a debt that must always be deferred, even at the price of survival.

As I indicated, distance should bear on inflation. Money, as science fiction writers predicted before economists, is essentially time. Marx measured money in terms of labour-time, but by this argument it should be measured in terms of the speed of acquisition. Thus inflation would be the measure of distance between the sources of energy and the speed with which they are consumed, a measure which intersects with reproduction, especially but not only that of labour-power.We will regard money, then, as the phenomenal form of the socially produced time of speed, rather than of labour-time as such. This retains some of the reasoning behind Marx's definition of money, although that definition conflated the social time of production with natural reproductive time, and it is these we are separating in this redefinition of the relation between value and price. The price of a commodity becomes inflated the further removed it is from its value, and especially inflated if its production has removed the source of value altogether. Once more, time, as money and speed, literally encapsulates the natural energy whose flourishing it must diminish. For if the quantity of use-value overall as the basis of surplus-value is diminished, as I have argued it must be, something has to take its place. This something, anticipating a little, is the creation of an artificial space-time.

Short-term profitability, with its inflated price, must lead to a diminution in long-term profit and productivity. In that the substantial material embodiment in productivity and profit has to be reduced or rendered unreproducible by the logic of production geared to speed, capital is its own worst enemy. How this is played out in total terms should be reflected in the crisis of capital, in its 'long waves' and 'laws of motion'. In sum, what Marx saw clearly and before all was the inherent contradiction in capital as a mode of production. He saw it in terms of labour and technology, or constant and variable capital, as he defined it, where the former, to keep pace, had to expand at the expense of the energy input of labour. The contradiction is recapitulated in this account, although its terms of reference have changed. Or rather, its terms of reference have been stripped of their phenomenal forms, so that the contradiction emerges as what it is essentially: one between substantial energy and artificial speed.

## HOW SPACE REPLACES TIME

Yet we have established that the contradiction between energy and speed is not simple. Two forms of time are at issue: the generational time of natural reproduction, and speed, the artificial time of short-term profit. Speed, as I have already indicated, is about space as much as time as such. It is about space because it is about centralization and distance. Speed, measured by distance as well as time, involves a linear axis, time, and the lateral axis of space. In this section, I will begin by emphasizing how, in the consumptive mode of production, the artificial space-time of speed (space for short) takes the place of what I am terming generational time. For to the extent that capital's continued profit must be based more and more on the speed of acquisition, it must centralize control and accumulation more, command more distance, and in this respect space *must* take the place of generational time.[21]

It is clear that generational time suffers because capital tends inevitably to speed up the production of all commodities, including naturally formed or agricultural ones. While there are countervailing tendencies in agriculture, and the very existence of labour-power, in scarce or apparently irreplaceable sources, the speed imperative will override them wherever possible. As production speeds up, it is also clear, capital will diminish or degrade the conditions of the specific or overall natural reproduction of natural and agricultural products. But

---

21 The same point is very well made by Altvater (1987) in the context of a discussion of thermodynamics, economics and time. This article is in part a creative, critical discussion of Georgescu-Roegen's thermodynamics-oriented 'bio-economics' (which argues, on the basis of Newton's second law, which it applies to space, that scarcity is inevitable). Georgescu-Roegen differentiated between time 'T' (a continuous sequence) and time 't', the mechanical measurement of intervals. Shades of Heidegger! Mechanical time lacks the historical sense that goes with a continuous sequence, and it is also opposed to historical time 'T', because it cannot be measured and predicted mechanically. For Georgescu-Roegen, 'a particular logic develops in the space and time co-ordinates (as in the social and economic co-ordinates): economic surplus production is guided by the quantitative imperative of growth by way of reducing the time spans of human activities (especially those of production and consumption). It does this by accelerating and transcending the quantitative and qualitative impediments in space in order to compress time, thus setting "T" into "t". There are thus two co-ordinating systems of space and time, which, in the form of two patterns of "functional spaces", are fixed upon a territorial-social reality' (Altvater 1987, p.63). Altvater goes on to conclude that 'the expansionist pressure inherent in the economic logic of surplus production has a territorial dimension (as production is necessarily always spatial). Surplus production is thus identical to the economic conquest - exploration, development, penetration, and exploitation - of space, i.e. the 'production of space' (Altvater 1987, p. 69). A different distinction between the two forms of time is made by Kristeva (1979), who distinguishes between cyclical and monumental time on the one hand, and historical or linear time. Cyclical time is the natural time of repetition; monumental time is that of eternity. The problem with equating historical and linear time is that the sequential nature of generational as well as historical time is downplayed.

this is not the only way that generational time is short-circuited by short-term profit.

As I have indicated in relation to fixed and constant capital, capital will also bind more and more living energy in forms which cannot reproduce themselves. The same is true of many commodities produced in Departments 2 and 3: commodities for the individual consumer's consumption. These fixed or bound commodities either cannot be recycled at all, or are out of time in that they can only be recycled at a pace far slower than that of other biospheric ingredients. The production of these kinds of commodities is the heart of industrial production, and this industrial heart has a temporal beat which we stressed at the beginning of Part II: the beat of instant gratification, a beat that gets more rapid by the minute. The substances in bound commodities are cut out permanently from the generational process of natural exchange, at the same time as they are inserted, in their newly acquired objectified or bound forms, into the process of commodity exchange. Of course, it matters to some substances more than others; trees lose more than rocks or minerals.

But what these erstwhile natural things lose in their ability to go on living, to reproduce down the generations, they gain in mobility. Not much of a gain, to be sure, for the things themselves, but a big gain for capital, which certainly requires the portability of commodities in Departments 2 and 3, and requires it to a large exent in Department 1. Moreover one cannot consume more products within production without having a market for those commodities outside production. So both processes of consumption have to be speeded up. The more directly consumable a product is, the greater its use-value. Once more, the easily consumable product is the one that is most portable, and that involves the least expenditure of energy in consumption (a dishwasher is more valuable than a bucket, and infinitely more valuable than a stream; a microwave meal costs more than the same ingredients bought separately and prepared). More time and energy are required to produce these products, and make them portable; less energy to consume them, especially if they come to you, and come to you as fast as possible.

In short, a commodity has to be shiftable, for it has to be able to come to market. Aside from pigs and their ilk, commodities can only come to market in a movable form, and this means that they have to be shifted, i.e. removed, from the circumstances in which they can reproduce themselves. The exceptions here are labour-power and animals. I noted that one of the distinctive features of the commodity labour-power is that it is portable of its own accord. Not only that, but labour-power, like other animals, can be portable without losing its capacity for reproduction. But humans and animals aside, no other natural substance can reproduce itself if it is uprooted or, more generally, removed from the earth. However, centralization requires portability and therefore uprooting; and it requires it more the faster production becomes, and the more the scope of centralized production extends. This should mean that, until and if something takes its place in a cost-effective way, the portability of labour-power becomes ever more important, both as a commodity which covers its own transportation costs and because of the part it plays in shifting things around. And the scope of centralization must extend as the extent of acquisition depends on it.

As we have seen, to extend acquisition one needs means of transportation in the first instance: either to bring the desired good to you, or for you to go to it. Extending acquisition to consume more goods in the process of production automatically entails two things. The first is an alteration in the scale of production. Production ceases, to a greater or lesser degree, to be local in scale, and this means the consumptive producers are more likely to lose track of the source of value, in terms of the time of natural reproduction. The second consequence of extending acquisitior has also been discussed, but I need to restate it as we are coming closer to the base role of the state in the process whereby time is made over in favour of space.

The second consequence of extending the means of acquisition is that the speed with which the goods have to come to the point of production also increases. That is how capital operates according to its own fantasmatic law of speed. Or rather, that is the operation of the process we are renaming centralized consumption, a process of which capital is the greediest and most efficient exemplar. The more things are brought together from out of their habitat and locale, the more networks bringing them to the place of consumption are needed. The more they are brought together, following the paths of centralized consumption, the more they are cut out of their habitat and locale. The more they are cut out, the less they can reproduce. The less they reproduce, the less they become. The less they become, the more substitutes for them need to be found. The more substitutes need to be found, the greater the centralization needed to find and transport them. Centralization, speed and spatial scope all increase because the newly produced goods have to be produced and distributed in accord with a time-scale that at least matches that of local production in order to compete with it, a time-scale that will of course aim at overtaking local production and same-scale competititors.

In other words spatial centralization creates energy demands and an energy field which can only sustain themselves by extracting surplus-value from nature. It is impossible for it to do otherwise: even without the imperative constantly to speed up to stay in the race, the additional demands that centralization makes on the reproduction of nature, through transportation, energy services (electricity, water) and so on means that more has to be extracted from nature than can be returned in terms of the time necessary for natural reproduction. This form of extracting surplus-value from nature is inexorable, for it maintains the *centralized* apparatus of the state *and* advanced technological production, regardless of whether the *mise en scène* is capital's, or that of state socialism.[22]

Thus the distance of production and distribution based on increasing centralization takes the place of time. Moreover, distance should take the place of time in inverse proportion to it, so that generally, lateral space will more and more substitute for the time of local generational production and consumption. Space will take the place of time by the denominator common to both: namely speed, and it will take time's place by increasing the speed at which the entities and substances traverse the means of transportation to the place of production, the speed with which they are consumed in production, and the speed at which they are distributed, in accordance with the scale in which they are consumed in production, and distributed for further consumption.

This speedy continuum of consumption for production and further consumption is the essence of why space has to override time in the CMP. In fact, the idea that centralization of itself demands that more be extracted from nature than can be returned demands a formula: the condensed distance and imposed directions of spatial centralization are paid for by the time necessary for natural reproduction. Is it the case that what any natural thing loses in terms of its ability to reproduce, it

22 This is not to minimize the differences between the two systems, although environmental critics almost invariably run them together (thus Bahro 1984; Kelly 1984; Porrit 1984; Sale 1985; amongst many others). Nor are environmental critics the only ones who do so. Goldthorpe's well-known critique of these 'industrialist' elisions is still pertinent. I provide some grounds for distinguishing between the two systems on environmental grounds below.

gains in portability? It was with this in mind that I suggested earlier that, where the speed of acquisition is unimpeded, the production of exchange-value is the consumption of use-value, via the imposition of portability.

We are left with a world in which centralized space, in general, is paid for by the sacrifice of reproductive or generational time. This world is made over on a lateral axis, which uproots to a vast extent the generational or 'linear' one. In this making over, capital carries on like a parody of natural production. Not only does it like to produce plastic oranges, Stepford Wives, and other imitations of the original. It has to have a means to 'reproduce' its products, to enable substance to turn into something else. In natural reproduction, this is the energy generated by the natural cycles themselves. We know that capital, like nature, uses energy to enable it to transform one substance into another. But it garners its energy by violent conversions, and these conversions follow rhythms that bear only an attenuated relation to the rhythms of natural production, whose temporal constraints they ignore.

In reproducing or producing its babies, capital has its own cycles and 'laws of motion'. Its parody of nature is almost complete. It plays God and redirects nature at its own speed and from its own subject-centred standpoint. It is playing with high stakes here, because it is literally altering the *physis* of the world, adjusting the inbuilt logic of nature and the spatio-temporal continuum to suit itself. By its will, it is imposing a direction on physical processes which is other than their own. As it creates this subject-centred world of objects, and the artificial pathways and laws of motion that reform the natural connections it breaks, it makes a fantasy come true. It establishes its own foundations, but it does so by consuming the real foundations, the logic of natural substances. Meantime the wilful subject, the agency affecting this, becomes more and more invisible in the diverse forms of power without accountability that mark the present era.

We return to the alteration of the *physis* in the next chapter. At this point, taking account of the speed factor as the intersection between the linear axis of generational time and the lateral axis of spatial reproduction will enable us to say something brief about: (i) the state; and (ii) the reproduction of labour-power and the positions of women and men, especially in the neo-colonial context. These comments, as I said at the outset, will be gestural rather than substantive.

## THE STATE

It is becoming increasingly clear that the momentum of capital alone is insufficient to account for the power of agency, 'the invisible hand', in this centralizing process, and I noted earlier that centralization is inextricably tied to the state, which provides 'the general conditions of production'. The more the emphasis shifts to portability and acquisition, and the more by implication it shifts to expansion, the more the issues of territorial control and transportation, one of those vague 'conditions of production', become salient. Which also takes us back to Lacan's emphasis on aggression in spatial dynamics. To extend centralization, and territorial domination, in which more territories are answerable and/or geared to the same centre, one needs means of transportation in the first instance and, for domination, means for war.[23] Spatial control and spatial expansion are the conditions of the invisible hand extending its grasp; in a sense they also *are* the state.

The state is part of the infrastructure of distribution, the outer sphere of consumption and exchange, all of which are not peripheral but central in this revised value-theory. Not only does the state lay the grounds for and regulate key variables in the speed of acquisition (through transportation, energy services, and other forms of extension). Together with capital it also regulates the law of substitution. For example, whether oil can substitute for labour-power in the production of certain commodities will depend on means of transportation, treaties governing imports, and so on.

While the costs of establishing centralized state control may not be of particular significance to use-value overall in themselves, they are none the less paid for out of that use-value, and consume it in the same way that capital does. This homology is, or was, striking in the recent stage of capital's development: state-monopoly capitalism, so-called because the mutually supporting interests of both parties seemed so great as to beggar separate description. But however unwillingly it did so, the state provided the spatio-temporal conditions of production from the beginning. In one respect, the periodization of the various 'stages of capitalism' in Marxist theory is incomplete because it does not recognize that the establishment of the modern state is integral to the historical process whereby space takes the place of time. The existing

23  If one doubts that speed of portability is a cardinal fantasmatic axis in capital and associated forms of foundational 'self-expression', one need only note the line which, to vary Adorno's metaphor, led from the portable troops on the straight Roman road to the portable nuclear missile.

periodization moves from competitive capitalism (first stage) to monopoly capitalism (second stage) to state-monopoly capitalism, otherwise known as late capitalism (third stage).[24] The third stage reveals the spatial imperative in all its munching glory, with its speedy circulation and its ever-expanding reach that cuts off the roots of reproductive time. But it greets this imperative as if it was a novelty introduced by capital alone.

While Marx noted that the state provides the 'general conditions of production',[25] he did not note the remarkable structural homology between these 'general conditions' and the requirements of production, let alone that 'production' is also a means to the state's self-expansion. Yet the homology is becoming increasingly apparent, although it is usually described as a trend. Thus Mandel:

> There is . . . an *inherent trend under late capitalism for the State to incorporate an ever greater number of productive and reproductive sectors into the 'general conditions of production' which it finances.*
> (1972, p. 484)

The question now is why, if the state's role is this fundamental, why have I devoted so much space to the economics of value-theory rather than the political analysis of the state? Certainly one could write at far more length of the state, in all its static majesty, but this would be to miss the real fundament: the essentially competitive spatial *dynamic* of extension and acquisition, with the demand for ever more fodder, that political economy reveals best. For capital, and the extraction of surplus-value, is the best means for executing the process of levelling time. In addition, as we shall see in a moment, while all states feed on time to some extent, they vary in the efficiency and extent to which they do so, and in the constraints that their various cultures and histories impose upon them. This variation is reflected in the uneven demise of state power, and states for that matter. The demise suggests that while the nation state was one form in which 'the

24 The periodization of capital is contentious, when it comes to the third stage. Mandel (1972) ties the idea of state-monopoly capitalism to Comintern strategy and prefers to see the present era as an accentuation of that of monopoly capital. Mandel insists that 'The era of late capitalism is not a new epoch of capitalist development. It is merely a further development of the imperialist, monopoly-capitalist epoch' (1972, p.10). See also Baran and Sweezy (1966) and Poulantzas (1968).
25 An area which Mandel notes has been neglected in Marxist theories of the state (1972, p. 48, p. 476).

conditions of production' were laid down, it may not be the only form that will sustain them.

Crucial here is the idea that standards of efficiency in denying time are set globally. For Gourevitch, it was a global economic pressure in the 1980s that made nations 'curtail state spending and interventions. Whatever the differences in partisan outcomes, all governments have been pressed in the same direction' (Gourevitch 1986, p. 33). Even more strongly: 'governments no longer possess the autonomy to pursue independent macroeconomic strategies effectively, even if they were to seek to do so' (Garrett and Lange 1991, p. 543). Moreover, it is argued that today state power should not be measured in terms of military force but economic capability (Rosecrance 1986; Nye 1989; Jervis 1991) and, at the same time, that the state's domain of economic efficacy is now shared with many international organizations (e.g. the IMF) (Cox 1987; Shaw 1991). Hall, Held and McGrew (1992), in an excellent discussion of this literature from which my examples are drawn, stress that while this economic direction may be a global trend, not all states are affected equally (p. 91).

One reason why they are not affected equally is this: while any form of state will embody the spatial dynamic to the extent that it has an apparatus of centralized control, some states embody it in a purer form than others. Indeed some states are constrained by other imperatives which make them manifestly inefficient when it comes to speeding up the sacrifice of time. This is where the effects of specific genealogies, specific traditions intersect with those of the totalizing spatial process. Britain, which is generally inefficient when it comes to traversing space, exemplifies well the conflicts between spatial extension and a tradition which gives too much weight (however misplaced) to generational, temporal rights; e.g. social position determined by birth, respect for queues, etc.

More dramatically, the collapse of Eastern Europe can be explained by the conflict between a form of state, and the dynamic whereby space replaces time, and the related desire for instant gratification. We shall come back to this briefly below: the fate of Eastern Europe, and the plight of the former Soviet Union, indicate why the spatial-power dynamic, rather than 'the state' or 'capital', is the overriding one.

We have to bear in mind the different roles various states play in providing and regulating the general conditions where space replaces time. Marx's analysis of how some states aid accumulation and expansion better than others (1867 *Capital* 1, p. 751) is appropriate here as an exemplar of how the modern state can be evaluated, albeit by different criteria. Some states are far better suited than others to the law of speed, and where the state fails to adjust its form to this law, or attempts to countermand it, there will be gigantic temporal hiccups. The form of centralized state which naturally works in harmony with the process of acquisition, and thence distribution, is a state with minimal checks on the abolition of the linear time of reproduction in relation to labour-power, and in relation to the environment.

This last point returns us to the reasons for blockages in the Eastern bloc. I am unable to deal with this question in detail here, or with reasons for the collapse of the ex-communist societies, but I will make some brief suggestions in the hope that another will either refute or verify them. If my economic theory were to be applied to Eastern Europe, this is what should follow. State communism, in so far as it did attempt some minimal redistribution of wealth to labour-power (which means to its reproduction cost), imposed a temporal constraint on a system designed to eliminate it; for any system of centralized consumption must work to increasing speed in relation to space rather than time, and this is a concomitant not only of competitive acquisition but of centralization. If a state has to introduce some guaranteed measure of distributive justice, this inevitably leads to hiccups if not major obstructions: distributive justice, as we shall see in a moment, is a temporal constraint which can be offset where labour-power is imported, but it remains a temporal constraint when it is honoured.[26] It sits ill where the elimination of time, and instant gratification is the end-goal of the game. It sits ill in a centralized CMP, the system where queues could signal the end of an era.[27]

26 Of course the collapse of Eastern Europe is a question for detailed study, but I will make some more very general remarks here. The more highly developed technology of the advanced heartlands is inextricably bound to a higher level of surplus-value extraction from natural substances overall. *In principle,* provided the country has enough natural wealth, this means that labour-power need not be exploited as much as it would be in the absence of that technology: there is no need to increase the rate of relative surplus-value extraction to countermand the expenditure on constant capital. Just as this makes the immiseration of the working class less likely in such societies, so may it increase it in societies without the same technological outlay *if they lack natural wealth.* Lesser technological outlay and fewer natural energy sources should lead (via the law of substitution) to increased pressure to exploit labour-power. But as labour-power has to be paid, and as it cannot be seriously overworked in an ostensibly socialist economy, then relative surplus-value extracted from labour-power can only be increased through degrading its sphere of consumption. In terms of the psychical dynamics discussed above, this must increase consumer aggression, the demand for choice and so on.

27 It also signals a tension between the size of states and communities which constitute themselves as economic and political entities on different scales. This is discussed in the last chapter.

## REPRODUCTION: PERSPECTIVES ON GENDER, NEO-COLONIALISM AND CLASS

The question of distributive justice and temporal constraints will be plainer after we have discussed reproduction, which bears on women and neo-colonialism. As with the state, the key to the following perspectives is the intersection of space and time. More narrowly, it is in how this intersection, itself established by speed, brings in the sphere of reproduction, especially of labour-power. For while my argument displaces labour-power from the absolute centre of value-theory in terms of production, it also shifts the emphasis to labour-power's reproduction, as it shifts it to that of nature overall. To a limited extent this shift was foreshadowed in debates about women's reproductive labour, which drew attention to the importance of this sphere's *indirect* contribution to surplus-value. But this debate foundered because it kept within the classical categories.[28] The shift to reproduction in my argument is structural. Reproduction of nature overall becomes the hidden ground of value and exploitation; capital drastically enhances its profit because it does not pay for reproduction at its temporal value, unless it has no option under the law of substitution.

From the perspective outlined above, the reproduction of labour is the perpetually odd element out in production. Labour-power is the odd element because the socially necessary labour-time required to reproduce it is fixed in part by nature. It is fixed in so far as socially necessary labour-time includes the reproduction of children and thus the next generation of labour-power. While the time necessary for the reproduction of nature, even of animals, can be short-circuited, that of labour-power cannot on the face of it be speeded up. Which means such reproduction is potentially out of step with capital's consumption-for-production, in which all things have to move faster and faster.

Now as the imperative to speed up other living entities and substances is so evident, and evident in everything from soil poisoned with fertility drugs to fantastic wingless chickens and legless cows, animals tailor-made to producing flesh at the expense of their own

28  With two exceptions the main contributors to this discussion all argued that women's domestic labour benefited capital (Harrison 1973; Dalla Costa 1973; Delphy 1977; Gardiner 1975). The problem was that if surplus-value depended on productive labour, and productive labour did not take place in the household, then how did women contribute to it? Humphreys (1977) in an outstanding historical study, argued that domestic labour was actually a support in and to working class struggle, that the working class was worse off if both spouses laboured outside the home as well as within it. See Brennan (1977) for the same argument based on migrant women in Melbourne industry. See the discussion in Barrett (1980) for an overview.

ability to reproduce, human labour-power's apparent exemption from the same speedy imperative becomes significant. But, always in the event that no other natural substance can provide what labour-power provides (the law of substitution), the apparently impossible end of speeding up the generational reproduction of labour-power can be accomplished in various ways. It can be accomplished by keeping the cost of that reproduction down in relation to the other elements entering production. However, if this means is ineffective in a given situation, where the labour required exceeds the short-term supply, then one is left with the apparently impossible alternative of speeding up the generational reproduction of labour-power so that it keeps pace with the other elements entering into production.

In fact, speeding up the reproduction of labour-power is not impossible, and this is plain once we turn to the alternative means by which human labour-power can be reproduced. In referring to 'alternative means' of reproducing labour-power, I am not invoking the panoply of science fiction and high-tech, of cyborgs and genetic engineering, although the proliferation of fantasies concerning the former and investment in the latter is not irrelevant. In part, it is perhaps a symptomatic recognition of an underlying quest to find a fast-moving replacement for humans, capable of what we distilled as their most distinctive functions: portability and the capacity to take direction. For that matter, all the carry-on over artificial intelligence has more obvious purpose and point, if capital seeks a tame direction-taker. And of course, such docile will-less things already exist, in the form of computers, which altogether lack the 'imaginative capacity for design' (Marx) in executing commands. But the computerized component in constant capital expenditure, and the ambition it encapsulates, is not the immediate question. The alternative means of reproducing labour-power I have in mind at the moment is what I will term the lateral reproduction of labour-power, meaning the migrations of workers.

What I want to propose here is that the lateral reproduction of labour-power will increase when the linear reproduction falls behind the imperative to speed up in other ways, and/or when linear reproduction becomes too costly. At the same time I want to propose that such increases work in tandem with an imperative to keep the cost of the generational reproduction of labour-power down, in lieu of the ability to speed it up. These propositions can be tested readily enough, keeping the law of substitution in mind. And in so far as they encapsulate the law of substitution, it should follow that where the lateral reproduction of labour-power is prohibited for some reason, the generational cost of reproducing labour-power will be forced down (cf. Balibar and Wallerstein 1988, p. 108).

Clearly, these processes involve international labour flows as well as national labour supplies, and national legislation affecting the cost of reproducing the next generation. All these are regulated by the state. And it should follow that a good welfare state will either be 'inefficient' or have ready access to guest workers; a state without this access will 'speed up' generational reproduction by keeping its cost down. The condition of an efficient and just welfare state is either that it is self-contained enough to keep to economies of scale, and/or that its natural resources make it rich provided they can be exploited fast enough (but substantially rich in the long run anyway). The production of surplus-value in a country which disregards a welfare state is enhanced anyway, of course, but enhanced either by speed or natural substance and energy: the United States is amazingly rich in natural substance, while Japan is leading the field of speed (which may bring the United States, rich through substance, into more economic conflict with Japan, rich through speed).

To return to reproduction as such. We are left with the question as to why people have children at all in these speedy times. In feudal and petty-bourgeois modes of production, the interests of social reproduction and the interests of parents coincide. In the CMP, they do not coincide automatically,[29] which means that the overall interests of social reproduction are not guaranteed; they are not in the necessary self-interest of either sex. The striking facts of the increase in single mothers and decline in fathered families may evince this conflict with self-interest for men.[30] But we are unable to explain women's persistence in having children in terms of self-interest, especially as the middle-man (the only generative middle-man in existence) is progressively cut out. We can only explain this, and explain the behaviour of men who want children, by (at least in part) their resistance to the economic logic of self-interest, and their persisting sense of generational time. On the other hand, one could deduce that an economic self-interest factor was working for women who had children and

29  The birthrate in the advanced heartlands of capital is declining while that in the neo-colonialist countries increases. These trends are at odds with demographic predictions which see a fall in birthrate as consequent on industrialization and agricultural modernization, no matter where and under what circumstances industrialization and modernization takes place.
30  See the discussion in Elliot (1991).

received a state benefit *when other economic options were few or virtually non-existent*. But this seems unlikely.[31]

What is clear is that the interests of social reproduction overall are best served by keeping the costs of the linear and lateral reproduction of the labour-force to a minimum. This means that two groups are likely to be impoverished: single women and/or women who are positioned low on the class spectrum (see below); and the vastly heterogeneous peoples from whom a lateral supply of labour-power can be drawn. If there is a structural connection between gender, race and the residual category of class, I suggest that this is it. In other words, the structural connection lies in the fact that all three groups are exploited for social reproduction, for keeping the cost of labour-power down. These forms of exploitation prop one another up.

The heterogeneous peoples who supply the migrating labour-force are far more likely to be those who are racially and ethnically stigmatized. Wallerstein and Balibar sum up:

> Racism operationally has taken the form of what might be called the 'ethnicization' of the work force . . . But while the pattern of ethnicization has been constant, the details have varied from place to place and time to time, according to what part of the human genetic and social pools were located in a particular time and place and what the hierarchical needs of the economy were at that time and place. This kind of system – racism constant in form and in venom . . . allows one to expand or contract the numbers available in any particular space–time zone for the lowest paid, least rewarding economic roles.
>
> (Balibar and Wallerstein 1988, pp. 33–4)

There is more incentive to migrate where there is unemployment or bare subsistence employment in the home country, and/or where there is over-population relative to job supply. Advanced capital would seem to be well served by over-population in the neo-colonialist countries, both in terms of a greater willingness on the part of the latter's populations to migrate, and in terms of greater competition for jobs within those countries.

Significantly, it is usually men who migrate or move in search of work (Tilly and Scott 1978, p. 77), while women with children remain

---

31 While the publicity given feminism may beguile us into thinking otherwise, the overall global *economic* situation of women *vis-à-vis* men appears to have declined this century.

fixed in place. This repeats a pattern evident in capital's seventeenth-century genesis, and in the non-metropolitan countries where capital's advent is relatively recent.[32] This pattern goes hand-in-hand with a major alteration in scale. It is not only the division between town and country that is affected here; it is also the household, as the site of production (Nicholson 1986, p. 3ff). Household production, or petty commodity production, as Marx and Engels termed it, accorded women a very different and generally better economic place. Their productive labour was not geographically divorced from their situation as mothers.[33] The significance of household production for women has been relatively neglected in Marxist debates about whether petty commodity production is a pre-capitalist form or an on-going form of capitalism (Scott 1986; Redclift and Mingione 1985). The idea that it may be a form opposed to it was proposed by Clarke (1919), but her remarkable thesis was not developed.

But the immediate concern lies elsewhere. Apart from indicating that the production of migrating men and single mothers is endemic to and a condition of capitalization, this pattern also reinforces the notion that these two groups have a great deal in common. They have in common their exploitation for social reproduction, even though their short-term interests are opposed. Or to say the same thing differently, they stand opposed in that one group advances lateral reproduction, the other linear reproduction.

In this context, we can consider the concept of class. This is now a problematic concept. It has been thrown into question especially by the debates and research which point to an increase, in the advanced countries, in the size of the middle class (Renner 1953). It has been put into question here by the realignment of productive labour with nature (and see the appendix). Earlier, I laid out grounds for arguing that the increase in size and the realignment of labour with nature were related. If nature is also a key source of surplus-value, then it would be possible within an economy overall (when its profit or surplus-value is conceived in total terms) for more people literally to live off the fat of

---

32 Tilly and Scott's classic study puts a general thesis on the effects of industrialization in the family economy, but concentrates on England and France in its detailed study. Their general thesis is borne out by the non-metropolitan studies; the pathbreaking work here is Boserup (1970). Anther significant early study here is Tinker (1974).

33 One of the striking and most impoverishing effects on women as mothers wrought by industrialization was the advent of the putting-out system. This meant women could work at home but without the protection of the social structure of the family economy or union regulation (Tilly and Scott 1978, p. 75).

the land, and the oil, and the sea, and the beasts, and even the lilies of the field. But where that is not possible, or less possible, 'people' will occupy the same position as nature, exploited at the level of production as they are at that of reproduction. In terms of production, they will be positioned like the will-less other of the fantasy; they will be those who serve more of themselves and their energy than they are served, those who are denied agency in production while they run down their bodily being.

Taking this more slowly: as noted above, traditionally Marxists have defined class in terms of whether or not labour is productive. The working class is productive, the bourgeoisie or ruling class unproductive, and debates have raged over the productive status of the petty-bourgeoisie and/or new middle class. I am suggesting that productive labour is that which is closest to other natural forces and sources, in terms of its inability to exercise will and design, direction and control of the production process. We have also seen that this inability is tied to scale; it is as production becomes centralized that the labourer loses a direct and imaginative relation to the product. We can add here that even after industrialization, it is women who are most significantly affected by the scale factor. In most sectors of the economies in England and France 'the smaller the scale of organization, the larger the size of the female workforce' (Tilly and Scott 1978, p. 68).

But by this argument, scale, centralization and distance have also figured in the production of surplus-value in another way: surplus value is measured against the speed of acquisition, which consumes energy: the energy of labour and other natural forces. I have also suggested that distance figures here, in terms of speed (how far the commodity to be consumed in production or outside it has to travel, and how fast, affects the energy consumed). And I have argued that surplus-value produced this way works on a different axis (space, related to price) from surplus-value produced by comparison with the time of reproduction (value).

The question becomes: where class is concerned, how does surplus-value measured by the speed of acquisition intersect with surplus-value measured by the time of reproduction? Remembering that labour-power is both a commodity that is consumed in production and one that consumes, we can begin answering this by noting that the speed of acquisition has been tied to a continuum of consumption, in an argument which makes consumption for production and further consumption integral to the production of surplus-value.

In this version of value-theory, social reproduction has become a means of adding value in itself. It has become this means precisely because of the emphasis on energy consumed in distribution and exchange, which of course involves the energy consumed by and in the reproduction of labour-power, at the level both of day-to-day consumption and of generational reproduction which is where, most obviously, women and domestic labour add value. Moreover, on the axis of acquisition and consumption, and from capital's perspective, labour's voluntary portability marks it out from other living substances, whose transportation and distribution costs are stood by capital. We have seen that, in terms of the lateral and linear modes for extracting surplus-value, labour-power provides a surplus in both respects. It adds value in the traditional way. And in covering its own transportation costs, it decreases price.[34] But does this make for a necessary tie between portability and productivity? Within the framework of the old value-theory, it does, in that labour-power's transportation costs are part of its own social reproduction costs, which have to be less than the value it adds in production. On the one hand, making social reproduction a value-adding variable in itself means that there is no necessary connection between traditional productivity and portability. They are both axes of exploitation. But when portability and reproduction are united, as they are here, as different sides of acquisition, portable labour-power is connected structurally to the 'fixed' reproducers of labour-power.[35] This structural connection solves the problem set out by Balibar which is how 'to keep "in their place", from generation to generation, those who have no fixed place. . . . For this, it is necessary that they have a genealogy' (Balibar and Wallerstein 1988, p. 213).

It is married women who stay fixed in place, and often suffer more

34  At the phenomenal level, this is a marker of class. Those who are furthest from the place of production, those with longest to travel of necessity (without, for example, parking places etc. provided) are those lowest down the class-scale. If you are adding more value than you get, if your means of subsistence are less than the energy you transmit in the process of production, you are probably covering your own transportation costs. If you are the consumer of labour-power, and therefore are non-productive in the technical sense, labour-power is a commodity that is desired and comes to you. Moreover, as capital, as a purchaser of labour-power, you will choose the labour-power which is readily available, rather than standing the costs of flying or in other ways transporting its labour to the point of production.

35  Despite attention to sexism and the invisible support of household labour earlier in their joint study (1988, pp. 34-5), Balibar and Wallerstein do not refer to it when discussing how the contradictory requirements of destabilization and maintaining fixity are to be met (1988, p.212). Nonetheless their identification of these two contradictory aspects to capitalist accumulation is of critical importance.

economically by doing so.[36] Their fixity here overlaps with, and is reinforced by, the fixing of a negative image onto them which we discussed in Part I. The individual energetic exploitation works with the social one. But once again, the same is true for ethnicity and race: the offloading of a negative image and the aggression that goes with it onto the different other establishes a fixed point with energetic gains to the colonist. The difference is that these ethnic and racial 'fixed points', when they are masculine, are free to move at the economic level. More accurately, they are frequently compelled to move. Their portability is often a condition of their survival. In both cases, enforced fixity or compulsory migration, the result is the economic anxiety that we analysed as the other side of the aggression that secures the subject's position. The spatial, psychical dialectic of aggression and anxiety is now an economic dialectic as well, with a tie to spatiality that extends beyond urbanization.[37] In this dialectic, those who are positioned as objects are once more the repositories of anxiety, who benefit the subjects, subjects whose position becomes more elusive.

Their elusiveness is the main reason why it is difficult to make more remarks about class position, especially middle class position. I am very aware of this difficulty, and in truth, think it arises because class as defined by Marxism is disappearing, but exploitation as defined by Marxism is not. I suppose one can say, schematically, that the ruling class can be defined as those who have maximum control and design of production, and whose social reproduction costs are entirely covered by surplus-value. True subjects they. But one can say nothing so schematic about the vast new middle class. We can note, however, that this class has been tied to the massive growth of the service industry (Renner 1953), which may give it a special connection with the foundational

36 On the different impact of industrialization on married and single women, see Tilly and Scott (1978, p. 88) and Douglas (1977, p. 56). Most women were married however, and the research on this inclines to the view that their position deteriorated more than men's, although the real contrast of course should not be with the position of men, but between women's position before and after capitalization. Tilly and Scott's comparative study supports the idea that the position of women invariably suffers (both in relation to their former position and in relation to men) with twentieth-century 'development' and capitalization. Clarke's sociology of women in seventeenth century Britain supports the same conclusion. So does Boserup's study of the effects of development on women in Africa. Ginsborg argues that it was the migrating men who suffered most in the Italian *miracole;* unlike the women, they lost the support of the traditional kin networks (Ginsborg 1990).
37 I suggest that both psychical and economic factors combine to produce the recorded result that 'The closer in time that a given household is to the experience of household production, the more likely it is that women will do productive work and that they will subordinate time spent in reproductive activity to that work' (Tilly and Scott 1978, p. 230).

fantasy, which I analysed in terms of commodities which seek to serve. In addition, the notorious instability of the middle class, and, for that matter, all who dream under capital, is exacerbated by the scrabble for the subject's position, to be the one who secures it, who is able to project fixity and delay onto the other. It is exacerbated by the way the foundational fantasy shapes consumption desires regardless of class position.

In a loose sense, it is obvious that consumers are divided into classes in terms of their ability to consume. In fact this ability is a significant if unreliable indicator of class position. It is also an indicator in the spatio-temporal terms which are fundamental in this rewritten value-theory, and it works in the following way.

The less the delay the consumer endures between desiring the object of consumption and acquiring it positions that consumer in spatio-temporal terms by definition. The commodity that comes to you is more expensive, and your class position will appear more substantial, if you can afford to have commodities come to you. If you can, or if you choose to seem as if you can, you act out the foundational fantasy more dramatically as a subject. This level of consumption - Departments 2 and 3 - is now evidently homologous with Department 1: instant gratification prefigures and demands speedier acquisition; the speed of acquisition makes for more instant gratification.

Of course the range of objects desired will be circumscribed in terms of what is fantasized compared with what is realistic, and this circumscription is precisely what makes the spatio-temporal in icator of consumption unreliable. In an economy which fosters credit, and whose permanent inflation is explained in relation to credit (by Marxist and non-Marxist economists alike), the delayed gratification that marked capitalization in its reality-testing heyday is increasingly undermined. Today you can have it now and pay later, and consumers are exhorted to do just this. Whether you can actually afford to have it now, but none the less *have* to have it now, are questions which need not be decided by income, provided credit is good. For this reason the limits on delay, in an increasingly fantasmatic economy, are set by the limits on credit. These limits are often countermanded by the credit masquerade, a masquerade of phenomenal marks of 'class'; they are also countermanded by aspiration. An aspiration, a dream, if not a goal-directed course towards being in the position where it all comes to you: this is probably the single most important factor disrupting and undermining any class solidarity or class definition.

Consumption reveals the homology between the individual foundational fantasy and the broader socio-historical process. More generally, we now have grounds for showing how a proliferation of economic, social fixed points works hand-in-hand with the repressed psychical ones. But before returning to the foundational fantasy, note that we have a definite connection between the exploitation of the environment and the process of surplus-value extraction.

The object which makes a profit is the object which controls the environment, in terms of speeding it up and moving it round, creating its own 'laws of motion'. In addition, we are able to see that the aim of capital is to create the conditions by which it is in fact able to control the environment. To a certain extent, it is successful, and its success is the condition of its profit. *Mutatis mutandis,* the object which makes a profit has to be that which controls the environment, remembering that this control has a very specific content. It is a content far more specific than that given 'control' by Heidegger, because of the precise way that control is geared towards speeding up time and collapsing space. I have given an account of the mechanism by which time, measured by delay, is progressively eliminated. This mechanism is surplus-value extraction, usually known as profit, which, in the portable world it generates, breaks down the constraints that kept the ego in check. It does so not only in terms of class and sex-identity patterning, but in terms, which we can now see are related to class, of the extent to which fantasies come true and gratification comes more rapidly.

As Weber saw so plainly, a temporal shift, of a different but related order to that the state effects, was crucial in capitalization. This was Protestantism's shift towards delayed gratification. While this shift appeared to take account of time, it did so by retaining a surplus extracted, in the final analysis, from generational time. Calvinism *conserved;* it did not throw its bread upon the waters, or anywhere else. But unlike today's subjects, the subjects of Protestantism were prepared to wait. The ability to delay gratification has now become the desire for instant gratification, with the means for that desire's gratification, if you occupy the right position in the right place.

# Chapter 5

# Conclusion: Time and exploitation

I find myself with three threads to pursue in concluding. I have divided these into sections. The first section pursues some loose ends left over from Part I. It is of interest to those who are curious about the concerns with history and the question of the fantasy's universality, which it discusses in relation to symbolization and scale. The historical question is elaborated in the second section, on the construction of imaginary time. The focus here is on the *physis*, the interaction between microcosm and macrocosm, and how the sense of history is constructed as things get faster and faster. The third section is about exploitation, and programmatic and other forms of opposition to the ego's era. The reader interested in what is to be done may wish to read this section first; it follows on directly from the last chapter's concerns with the applicability gap, and the question of who gets to be in the right place at the right time.

## NOTES ON THE FANTASY'S HISTORY: SYMBOLIZATION AND SCALE

Part I of this book concluded with the idea that the ego's era is born of patriarchy, a system of social life which moulds the foundational fantasy into an acceptable expression, at the same time as it fosters some of its fonder delusions. To the extent that this book contributes a theory of history and modernity, this notion is fundamental. It is basic to the political and ethical implications of my argument. For if the psychical affinity between modernity and its patriarchal sire is forgotten, it is relatively easy to mistake the constraints that feudal patriarchy imposed for solutions to the anomie and fragmentation that mark postmodernism. The longing for the past, the seeping nostalgia that characterizes key theories critical of the modernity that leads to postmodernism, is prompted and then justified by a limited insight, limited in that it sees the patriarchy that preceded the ego's era and kept it in check as its solution, not its precipitate. The idea of the ego's era, the notion of the culture of narcissism (Lasch 1978), the belief in the corrosion of the lifeworld (Habermas 1968; cf. Fraser 1990), all imply that we should go back to patriarchal hearth and home.[1]

We reach other conclusions if we retrace the relation between the foundational fantasy described in Part II and its patriarchal enactment. By the foregoing account, the ego comes into being and maintains itself partly through the fantasy that it either contains or in other ways controls the mother; this fantasy involves the reversal of the original state of affairs, together with the imitation of the original. When recognition of the other is unavoidable, the ego's first response is that it is not the dependent child. In patriarchal societies, the fantasized reversal of the original state is actualized to some extent in the relation between the sexes. Herein lies the importance for a man of the need to take care of the other, to be the breadwinner, a matter whose significance may lie in the distance between the extent to which he actually gives of himself, and the extent to which he relies on the other's giving him an image of himself as giving, regardless of the reality of whether he gives or not. But more to the point: the truly patriarchal society is on the decline. While it might be thought that in such societies the psychical fantasy of woman expressed the splitting that founds subjectivity in an acceptable form, it also reinforced the fantasy of controlling the mother, whose capacities it denied in theory. This theoretical denial (while it was contradicted by the practice of pre-modern women) laid the grounds for denying any notion of indebtedness or connection to origin. As patriarchal society (not the same thing as sexism, not in the least) dies out, this denial persists and extends its reach, via the imitation of the original embodied in commodities and the nature-consuming conditions of their production.

Any strategies let alone solutions to the ego's era thus begin with recognizing the explicitly maternal nature of the origin that is denied. But while they begin there, they do not end there. The construction of sexual difference along patriarchal lines is not the origin of the foundational fantasy. Rather it seems that, in patriarchal societies, a far more ancient conflict is played out in the arena of sexual identity. How

1 Nancy Fraser's (1990) scrupulous critique of Habermas makes the inherently patriarchal longing at base of his lament very plain.

universal this conflict is is another question; so is the question of whether the fantasy is inevitably patriarchal in its expression. As these questions bear on the historicity as well as the political implications of this argument, they need to be considered.

We had good reason to place the fantasy well before its technological reinforcement. But we also had good reason to limit any claims about the fantasy's historical generality. I shall review the elements of the foundational fantasy one by one, beginning with the notion of subjective containment. It is evidently historically and culturally variable, and probably historically restricted. Alternatives to it were symbolized in the premodern West, and are symbolized in other cultures. Generally, this alternative symbolization features in cultures which are not marked by extensively technologized and urban, built environments. In these cultures, production is local in scale, the relation to nature physically closer. This is not, it never is, to reduce symbolizing alternatives to local scale and closeness to nature. It is however to stress that thinking and experiencing oneself as an energetically contained system is more likely in a culture in which fixed points proliferate. It is also to stress, simply, that alternatives to this and other elements of the fantasy *can* be symbolized, and this fact reminds us that our psychical being and ethical possibilities are not confined to foundationalism. We are always more than that, but the circumstances in which we become something more, and the duration for which we sustain that becoming, are constrained by the interactive economy, the fixity of the environment we inhabit.

Turning to the next element in the foundational fantasy: the subject–object distinction. The idea that this is universal, and the related preference for visual and 'object'-oriented thinking, is also highly dubious. The distinction comes to power under the same circumstances as the notion of containment, although, like that notion, it long preceded the technological circumstances favourable to it. An enlargement of scale does not *produce* subject–object thought, but it does enhance its dominance. Other elements in the fantasy have more claims to cultural universality, although they vary in intensity.[2] The factors

2 A probably obvious aside. Many of the desires which seem universal register their universality culturally, not in terms of individual behaviour. Thus if one thinks of the psychical permutations of devouring, one might think of Thyestes being served his son at dinner, not of Ancient Greeks sitting down to filial meals as a matter of course. Whether we attribute the power of various myths to their touching an unconscious chord in each of us, or see them in terms of an intersubjective unconscious which may or may not register in separate persons, does not matter to the extent that in both

of envy and sadistic aggression are presumably universal this side of paradise. The more specific desires to devour, poison and to dismember also have good general claims, as do the ethical codes which forbid these desires' naked expression. But the desire to dismember or destroy *in order to know* is something else. As with much else in the Faustian repertoire, this seems Western. The desire for instant gratification, the desire to be waited upon, the envious desire to imitate the original, are more troubling, in that their universality is more difficult to locate. At one level, imitating the original is as universal as children playing parents,[3] and men imitating mothers at one remove.[4] But whether envy is a necessary corollary of imitation is questionable. Imitation can also be accompanied by envy's opposite – admiration. We might say that imitation can be gauged envious where the original is denied, by any of the mechanisms of denial (from trivializing to trashing). The desire to be waited upon is manifest in any assertion of power which involves the one's *going to* the other. But the close relative of this desire, instant gratification, again seems heavily culturally modulated in Western terms.

In sum, some elements of the fantasy are universal, although their strength can be reinforced or negated. On the other hand, the desire to know by dismembering, destroying, the subject–object thinking tied to hallucinatory envious denial, and instant gratification, or the denial of time in relation to power and control, seem slanted to the West. These are also precisely the desires that are most reinforced in constructed technological inertia. The shift from a genuinely patriarchal feudal society to a sexist capitalist one is also the shift from a society with a limited technology to one that is capable of satisfying the desires in the foundational fantasy with more precision. Thus it is more likely that

cases the social nature of the foundational fantasy is confirmed, although the choice of options would influence the causal weight we give the social manifestation.

3  There is a small anthropological literature, and some historical discussion of, children's play. The main difficulty with evaluating the anthropological material is the extent to which children conceive of themselves as children, or alternatively, as small people. Cf. Aries (1962) and Foucault (1976).

4  While I suspect the fantasized attacks on and denigration of the mother's body are universal, I do not want to claim that they are universal without the monumental cross-cultural research that would need to be done to substantiate the claim. However, one immediately thinks of the anthropological line of enquiry extending from Mead (1950) through to, for example, researchers such as Gillison (1980), and one waits for the book. Gillison's research on the Gimi in Australia is wonderful fodder for a psychoanalytic interpretation. During male initiation rites, flutes which Gillison describes as 'symbolic penes' are shown to the boys, and (a secret kept from the women) the boys are informed that 'in truth, it was once something that belonged only to women. It wasn't ours! We men stole it!' (1980, p. 156).

pschoanalytic case histories will uncover the desire to poison the mother (read: nature), rather than revere her in the infant psyche of today. But that the desires existed beforehand is not open to doubt. A few other remarks on their proliferation, and their aims, are in order.

The less technologically efficient or controlling the culture, the less nature can be denied as source, although it can certainly be railed against. There has been more railing in the West than outside it; in some non-Western cultures, nature can also be symbolized with something like affectionate regard, a partner to be worked with rather than feared and subjugated (Plumwood 1993). However the same regard need not be extended to women. Joint expressions of the desire to control the mother and control nature again keep harmonious company in the West especially, as does the wish to make both mother and nature passive while becoming the agency of control. The explicit idea of indebtedness however, meaning the acknowledgement of an origin to which one owes one's existence, features in any theistic or deistic culture, which means all cultures other than a predominantly middle-class section of the culture (broadly conceived) in which I am writing; obviously there is no corollary between acknowledgement of the mother's creative agency and believing in creative agency as such. Nonetheless, there is a corollary between denying the mother's agency and denying creative agency *tout court*. This is apparent if we consider the role that the denial of the father's agency played in the transition from patriarchy, as a modified omnipotent claim, to the rampant omnipotence of the ego's era. While a patriarchal culture formally denies the mother, it stops short of denying any indebtedness at all. It of course accords considerable recognition to the father's creative agency. The point at which a patriarchal culture in the West begins to give way to a liberal-democratic one, is the point at which the power and claims made in the name of fathers begin to be limited, in favour of 'individuals' without a past, without an origin. It is also the point, as we have seen, where the notion that individuals are contained systems, in energetic terms, comes into being.

This transitional point deserves attention. Liberalism cloaks the desires in the foundational fantasy with a more acceptable vocabulary, a vocabulary that is confusing, because it amalgamates foundational thinking with the appeal to tolerance. And this appeal, together with the injunctions to *judge not*, to do unto others as you would be done by, constitutes the most enduring opposition to the projected aggression that lies at the heart of the ego's era. But while the earliest vocabulary of liberalism embodies this amalgam, it also recognizes dominion. It stakes out territory free of fathers and God slowly, and often reluctantly. Thus the foremost exponent of the origins of liberalism, John Locke, was himself 'for a fleeting moment' (Dunn 1978, p. 40) caught in the tensions between the absence of God as a possibility and the requirements of Locke's own Christianity.

> A dependent intelligent being is under the power and direction and dominion of him on whom he depends and must be for the ends appointed him by the superior being. If man were independent he could have no law but his own will, no end but himself. He would be a god to himself. . . .
>
> (Locke quoted by Dunn 1978, p. 40)

Dunn, after quoting this passage, goes on to add that 'when God in due course died, man, an intelligent being, no longer aware of any other being on whom he *was* dependent, set himself to try to be [a god]' (1978, p. 40; see also Dunn 1969). And there we have it precisely. As long as the vocabulary of dependence, dominion and direction was retained, the implications of an egoistic liberalism were not spelt out.[5] At the same time, the insistence on that vocabulary points to the opposite possibility: a being without ties, dependent on no-one. In the logic of denial then, the first step in the denial of God is in the denial of the mother's agency, the second the denial of the father's. However, the denial of the mother's agency was no simple step. The Protestant rejection of the Virgin's status buried an acknowledgement of the maternal that had compensated somewhat for the other forms of denying the feminine. In the medieval times before subject–object thought, Mary had even been associated with logic (Southern 1953).

Nor was the denial of the father's agency straightforward. God took time in dying, and the liberal rejection of dependence was aimed initially at the indebtedness presupposed in the patriarchal, feudal social contract. Pateman's argument that the social contract of Hobbes and Locke was essentially a fraternal contract is based on the idea that liberalism in its origins denied its dependence on the father in favour of a post-patriarchal orientation of man towards his equal brothers (Pateman 1988). MacCannell's wonderful study shows how the 'regime of the brother' (MacCannell 1991) ushers in the death of God

---

5 Dunn's broader thesis, that it was possible for Locke to think as he did *because* he was a Christian does not of course abolish the fact that Locke thought as he did.

and superego, together with a sexist system of power without accountability. The individual brothers answer to no one. By the twentieth century, man has become 'a prosthetic God' (Freud 1929). His technology abets his deification, as did the discovery that his origin was a Mendelian accident. The puzzling popularity Darwin enjoyed in his own times (Rorty 1993) ceases to be problematic if it is situated on a continuum of increasing narcissism. So situated, Darwin's theory represents a confirmation of the idea that we humans are the most intelligent beings existing; not in God's image, but accordingly without peer. But man's politics and his related if anterior endorsement of a distinct *interior* identity anticipate this claim. The abolition of any mediation between man and God takes us that much closer to the godhead craved. 'Capitalism' and its technology is evidently not the sole cause of man's newfound godhead, but the process of capitalization is critical to the physical alterations which make atheism less of an intellectual decision than a position based on affectual resistance to its alternative.[6] For myself, stepping for a moment into the benighted genre of personal criticism, my intellectual convictions here conflict with a resistance to the idea of an easy way out, and I suppose this is standard.

But on the continuum of increasing narcissism, feudal patriarchy remains a mid-way step between what the fantasy denies and what it

6 While the concern with the psychical origins of atheism is not of particular interest to them, the question of divinity and more generally spirituality is returning in some of the feminist writing I have already mentioned. Both Kristeva and Irigaray see some form of divine representation of the 'feminine' as critical to counteracting the worst effects of patriarchy and the patriarchal social contract. Thus Kristeva sees the Virgin Mary as a figurative check on the 'powers of horror', while Irigaray sees a symbolic feminine Godhead as a means of guaranteeing woman's origin and thence identity. See Kristeva (1983, pp. 374 ff.) and Irigaray (1984). The difficulty with these writings is less with the writings as such than with the commentators' attempts to deal with the embarrassment of having an otherwise admired thinker apparently endorsing God. Both Whitford (1990) and Grosz (1986), for whose outstanding deployments of Irigaray I have the greatest respect, conclude that Irigaray is not so much a believer as a strategist. Her appeal to the divine is read as a 'strategy' for undermining the existing symbolic, as well as a means for women counteracting the death drive through faith in female and feminine worth and goodness. The problem with seeing the advocacy of faith in a maternal or feminine divinity as a strategy is that one has to ask the question: strategy for whom? If *we* know that God does not exist but *they* need to believe that She does, what precisely are *we* saying? And if we see it as a strategy, from where will we derive the power of conviction in our own female worth which would protect us from the death drive, to which we are also liable? In this context, note too that Irigaray is also conscious of spirituality and divinity in terms of the fact that the idea has been so split from 'matter'. 'Our so-called human theories and our most banal discourses are moving away from these things, progressing through and with a language which forgets the matter it designates and through which it speaks' (1986, p. 1). I could not agree more with these sentiments, as the above should make evident.

seeks to accomplish. Yet this is no uninterrupted continuum. It is riddled with discontinuities. A close study of these discontinuities would, I think, show something very important about the question of scale. Part of the problem with the disputes over whether economic shifts preceded ideological shifts in the rise of capitalism is the relative neglect of scale. We have seen that there were pockets of small-scale capital within the larger scale feudal economy. We are aware that demands for liberty, individual rights, and individual conscience (the protestant ethic) were articulated before capital becomes the dominant economy. If we take account of scale, we may at some future point be able to trace a dialectic between small-scale shifts to capitalization, and an increase in the articulation of subject-centred demands, where the symbolization of the demands in turn enforces the power of capital.

Overall, scale is obviously critical in this argument, which is built on interpreting the relation between microcosmic and macrocosmic expressions of an identical egocentrism, or subject-centredness. It is also built on the idea that the extent to which the fantasy takes hold subjectively or psychically depends on the extent to which it is materially acted out. Thus the burden of this analysis is that attempts at symbolizing alternatives to the fantasy in the present will fail without alterations in economic scale, because the monetary economic dimension is the key to its global dominance, its *increasing* materialization (it is always material).

But of course any increase in materialization depends on the fantasy's symbolization at some level, even if the level is only that of articulated subjective desire. Moreover, in discussing the foundational fantasy's universality in the past, we are only able to refer to its symbolization. I do not dispute this limitation. But this limitation, the limitation imposed by the inscribed record, means that symbolization itself is sometimes taken as the sole cure for present ills. This of course I do dispute, because it discounts the interaction between symbolization and scale, and the complexities of what should not be symbolized, as well as what should. Thus Skinner: 'To see the role of our evaluative language in helping to legitimate social action is to see the point at which our social vocabulary and our social fabric mutually prop each other up' (Skinner 1988, p. 132).

As I said at the outset, the power of a psychical fantasy depends on the extent to which it is reinforced or negated by social practice and the language of the times. If a psychical fantasy has a relative autonomy from socializing forces, practical strategy needs to take account of what has to be negated as well as celebrated. Skinner's overarching point, that the available vocabularies of agents and the meaning they have act as a constraint on their action, (Skinner 1978, pp. xii–xiii; 1988, p. 132) works both ways here. We need a vocabulary which constrains manifestations of a destructive psychical fantasy, as well as one that symbolizes the relation to maternal origin. For of itself, this symbolization does nothing to oppose certain elements of the fantasy (the objectification of the other by means ranging from devouring to dismembering, the denial of agency and conation in matter, the omnipotent control that would have it come to you without delay): elements which, when acted out on larger scales, result in a world in which more and more occupy the psychical and economic position of objects, reinforcing the crazed whims of an unseen subject, whose position they, or we, aspire to even against our judgement.

In the world of objects, the historical discontinuities, the breaks in scale and symbolization, are overridden more and more by an homogenizing force, in which both scale and vocabularies manifesting the fantasy reinforce one another. We now exist in a world in which the desires of the fantasy have ever more licence. Their claims to be human nature, or common sense, are ever stronger. What is also clear is that while an articulation of these demands could and still does erupt in small locales (the demands of smaller scale economies are fateful in Eastern Europe today), those demands are now becoming global. This is a necessary consequence of acting out the fantasy with ever-larger precision, because this extends the physical grip of the fantasy on individual persons. It remains to see just how it comes about.

## IMAGINARY TIME

Our task in this section is analysing how history is constructed as a *material* narrative. In turn, this depends on analysing the slower time and wider space over which the ego's era is played out, thereby completing the account of how a psychical fantasy comes to be played out on a scale with an ever-enlarging compass, and how techno-economic dynamics reinforce the desires in the fantasy at the expense of other psychical possibilities. In other words, this reinforcement alters the *physis* in ways which make it harder to act if not think outside foundational terms, precisely because of the energetic changes they effect. In this connection, we can consider Jameson's contention that alterations in the sense of temporality lead to changes in language use (Jameson 1991).

The key to the alterations in the *physis* lie in the terms time and space. Time and space are basic to the dynamics whereby the foundational psychical fantasy is generated. We want it now, and we want it to come to us. On the social scale, by inventing technologies that bring whatever it is we want to us, and which do so immediately, we are abolishing time. But paradoxically, as we have seen, this entails extending the fantasy in space, and for a reason yet to be determined, giving it more time to play itself out: instead of a lifetime, or the years of an individual psychosis, the ego's era spans a few centuries. The only way of resolving this paradox, and the tautology that this argument becomes without that resolution, is to suppose that as we extend the fantasy in space, and make it immediately present, we simultaneously slow down time. In turn, this means supposing that the mechanism by which we make the fantasy present and extend its spatial coverage also congeals or slows down time. What is this mechanism, and how is the paradox to be resolved?

We have established that the paradox is resolved in the case of infancy and the birth of psychical reality in this way: what prompts the hallucination is the desire that the longed-for object be present here and now. Hallucination not only introduces instant gratification (in theory); in practice, it also introduces delay. In the social case, technology constructs the commodities that satisfy the fantasy of instant gratification and service, but how do these constructions simultaneously slow things down, especially as production is getting faster and faster? The key here was the notion that the ego's own hallucinated responses constitute the first point of resistance. We supposed that the construction of a commodity also binds energy in the same way that it is bound in the repression of an hallucination. In both cases the energy is attached to an image, fixing it in place. The commodity, like the hallucination, constitutes a point of resistance, in that it encapsulates living nature in forms which remove them from the flow of life, just as the repressed hallucination traps psychical energy in a constructed, contained, boundary that founds the subject. In other words the fixed points of commodities function analogously with hallucinations and fantasies in that they bind living substances in forms which are inert, relative to the energetic movement of life.

I broke off this investigation of the parallels between the commodity and the hallucination to investigate, or to concretize, Heidegger's assumption that 'humanity' was establishing global transitions in shorter and shorter timespans, compressing time in the process. The labour theory of value without the subject–object distinction shows how these still points must accumulate ever more rapidly, relative to the movement of life, which has to be cheated on, in order to make a profit. The more of these relatively inert points there are – and they are of course more significant, more fixed, when the commodity produced is not biodegradable – the slower the movement of life becomes. Thus the notion that points of resistance slow things down provides a critical principle by which to gauge what should and should not be constructed. That gauge is – how readily can these constructions re-enter the movement of life?

The notion that points of resistance slow things down also means we can account for the paradox whereby the infantile fantasy takes more time to play itself out, in a way consistent with the idea that the fantasy simultaneously extends itself in space. It takes more 'time' to play itself out in the sense that it uses more living energy, as it systematically extends itself in the spatial conquests necessary to supply the living substances by which it sustains itself. However, it also follows from this argument that the 'time' it takes to play itself out is itself a constructed phenomenon, in that this 'time' consists of the accumulation of 'points of resistance' or commodities. Moreover this 'time' has its own direction.

The construction of one commodity (using the term in the broadest sense)[7] fixes a relatively inert or still point. This point (let us say it is a factory, even a town) then functions as an inert point of reference from which distances are measured and pathways built. They are built, at least in part, as a means to further the consumption, and free enterprise competition is always a race, of more living substances in the process of production. Of the different characteristics that mark the networks established by these means, there are two that need to be recalled here. The first is that to stay in the race of efficient consumption for production and further consumption, these networks need to facilitate the most rapid transport of energy possible. This applies to energy of any order: the natural substances consumed in production, and human labour-power. The means by which natural substance or labour is extracted and conveyed from $a$ to $b$ has to be

7  A commodity varies in scale depending on the position of the consumer. From the standpoint of one consumer, it could be a small-scale consumer good. From the standpoint of another, it could be ICI.

speeded up. This is why, at the level of constructed space–time, everything seems to be getting faster and faster. The second point about the networks constructed in relation to still points is that at the same time as they partake in the process whereby natural reproduction is actually slowed down, they must, like the still points themselves, have their own physical energetic effects, effects additional to those noted by both Lacan and Benjamin. These effects are also physical in the sense that commodities function as points of resistance to natural rhythms so that, in reality, things get slower and slower.

As the networks between these points extend, creating more still points in the process, the expanding spatio-temporal construction that results has a pattern of its own. There is every reason for supposing that this pattern presents itself to us as temporal causality (Cf. Cornell 1992, p. 124ff.).[8] Temporal causality is the process whereby one thing appears to lead to another across time in an apparently irreversible manner. This taken for granted process is of course at issue in physics, where the asymmetrical nature of time, the puzzle as to why time only goes one way, or why time is irreversible, is regarded as something to be explained. By this account, time could be understood, in theory if not in practice, as reversible, provided that all the points of resistance out of which space–time is constructed and connected were systematically undone, and if their component natural substances re-entered the natural rhythms of production, from which they were initially, physically, 'abstracted'. This understanding of time also accords with the deconstructionist idea that causality is a construction, a line of reasoning we impose on events. Except that, by my argument, the causal construction really has been constructed. The fact that the construction has a fantasmatic origin makes it no less physical in its effects. In other

8 Drucilla Cornell's comments on temporal causality are developed in the context of a critique of Niklas Luhmann. Luhmann recognizes the Parsonian point that a temporal social system can only be compared to something that is not temporal (Luhmann 1975, p. 292). He even says that it can only be compared to something that is 'immediate', that is to say, timeless. But having had this insight, he then goes on to neglect its implications altogether. He forgets the existence of the 'immediate' something, and argues instead that a temporal system can have nothing outside itself, and thus that there is no point against which an alternative future to the one already contained within the present can be built. From the perspective of this argument, of course, that alternative point is present in the natural world. Moreover, as I imply in the text, if the 'immediate' something is the physical world, if the physical world is also spatio-temporal, from whence does it get its temporality, if not from the social world? Cornell criticizes Luhmann's 'privileging of the present' from a Derridean perspective, (Cornell 1992). The significance of time and space in social organizations generally, and the shift from modernism to 'postmodernism' in particular, is the central theme of Giddens (1990).

words, to read causality as a mere illusion, which could be done away with by refusing to impose causal reasoning in theory, accords with and therefore does nothing to counter the galloping construction of causality in the physical world. By the same token, to read narrative as a mistaken imposition of a linear discourse on a situation whose polymorphous facticity will not brook it, is to overlook the extent to which a narrative line has been produced as a physical, material reality. That narrative owes its existence to a process in which an infantile fantasy appears to have shifted itself from the realms of a transient moment in individual life to make itself dominant across time, but the present effects of that process are such as to make it difficult to trace the narrative.

The dynamics described in this process must be cumulative, not only in the sense that, as things get faster and faster at the level of constructed space–time, they get slower and slower in relation to the natural logic they attempt to rival. The dynamics must also be cumulative in terms of the extent to which the causality constructed presents itself to us as an historical process.

'History', as the sense of the sequence of past events, is increasingly moulded by the extent to which a foundational psychical fantasy makes itself materially true, and by its consequent material effects on the individual psyches that entertain the fantasy. This is why grasping the fact that the fantasy has become a material narrative across time is so critical, if so difficult. It is critical in creating a monolithic view of history which has a material basis in the present, but which had to cover over all sorts of local differences to attain supremacy. Even so, these differences still erupt, in uncovering what the written record has not included hitherto. In this respect, scholarship, as the uncovering and correcting of what has been omitted or distorted, is always anti-foundational.

As we have seen, the materialization of the narrative is also critical in creating, and then undermining, the historical sense as such. The postmodern oblivion to, if not its condemnation of, history has a predecessor. 'Thinking historically' has not been always with us, only to be abandoned in the present. At first glance, it seems that it is only as the shifts in social organization become sufficiently marked as to be memorable within an individual lifetime that the historical sense is born. The problem with this is that dramatic changes had occurred within the span of individual lifetimes hitherto: had I been born in France in the thirteenth century, been a mercenary or a saint or even a literate priest, I would have witnessed the departure of one king, the reinstatement of another, etc. On the other hand, one could reply that such shifts in social organization were not sufficiently wide-reaching or fundamental in their effects to have brought a historical consciousness into being. Yet this only mitigates the objection that changes occurred in individual lifetimes beforehand. It does not resolve it. One can only explain why rapid shifts infiltrate consciousness and intellectual aware-ness with more power, why the sense of stasis declines in and especially after the seventeenth century – although that static sense survived major historical alterations hitherto – if the power of the historical sense is understood literally, as a physical force. It can be understood in this way if the shifts in social organization result in a sense of the passage of time that propels one to locate events and experience in time and space. Yet what would such a sense involve? It would have to have two ingredients. Any sense of time has to be based on a feeling of motion. To feel motion, one has to have a fixed reference point, fixed relative to one's motion. (Or one can be that fixed point, and feel the other's motion.) The second ingredient is that this feeling of motion has to be rapid enough to mean that there is a need to locate events and experience. And these can only be located in fixed points of reference. In other words, the historical sense requires not only motion, but fixed points that do not change. From this perspective, it seems that where energy boundaries and technology are concerned, we are dealing with something like a three stage process historically. The first stage is charted in the pre-Renaissance writings discussed in Chapter 3; the second stage is embodied in the notion of a self-contained, interiorized consciousness; the third is the return of the repressed, the idea of energetic connection. In other words, the notion of the contained individual marks an interregnum, which is also characterized by interiorized thinking and historical consciousness.[9]

9  Thinking historically appears to gather steam with the social changes that pre-date and accompany technological shifts. For instance it is only in the late sixteenth century that the first histories, as the description of particular periods, begin to be written (Weiss 1967). Lévi-Strauss's (1963) classic distinction between cold and hot societies is a distinction between hot societies which have internalized their historicity, and cold ones which seems timeless. If Evans-Pritchard was right, a rise in historical conscious-ness requires (in effect) a memorable change in social structure and occasions for social mobility. It is when the social hierarchy is unchanged, when the same number of social places are available, that the 'distance between the beginning of the world and the present day seems unalterable' (1939, p. 108).

Yet the technological correspondences of these stages break down, in that the first stage refers to a less technological or built environment; the third, which is apparently similar to it, to a highly technologized context. However, this similarity can be explained to the extent that both the technologized and untechnologized environments affect the sense of history and passing time. The untechnologized environment has been correlated with stasis, with the sense of no-change: in this sense it is opposed to an historical consciousness. The highly technologized environment has been correlated with change that is so rapid that it also has negative effects on historical perception. I am presuming these effects are energetic, and that they impinge on perception not just because of their content, but because they also impinge on the boundaries by which the subject maintained its material illusion of containment.

Both the first and third stages are marked not only by the ideas of connection and transmission, but by perceptions which would now be styled paranoid. In the contemporary West, any perception of an ideational force on the subject that comes from without is liable to be designated this way. But it will be designated this way, in part, because it conflicts with the inherited and hegemonic symbolic. Thus one of the things this analysis points to is the importance of symbolizing the notion of interconnecting forces, and thus understanding their material effects.

If these material effects are taken into account, the extent to which the fantasy takes hold individually, and thus the extent to which individuals act in accord with the fantasy's constructed causal direction, should be cumulative. At this point I return to Lacan. When he discussed the ego's era, Lacan noted that it was accompanied by increasing aggressiveness and anxiety. He explained this in terms of the spatial constrictions of the urban environment. The more spatially constricted the environment becomes, the greater the anxiety and the greater the tendency to project this anxiety outwards in aggressiveness. Lacan's account of this process is as allusive as his account of objectification. Here again, a link needed to be made between aggressiveness and the other dynamics of objectification revealed by the analysis of the commodity. At one level the link was always evident. If a vending machine fails to produce, its chances of being kicked are high. At another level, the link had to be established in spatio-temporal, physical terms. Lacan's emphasis on spatiality provided a physical pointer, which can be extended in terms of the speculative account of still points of resistance offered here. These still points are inanimate, whether they are constructed commodities or internal fantasies. What I want to suggest now is that just as its own fantasies weigh heavily upon the ego, so does a subjective if subliminal sensing of what is animate or inanimate in the surrounding environment. The less animate that environment is and the slower time becomes, the greater the ego's need to speed things up, its anxiety, its splitting, its need for control, its 'cutting-up' in its urge to know, its spoiling of living nature, and its general aggression towards the other. But of course, as with any paranoid anxiety, the ego by these processes only accelerates the production of the conditions that produce its fears.[10] It constructs more still points which start, or speed up, the whole show again. At the same time, it uproots itself and its anchors in the interpersonal still points which defined it hitherto, which also short-circuits its memory. And by this very uprooting, it breaks down the identity barriers which preserved some form of individuality, leading to the psychotic anxieties, if not psychotic experiences, that mean we can speak of the outcome of the ego's era as a social psychosis. This psychosis is exacerbated by the failure to symbolize energetic connections, connections which are experienced fleetingly as displacement removes the anchors which barred knowledge of them. This failure to find a vocabulary of connections, to symbolize them in terms which are not subject-centred, means that any feeling of connection will only be experienced through the ego's lens, assimilated to a subject-centred world view. This is the essence of a major symptom of paranoia: the awareness of energetic forces in the environment (an accurate awareness), accompanied by the belief that these forces are focused solely on one's individual self (not an accurate belief).

The minor symptoms of the psychosis, on the other hand, are reflected in how symbolized ethical codes break down to accommodate an increasing incapacity to tolerate delay, a greater demand for service, a more extensive need for domination, a horror of inferiority contingent on escalating envy and the constant comparisons envy demands. These things are accommodated, but within vocabularies or codes of symbolization which are more concerned with flattery than courtesy, ranging from subject-positioning encounters in the everyday

10 There is a striking account of the paranoid's collusion in the production of the conditions it fears in Bersani's discussion of Thomas Pynchon (Bersani 1990, p. 188).

(Yes sir, right away sir, did you enjoy your meal?) to judicious quotation. In writing, they are reflected in a rhythmless prose, bearing the marks of dead fixed points. In theory, they are also reflected in an ever-rising flight away from the concrete and the flesh into the fantasmatic world of the abstract. It is this last flight that makes the sometimes obvious nature of the processes recorded here elusive.

The originating foundational fantasy situates the mother as a passive natural entity responding to an active agency located elsewhere, but this is becoming, or has become, more than an ephemeral fantasy. The extent to which active agency really is located elsewhere increases as the material means to control the environment increase, as they do when the fantasy is acted out. To the extent that this active agency results in the imposition of a direction on the environment which goes against, rather than with, natural rhythms and their own logic, the force of the latter figures less in any calculations made about what causes what, especially in the realms of social theory. At the same time, the active agency, the will at issue, is reduced too readily to individual actions. In fact the location of this agency is problematic in the extreme. A direction which goes against natural logic and rhythms is imposed, but while individuals strive for the subject position, it eludes them. They are constituted as objects unable to sustain a direction of their own, who labour under perceptions which reinforce their strivings for the subject position, while affecting their perception in ways which make it difficult to analyse the basis of the strivings.

By this argument, the subject's sense of connection with the world is physically altered by its physical environment. And if the physical points of resistance embodied in commodities function after the manner of fantasies, closing the subject off to the movement of life, they are also visual tangible evidence of a different physical world which, however fantasmatic its origin, makes the subject more likely to see what it has made, rather than feel itself to be connected with, or part of, what has made it.[11] This constitutes the main limitation on any

11 Luce Irigaray (1984) argues that any epochal change also requires a change in how space and time are perceived. The difference between her observation and this argument is that Irigaray sees the change in space–time perception solely in subjective terms, rather than attempting to explain it as a change that is physically produced. For a good discussion of French feminist theory and spatio-temporal concerns, see Grosz (1988). It should be added here that many feminist philosophers of science have suggested that the boundaries of the physical sciences and their underlying assumptions should be thrown into question; there is no reason why the physical sciences should have escaped gender-blindness, when the social sciences have not. But there is a difference between noting that the physical sciences should be questioned, or even

wholesale endorsement of Spinoza's theory. The equation of God and Nature is limited by the fact that nature is perceived, from a human subject-centred standpoint, in terms of visual and tactile extension. Spinoza himself noted the limitation, insofar as he noted that while the One Substance had infinite attributes, humans perceived only two: extension and thought. But for this very reason, there is always a 'beyond' to what we perceive. My point here is that while this 'beyond' is never immaterial, while it is always physical in some sense, it cannot be limited to 'nature' as we perceive it. Thomas Aquinas's parallel point is that nature does in restricted terms what God does in unrestricted terms. Yet if Nature is restricted in my argument, it is restricted even more as we progressively make our restricting, subject-centred perspective of the world more concrete. For in modernity the visual hallucination which denied feelings of unpleasure is now a concrete thing, and the various senses which otherwise connect the subject with the world stand back in favour of the visual sense.

The idea that the subject's sense of perception is physically altered by its physical environment, and the related idea that the concrete imposition of a foundational psychical fantasy has altered that environment, raise the possibility that different physical theories and theories of perception are more true for their times than they appear with hindsight, precisely because the times physically alter what and how we perceive. When commenting on how temporality has been displaced in favour of spatiality, Žižek (1992, p. 64) suggests that it is 'probably more than a coincidence that . . . the theory of relativity paved the way for a notion of the universe as a time-space continuum, i.e., for a "static" picture of the universe where time is conceived as the fourth dimension of space'. Žižek's point has even more weight if we consider that fourth dimensional thinking was several decades ahead of Einstein, as was the acceleration of the industrial process whereby space replaces time.

If the parallel drawn here between psychical and socio-historical temporal interference is correct, if the construction of more and more commodities slows down real time while seeming to speed it up, then this means that the physical reality in which we exist, the physical laws under which we live, *are being and have been altered*. By a socio-

showing that a more empathetic approach to science is possible – as Evelyn Fox Keller (1985) does – and proposing an alternative, speculative, physical theory. This is not the exhortation. This is the act.

historical process, have we contributed to the chaotic *physis* we now discover, the uncertainty we now remark (Heisenberg 1958), as if it had always been present? For if we have, we have done so by enacting a psychical fantasy which, because it relies on a divorce of mental and physical activity, reinforces the prejudice that the psychical process and its socio-historical parallel have no effect on the physical world; this prejudice in thought may be why it is difficult to get clear information from a scientist to the question just posed.

But while different theories of physics and the natural order may have more relevance for their times than they appear to have from the present standpoint, retrospectives on paths to the present, theories of social and historical change, will be limited by the blindspots of the present. Marxism partially explained the process involved, and this was the immense appeal of this most successful of master-narratives. It failed as a narrative not because it was a narrative, but because it began the story in the wrong place, and left something vital out. It left out the fact that 'materialism', meaning the quite literal concretization of the fantasy, its physical enactment with its physical effects, has increasingly made itself into a determinant reality, a reality that overrides that of nature.

Had it been a theory of how the economic is increasingly determinant of the character of this epoch, Marxism may have extended its explanatory reach. Socialism, as a programmatic solution to the ills of capitalism, misses because it half counters the fantasy we have analysed without fully knowing why. It remained bound by the gigantic scale that the old system of production demands. In part, this was because in attempting to mark out what makes labour distinct from nature, Marx ran together the ability to imagine and design with the ability to create value. To say the same thing, he ran together the general properties of labour across time with the specific properties of productive labour under capital. At the same time, Marx's theory shows how subjective capacities, themselves appropriated in the first instance, are then reappropriated or alienated by capital, and removed from the new class of human objects. They are appropriated in the first instance in that it is the fantasmatic belief that it is the source of agency and direction that brings the subject into being (cf. Chapter 3). The labour process under capital replays the dynamics of this appropriation in every detail where nature is concerned, and the extent to which it replays it with people positions them in class terms, in terms of exploitation.

## EXPLOITATION AND ITS OPPOSITION

By this book's argument, exploitation always involves an energetic transfer. In fact we can define exploitation on this basis; where there is no energetic transfer that depletes one agency while enriching the other, there is no exploitation. But exploitation in these terms does not only work at the economic level. It works at the interpersonal level as well, the level experienced in everyday personal and social life. In personal life, the wrong sex can assign one to a draining emotional tie, and an inexplicable fixity or inertia. In social interaction, this exploitation may be brief or glancing, but it is pervasive: the wrong accent, the wrong colour, the wrong sexuality can lead to a thousand slights in brief encounters, all of which give a temporary leverage to the subjects on the other side of them. As Patricia Williams has it, prejudice *is* violence (Williams 1991, p. 61).

What I am terming interpersonal exploitation is not reducible to economic exploitation. But we can now see that these forms of exploitation are related. Interpersonal benefits accrue to the subject in the same way as economic benefits. In both cases, the one is empowered, subjectified, by the energy of the other. At the interpersonal level of image, and imaginary fixing, one 'makes it to subject' by directing aggression and a negative image outwards, freeing oneself to move. Such movement is enhanced by the attention directed towards the subject by the one who is fixed, seeking the affirmation that it is in the subject's energetic interest not to give. It is this 'attention', the intelligence, energy and direction it embodies, that is appropriated by the subject. At the economic level, the same capacities are appropriated to greater or lesser extents, and the extent to which they are appropriated is inversely proportionate, roughly speaking, to the wage. But they are appropriated, usually, on a different scale, and the subject who benefits is accordingly harder to locate; the object position, the position of the objectified other, is easier to identify.

Whilst the subject is harder to locate, we can make the subject and object positions the key terms in the dynamics of exploitation, and we can redefine the relation to exploitation in terms of the two levels they operate on. Those who occupy the object position in interpersonal and economic terms are doubly exploited. These are most likely to be women and people of colour. But the *degree* of exploitation at either level also matters here, for exploitation at one level invariably shades into the other: a woman exploited in interpersonal life will find her economic power deteriorating, if for no other reason than that her confidence, her sense of her self as subject, is systematically eroded. The working-class man, denied the economic subject position, may find aggression giving way to prolonged depression. The aggression follows on from the fact that a person positioned as object economically will have a strong psychical drive to play subject in an interpersonal context. But the opportunities for discharging this drive are rarely sufficient to protect the part-time subject from depression, or to pre-empt it. Depression, if it is experienced only cyclically, or contextually, for an hour here or there, is another manifestation of the object position. This does not mean depression is always bad. It can be the moment at which the empowered subject becomes human, alert to the suffering of others. But I will leave for another place the question of how much gentler and kinder people are when their status as overweening subjects is in doubt. The point is that we are all of us at some moment objects, which will help explain why a privileged man may still experience himself as powerless and lacking. The limits on 'experience' (cf. Scott 1992) as a category are evident if this man's circumstances are viewed comparatively. Then any claims he makes to this effect are ludicrous. Yet such a subject will not be comparing himself with others; he will be comparing himself with a super-Subject, some fictional character who receives more recognition and lives out the foundational fantasy's omnipotence more than he does himself.

By whatever yardsticks, everyone then is positioned as subject and object in a variety of contexts. But these contexts add up to an overall situation. Our task, to borrow Spivak's formulation, is to 'make visible the assignment of subject–positions' (Spivak 1987, p. 241). While the different levels of exploitation cannot be reduced to one another, their homology means we can define subject and object positions in terms of both economic and interpersonal recognition. Both make people rich or poor in a currency of empowering images and coins alike. Taking account of homologous levels of exploitation not only makes it plain why the object-position is more likely to be occupied by the unwhite, the female and the economically class-exploited; it also shows how it is occupied in a way which aligns its inhabitants with nature.

The alignment with nature is all the more crucial because unless it is stressed, we shall continue to want to be subjects. We will want to be subjects even against our wills, because there is a politics of exhaustion being played out in relation to the fantasy on the global scale. We will want to be subjects to garner the energy needed to move – whether it is through the attentive recognition and labour of others, or those expensive 'labour-saving devices'. The consequence of living in the high-tech built environment is that one almost has to be a subject to repel its deadening effects. As I hope I have shown, these deadening effects are deceptive: the world from which they emanate appears to be a world of more rapid motion, with a rapid pulse that can for a time be taken as energy itself, as it speeds up one's conscious tempo. But the price of this temporary excitement will be paid somewhere. Even if it is not paid by the subject who benefits, the deadening effects of this environment more and more make each and everyone an object. That is what lack of love, in Eagleton's terms a political as well as personal affair, will always do.[12] So will lack of connection.

Still, as ever, the process of becoming either subject or object is complex, invariably overdetermined. The urge to resist objectification is very powerful, the life-drive more enduring and effective than its fantasmatic parasite. I have indicated that resisting the object position can be done in two ways: by striving for subjectivity through the exploitation of others, or by seeking to release the life-drive by other means. But, as Bernard Williams puts it (in effect), there is no immediate penalty for exploitation. Exploiting subjects often thrive: they are 'by any ethological standard of the bright eye and the gleaming coat, dangerously flourishing' (1985, p. 46; cf. Poole 1991, p. 139). Nor is there any guarantee that the exploited will opt for a non-exploitative release; we are now familiar enough, for example, with those flourishing female subjects whose feminism goes all the way to the bank but no further.

That aside, the relation between increasing objectification, and the positioning of the white, masculine subject is unclear. But it is clear the man is more likely to occupy the object position as the burden of fixity produced by his environment increases, and as his traditional others become less willing and less able to accept the object position, with the burden of fixity it entails. At first I thought that this heavier burden would lead to more objectification of the other by those still clinging to the subject position, and that racism and sexism would increase

12 Cf. Eagleton: 'Modern ethical thought has wreaked untold damage in its false assumption that love is first of all a personal affair rather than a political one. It has failed to take Aristotle's point that ethics is a branch of politics, of the question of what it is to live well, to attain happiness and security, at the level of a whole society' (cf. Eagleton 1990, p. 413).

accordingly. I am now less sure, and think there are two or three trends at work here. Probably the objectification of the other by those clinging to the subject position is increasing; but so are the counter-projections of those aspiring to that position, and/or rejecting the object position by other means. In the relations between women and men, there does seem to be an increasing antagonism, escalating projections, and a level of paranoia which makes trust difficult to sustain for more than short bursts. While the paranoia in contemporary sexual difference deserves more extended treatment, the point here is that this paranoia is but a stage in an overall objectifying process which targets everything living. As and if this process becomes clearer, so will the fact that the economy of the large scale is making a fiction of the subject position. Aspire to it as they may, fewer and fewer attain it.

What then are the alternatives to that subjection, the means for seeking release which do not replicate its dynamics? It is clear that these alternatives would have to hold at the level of interpersonal life, the realm of ethical decision, as well as at the level of organized resistance. For one implication of this analysis is that struggle on the inside must deal with the same conflicts as struggle on the outside. Resisting the acting out of a foundational fantasy on ever larger scales is one arena for action; dealing with the fantasy in personal psychical life is the other. The burden of this book is not only that the force of the fantasy in both areas increases simultaneously. It is also that resistance in one area will affect the other. This is so because we begin from the indissolubility of thought and matter, individual and environment. If this is taken completely seriously, every action, every thought, has an effect. On the one hand it is vital not to side with the deathly, to avoid, as Wendy Brown puts it, making a virtue of powerlessness (1991: 77). At the same time, the decision not to project a moment's aggression, not to impose a negative image on the other or in other ways manipulate for subjective advantage, these decisions resist and reverse moments of objectifying aggression. Like the aggression they resist, these decisions may reverberate throughout the cosmos, like Lorenzo's butterfly. They are also the moments at which 'choice' and the individuality it is meant to reflect become real, moments in which personal distinctness manifests itself in the soup of the ego's era. If I have given no attention to individual distinctness, this is because recognizing the common connections between us, connections that work for good and ill, is more the task of the times. It does not mean that people, any more than all the elements of the natural order, lack the distinctive beauty that marks each single snowflake. It does mean that they are less likely to reveal this distinctiveness when they parrot the rhetoric which homogenizes difference in the name of the ego, a rhetoric of me and mine which makes us all sound the same, even or especially when we chatter about difference.

But if one can resist one's impulse to dominate in the name of the ego, how does one resist being dominated? For that matter, and crucially, is there a structural basis for resistance? These questions are related, and the relation between them depends on reasserting the claims of generational time against the megalomania of the punctual self (Taylor 1989). More specifically, Marxism discerned a structural basis for resistance, wrongly, as it turned out, in the development of the productive forces; for Marx the larger scale would work towards undermining capital, by increasing working class solidarity, amongst other things. While the theory was wrong, it has left a legacy in the form of a strong radical predisposition to seek grounds for the structural undermining of the system. It has also left a labour movement history of solidarity, which no modern movement of resistance should ignore.

Organized working-class action has often exemplified forms of resistance which refused to give away intelligence and direction, without assuming a subjectivity which humiliates and denigrates others as people. It has done so through the solidarity or collectivity of its members, through the opposition to individualism, an opposition which can be the best protection available to personal integrity, when it does not seek to demean that other's difference, but embraces that other's likeness. In this, it serves as a model of action for other movements; solidarity can have force without destructiveness. At the same time, that solidarity has been most real, union resistance most effective, when mind and body were not drastically separated in the industry at issue (thus mining), and where the scale of action was such as to mean contact between people was other than superficial.

Keeping this in mind, I turn to the structural question. The main criticism of theories advocating an environmentally-focused restructuring of the economy is their utopian nature: 'utopian', in that they may ignore the structural realities of the present. Thus for example Hayward argues that works on ecology 'tended to jump too quickly from warnings of environmental crisis to political and philosophical conclusions ... oscillating between catastrophism and utopianism'

(1990, p. 2). Boggs (1986) argues that even the more thoughtful environmentalists such as Porritt (1984) miss 'a dialectical understanding of change' that connects the vision of the future to the economic structures of the day. 'Without this sort of linkage there can be no really efficacious practice of a *transitional phase* that involves a long and difficult shift in the nature of class and power relations' (Boggs 1986, p. 894). In fact huge social changes have been accomplished by spiritual and religious movements empowered by conviction. But the question of whether such movements can sustain their action effectively without a strategic, structural awareness remains.

One of the aims of this book has been to contribute to this awareness by drawing out the dialectical implications of capital's spatial expansion in relation to nature. This makes the question of economic scale paramount rather than incidental. It means that any opposition to the dominant economy of the day cannot call simply on socialism; it has to call on an alteration in scale. And while it is the topic of another book, there is a structural economic basis for resistance in the smaller-scale economies. These may have aided megalithic capital since its inception, but they can also abet its demolition. But to draw this out we need to take account of the fact that the small-scale businesses in the advanced heartlands are not the only form of small-scale production. The other is the subsistence or 'sustenance' economy (as Shiva (1988) renames it) that is daily eroded in the third world.

There are some points I need to make about this sustenance economy before returning to the structural basis for economic resistance in the West. Shiva (1988) has argued that, in this economy, the labour of women is geared to the preservation of nature; both the economic position of women and the regard for nature's replenishment are better protected by the small scale of the sustenance economy. Here, another structural basis for resistance already exists; the point is that it is eroded in the name of development, which confuses the question of scale with the question of technology. Needless to say, technology can be improved, and life enhanced through it, without these improvements necessitating the increase in scale which relegates women as mothers to the economic margins as it hastens the overconsumption of nature (cf. Chapter 5). The problem is that women in sustenance economies may be working in structures which potentially oppose the monster of economic scale, but the social and political power needed to implement that opposition is lacking. This lack has to be countered in any theory and practice of transition. Let us note immediately that these third world women also labour under systems of public symbolization (especially religion) which denigrate women. In this their position is similar to that of Western pre-industrial women. On the one hand, both non-metropolitan and pre-industrial women have far greater economic power. On the other hand, the practical position of these women is at odds with their symbolic description as weak of intellect, passive, and so on. The acting out that gave that designation more credibility came later. The written or religious record is one thing, the agency of and recognition accorded women off the written record is or was another. Historically, any such recognition lacked a vocabulary in which it could be expressed. Much of the confusion in the progressivist thinking that accompanies foundationalism, and lends itself to the illusion that the position of women has improved, stems from the disjunction here between the visible and symbolic record and the invisible practical realm. Still more confusion results from the fact that it is the economic power of women (who simultaneously occupied the position of mothers) that is occluded. Because in the pre-industrial division of labour, the connection between home and workplace meant that women were or are economically effective at the same time as they occupied that position. The position is a long way from the solitary mothers, the impoverished fixed points, of the last chapter. Making the (relatively) economic empowered woman-as-mother invisible is in some ways the essence of the foundational fantasy. And while the power of the woman as mother was denied officially before the seventeenth century, the denial could never be as thorough-going as it is when the woman's position becomes an economically dependent one, closer to the infantile one in fact.

Today in the third world, the marginalization of women through inappropriate technologies is the more possible precisely because of the patriarchal symbolic traditions which denied the agency of women, long before this denial was acted out with capitalization. As I have stressed, feudal patriarchy could only give birth to the ego's era because it denied the mother's agency. There was no 'vocabulary' in which this agency was expressed. Any process of economic reversal from the large scale to a smaller one, any attempt at retracing the steps that led to the ego's era can only be effective in the long term if it dispenses with the blind spot concerning maternal agency, if it acknowledges the maternal forces it draws on. For the same reason, in the third world today, the symbolic continuity between the theoretical denial of women, and the techno-economic practice which benefits from it, has to be broken. But attempts to break it will be ineffective without an effective limit on imperialism, and this takes us back to the potential political role of the small businesses in the advanced heartlands of the West.

The sustenance economy is a long way from these small businesses, but the distance is less if one sees the latter as the heirs, at the level of scale, to a similar if long departed sustenance economy in the West. Historically, to some extent, these small-scale pockets grew out of household economies, in which men and women were economically interdependent, (cf. Hilton 1973; Duby 1973; Stone 1977; Tilly and Scott 1978, p.15). The small-scale business economy can be viewed as a mini-version of mega-capital, or a mode of production in competition with it. Pockets of small business helped the rise of large-scale capital, but later they become its victims. If the small business mode is seen as a competitive one, it can be seen as a structural and strategic basis for resistance. The sheer number of people already self-employed in this mode of production is a force in itself. It is a force that could be mobilized in opposition to the large scale, if the question of scale in business is made an explicit issue. In other words, by focusing on scale, the small-scale entrepreneurs could be called into an alliance with the other forces opposed to corporatism, such as the union movement.

Small-scale entrepreneurs constitute an unreliable class for the classical Marxist. And naturally, if they are asked to choose between large-scale capitalism and large-scale socialism, these small-scalers will be unreliable. But if asked to choose between legislation which enhances and advantages small-scale businesses and a vague monetarism which eulogizes all competition, they would choose wisely.

What follows from this is the idea of setting political limits on gain, the *appetitus divitirum infinitus*; by the last chapter's analysis, setting limits on gain is the same thing as setting limits on scale. To restrict scale, and limit gain, does not denigrate the entrepreneurial factor, but it limits the negative effects of large-scale competition. It should increase the opportunities for creativity for more people. By cutting back the territory of production currently occupied by the megaliths, it expands the potential opportunities for more people to join body and mind together in labour having a direct relation to their product. Moreover, by limiting the scale of business in the West, we would automatically be limiting the power of the multi-nationals, and thus limiting imperialism. We would be implementing a programme in the West which assisted the third world in the preservation of its own sustenance economies. We would also be aiding the protection of the environment at the structural level. If all this is accompanied by a stress on how the denial of women, nature, and the connecting forces between them makes us blind to what we receive and what we owe, it will have more symbolic strength, a strength that depends on the unity fostered by its symbolic truth.

Of course, by no means all small-scale enterprises are environmentally desirable. The extent to which they are ecologically viable has to be considered. The point is that their scale means they are more likely to be environmentally friendly. We have seen that to maintain the speed necessary for effective competition, large-scale capital needs to be able to bring its natural raw materials from ever larger distances. If it is unable to do this, the close-to-hand environment has to be preserved, and generational time respected.

In terms of practical programmes, setting limits on gain and scale is something that can be done through the existing social democratic parties, as an integral part of any attempt at distributive justice and environmental reform. To some extent, it means recrediting national, or federal, boundaries, for limiting scale means aiming for self-sufficiency in restricted areas. And contra the revolutionary road to socialism, any such programme would mean using democracy in full awareness of the conflicts that will arise with the megaliths. But it also means using democracy with some economic resources on our side. This has always been a problem for those advocating the peaceful parliamentary road to socialism.

To think in terms of limiting scale is to think in terms that at one level have been thoroughly thought out by certain democratic theorists. For instance Held has argued that democracy is chimeric unless it is tied to an alteration in economic scale (Held 1987, p. 286 and *passim*). This programme does not mean turning one's back on the existing parties or states; the state itself need not be 'smaller'; it could be 'broader and thinner' (Connell 1990, p. 538). The state would become thinner as it limited its alliances with the megalith; it would do this as it limited the consumption of nature, as it withdrew the unbridled political licence by which the gobbler gobbles. But for the state to do this, it obviously has to exist and be the subject of democratic contestation between parties. It can be used, just as the city can be used. Both state and city have great costs, but we can attempt to make of the first an agency of protection, of the second, the place of a gathering, a meeting ground for the opposition.

For of course there is an opposition, 'oppositional' practices (Haraway 1985) that extend far beyond the small market and union hall. If this opposition is not known to itself, this is because the foundational fantasy splits people from one another. The splitting that secures subjective identity is replayed at all the levels on which the fantasy is acted out. The splitting in the fantasy obscures the common grounds for opposing it, the means for uniting its fragmented opposition. Yet while splitting is endemic to the fantasy, and subjectivity as we know it, its force varies, just as the fantasy varies in its impact. Splitting, at present, riddles all levels of political life. To resist the urge to split, the urge to ridicule those elements of the opposition to foundationalism one does not identify with, this is something I for one find extremely difficult. The tendency to think in terms of existing binary categories is very powerful. It is especially problematic to think in terms which try to run an emphasis on holistic connection together with historical economic analysis without giving in to the long-standing tension between them. But some days are better than others; the demons do not always win.

What this analysis does is remove the grounds that divide the opposition to various manifestations of the fantasy. It does this by symbolizing the maternal living force which is rivalled by the fantasy, and by delineating the fantasy and its acting out. Delineating the fantasy shows how common evils are intrinsically connected; this in turn permits us to symbolize connections between common goods, or the concerns of movements which, while they may be oblivious to notions of maternal origin, none the less *act* against various manifestations of the fantasy. Thus the stress on loving one's neighbour as oneself is aligned here with the opposition to sexism, racism, and to other projective fantasies that seize on sexual orientation as an excuse for offloading aggression. These things are allied with the opposition to any economic system that degrades human creative potentials, and takes more from than it gives back to nature. The counter-cultural stress on spiritual connection is aligned here with the union movements which struggle for rights for migrant workers, for different ethnic groups, and the welfare state politics of single mothers. Acknowledging one's indebtedness to and dependence on the extraordinary creativity of the 'God as Nature' is aligned here with the opposition to power over others in any form; the feminist concern with symbolizing divinity in maternal terms (Irigaray 1984) becomes an imperative, but it is an imperative that is aligned with the advocacy of tolerance that lends liberal vocabularies their good sense as distinct from their egoism. The intellect is allied with the living spirit, for it is the intellect's task to labour against the fixed points that block thought and the resurrection of the body. The fact that so many movements embody aspects of this alliance, the power of the life drive evident in all of them, is grounds for real optimism. Together these movements constitute an opposition to the acting out of the fantasy in all its aspects. But at present, these movements are undermined by the fixed points of ridicule that stand between them, fixed points that divert the life drive into deathly paths. It can be said, and rightly, that the aggression against the other that secures subjectivity through these fixed points will not just go away. But this aggression can find a more suitable object; it could and should be the foundational fantasy and all its manifestations. The more the fantasy comes into focus as the common opponent, the less the opposition will be divided amongst itself.

Apart from the effects of splitting, the opposition is undermined by the imitation of the original, which makes it hard to trace the fine line between what to oppose and what to advocate. This holds especially at the level of theory, the two-edged enquiry that discerns and colludes simultaneously. The imitation of natural logic by a constructed foundation makes it easy to confuse the question of subjective foundations with any foundations, to confuse the totalizing trend we confront with theories that appear to totalize, to confuse the history of a monolithic takeover bid with history as such.

Just as the ego will deny the history of any significant other (Fanon 1952, p. 34), so it will deny its own. This makes it necessary both to recognize differences, and recognize and understand the common enemy that would obliterate them. If there is an ego's era, then some poststructuralist tendencies can be read as countering that era's direction. The distrust of foundationalism and totality, the simultaneous suspicion of the ocular that dominates in the *lingua franca*, and particularly the defence of difference, go against the ego's desire to make the world over in its image. Other postmodern notions can be read as partial collusions with the dynamics of the ego's era: the distrust of history, the confusion of 'totality' with logic and consistency, the insistence that we can only know what is on the surface, and the belief that there are no guidelines, no basis for ethics or actions outside us. These collude with the ego's tendency to deny its own totalizing history, and its fantasy that it is the source of life.

Although the process of imitation constructs a complex physical alternative world which papers over the original, and makes it hard to see the forest for the trees (or even to find a tree), this should not blind one to the existence of the original. It is true we cannot know this original with certainty. But if I am right, it may be that we can learn more about the workings of the original through tracing the inverted path of the imitation. This is more likely to be so if the imitation does in fact compete with the original, so that an unconscious knowledge of the original informs the direction and content of its competitive contender. By reading the inverted path of the imitation, which is envious and fragmenting, we can deduce that the original is generous and cohering: if the imitation is repetitive, the original only makes the joke once; if the imitation seeks to abolish time, we can conclude that the original is timeless; if the imitation seeks to be everywhere at once, by instant telecommunications and most rapid transit, we can deduce that the original is everywhere already. If the imitation is always trying to be something, and cares desperately for its status, the original is really something, but does not care.

# Appendix: The labour theory of value and the subject–object distinction

There are four areas in my chapter on political economy in which more textual reference to Marx might be helpful. The first is the temporal dimension in value theory, and the theory as such. The second is the subject–object distinction. The third is the distinction between labour and nature. The fourth is the question of centralization, which bears on objectification. These are addressed here in turn.

## THE LABOUR THEORY OF VALUE

I will retrace Marx's labour theory by two routes. The first follows the path of time in Marx's value-theory; the second, the fate of energy.

### The path of time

To produce, 'our capitalist', as Marx liked to call the agent in question, has to acquire the instruments (tools) and raw materials (culled from nature) of labour, and the labour-power necessary to use the instruments to act upon the raw materials transforming them into commodities for exchange. In terms of Marx's explanation, our capitalist purchases the instruments of labour (machinery, equipment and so on) at their value, he purchases the raw materials at their value, and labour-power at its value. He makes a profit because labour-power is unique among his purchases, because it adds more than it costs. Labour-power adds value to the raw materials because it transforms them into a commodity, a new product. In the act of transformation, it embodies itself in the product, and the value it adds by this transformation within a given time is greater than the amount and time required to reproduce labour-power as a commodity. This extra value was called by Marx surplus-value. Surplus-value, rather than unfair wages and clever market manoeuvrings, was the real secret of capitalist profit. But Marx's capitalist does not cheat. He purchases all the elements of production, including the commodity labour-power, at their correct exchange-value.

As labour-power, like any other commodity, is bought and sold at its value, this value needs to be measured. The measurement approximates to the amount required to produce and reproduce the labourer. As this amount will vary historically, it is termed the historically given level of subsistence, and it is roughly expressed in the wage. The wage, in other words, should reflect the exchange-value of labour-power.

The exchange-value of commodities is the ratio in which they are exchanged for one another. $X$ number of shirts are worth $Y$ number of coats, or so much money. But the real determinator of equivalence here is not money, which is only a marker of it. The exchange-value of a particular commodity is set by the amount of *socially necessary labour-time* required for its production. Socially necessary labour-time, in turn, is based on the average amount of time required to produce a given object at a given level of technology. It is fixed by technology, not labour, because the available state of technology determines the time it takes to produce a given commodity.

> The labour-time socially necessary is that required to produce an article under the normal conditions of production, and with the average degree of skill and intensity prevalent at the time. The introduction of power-looms into England probably reduced by one-half the labour required to weave a given quantity of yarn into cloth. The hand-loom weavers, as a matter of fact, continued to require the same time as before; but for all that, the product of one hour of their labour represented after the change only half an hour's social labour, and consequently fell to one-half its former value.
>
> (1867 *Capital* 1, p. 47)

For some commodities, labour-time is also fixed by nature. Thus while the 'socially necessary labour-time' of labour-power is measured by the cost of consumption (and will increase to keep up with consumption), it is also measured by a more natural 'yardstick'. The cost of labour-power's means of subsistence should include the cost of rearing children (1867 *Capital* 1, p. 168).

The point here is that, in the determination of value, the time taken to produce a commodity overrides the quantity of labour it embodies, in that a certain length of cloth woven on a hand-loom should have no more exchange-value than the same length woven on a machine-loom, although the latter takes half an hour and the former an hour. Despite the fact that the hand-woven cloth involves a far greater expenditure of labour, these lengths of cloth are of equal value when they are measured by 'labour-time', a concept that elides labour and time, and to which we return. Thus exchange-value is determined not only by the amount of labour expended on the commodity in the production process, but by the amount of time it takes to produce it.

While this temporal yardstick holds for labour-power as much as for any other commodity, labour-power differs from other commodities because of its apparently unique capacity for giving more than it costs. It can give more in different ways, so that skilled labour-power will cost more than unskilled labour-power, because it costs more to produce labour-power that is skilled. It can give more in terms of either 'absolute' or 'relative' surplus-value. Absolute surplus-value is realized by increasing the total value with no change in the labour necessary for production. This can be done, for instance, by increasing the length of the working day. Relative surplus-value is increased either by technological changes that reduce the socially necessary time of producing a particular commodity; or by reducing the socially necessary labour-time determining the cost of labour-power; which means altering consumption patterns: if labour-power eats less, it costs less.

But the critical point is that the difference between the value of labour-power and the value of the commodities produced by labour in the production process is the gain made by capital. This gain is possible because capital purchases labour-power for a definite time. How that labour-power is deployed within that time varies, but it is certainly longer than the time taken to produce the value equivalent of the wage in the form of commodities for subsistence. In other words, the wage paid to the worker (the value of labour-power) is less than the value of the commodities produced in the production process (labour as such), provided capital adheres to the dictates of socially necessary labour-time in production.

## The fate of energy

To avoid any misunderstanding here, I will retrace the steps that led Marx to the conclusion that surplus-value depends on the difference between the time taken to reproduce labour-power and the value labour adds in production within a given time by a different route, beginning where he began. Beginning here will introduce the energy factor, for Marx of course began with the analysis of commodities, as I have done; in doing so, he stressed that all commodities must have a use-value, which meant they had to be formed from natural substance and material energy. Marx is emphatic about this: nature is the source of all use-values because (here Marx quotes Lucretius) 'out of nothing, nothing can be created' (*nil posse creari de nihilo*) (1867 *Capital* 1, p. 207 n.1).

In the specific epoch Marx called the capitalist mode of production, the capitalist produces commodities destined to be sold. Commodities must have a use-value, which not only means they have to be made out of something rather than nothing; they must also have a use for the consumer. But given that our capitalist is producing saleable commodities, his interest is in their exchange-value. His only interest in a commodity's use-value is the fact that use-value is the indispensable depository for exchange-value.

For Marx, the use-value of a commodity is a qualitative value, in that it pertains to a particular quality or property of a commodity. The most useful form of the object is the form most appropriate to consumption. The most obvious examples are food and clothing, and it is clear that what Marx had in mind here as the most easily consumed and therefore the most useful objects are those which directly satisfy individual human needs and wants. Unlike qualitative use-value, exchange-value is quantitative. From the point of view of exchange-value, it does not matter whether a want is real or fanciful; it is enough that the commodity wanted has a use for the subject who wants it. Nor is Marx concerned with how the commodity comes to satisfy these wants, 'whether directly, as means of subsistence or indirectly as means of production' (1867 *Capital* 1, p. 43). It is necessary to note these factors, for while Marx deliberately abstracts from them, they nevertheless affect his analysis.

When our capitalist purchases labour-power in the market, he purchases it as he would any other commodity for exchange, except that he also purchases labour-power as a use-value, the purpose of which is to create exchange-values. This creation means that all commodities can be measured quantitatively, and their potential equivalents gauged, in terms of the socially necessary labour-time required to produce them. Yet this concept labour-time, in which time and labour are elided, only becomes salient after Marx investigates the equivalent value of commodities in more general terms. While the exchange-value of a commodity is measured by the 'magnitude . . . the quantity of the value-creating substance, the labour, contained in the article . . . the quantity of labour . . . is measured by its duration, and labour-time in its turn finds its standard in weeks, days and hours' (1867 *Capital* 1, p. 46). Even more explicitly, 'Commodities . . . in which equal quantities of labour are embodied, or which can be produced in the same time, have the same value. . . . "As values, all commodities are only definite masses of congealed labour-time"' (1867 *Capital* 1, p. 47).[1] Still, labour-time is absolutely critical to the whole theory, and especially to Marx's agonies with the famous 'transformation problem' (how value is transformed into price). It is critical because it is the bridge between exchange-value and money. 'Money, as a measure of value, is the phenomenal form that must of necessity be assumed by that measure of value which is immanent in commodities, labour-time' (1867 *Capital* 1, p. 97).

Yet money, for Marx, is misleading precisely because it is only the phenomenal form of another quantitative relation: exchange-value.

> The common substance that manifests itself in the exchange-value of commodities, whenever they are exchanged, is their value . . . exchange-value is the only form in which the value of commodities can manifest itself or be expressed.
>
> (1867 *Capital* 1, p. 46)[2]

This needs more elaboration. Marx reasons this way: any equivalent or quantitative relation presupposes that commodities have a property in common. Writes Marx, in a silent disavowal of Descartes, this common 'something' cannot be either a geometrical, a chemical or any other natural property of commodities.

> If we make abstraction from its use-value, we make abstraction at the same time from the material elements and shapes that make the product a use-value . . . Its existence as a material thing is put out of sight.
>
> (1867 *Capital* 1, p. 45).

Such properties claim our attention only in so far as they affect the utility of those commodities, make them use-values. But the exchange

---

1 Marx is quoting himself.
2 What is more, something, however useful it is, is not a commodity unless it is an item destined for exchange.

of commodities is evidently an act characterized by a total abstraction of use-value. Exchange-value is the only form in which the value of commodities can be expressed, but this value is not manifest; it is not substantial. Accordingly 'the value of commodities is the very opposite of the coarse materiality of their substance, not an atom of matter enters into its composition' (1867 *Capital* 1, p. 54).

In the act of exchange, one use-value is just as good as another, provided only it be 'present in sufficient quantity' (1867 *Capital* 1, p. 45). Marx then goes on to say that: 'If then we leave out of consideration the use-value of commodities, they have only one common property left, that of being products of labour. . .' (1867 *Capital* 1, p. 45). It follows from this, and the abstraction concerning use-value and exchange-value, that human labour-power, as the expenditure of human labour-power in general can be considered in terms of 'abstract labour', while the labour involved in producing a particular use-value (as all abstract labour must be by definition) is 'useful labour' or 'concrete labour'.

In sum, having put aside the materiality of commodities, Marx concludes that their residue

> consists of the same unsubstantial reality in each, a mere congelation of homogeneous human labour . . . . All that these things now tell us is that human labour-power has been expended in their production, that human labour is embodied in them. When looked at as crystals of this social substance, common to them all, they are – Values.
>
> (1867 *Capital* 1, p. 46)

Despite the emphasis on an immaterial quantity, Marx insists that every useful thing may be looked at from the point of view of quality and quantity. Indeed, from capital's perspective, useful things are considered in terms of their qualities, rather than their quantities. This might seem paradoxical, given that capital depends on exchange-value and exchange-value is a quantitative summation, but it comes about precisely because the utility of a thing makes it a use-value, and 'use-values become a reality only by use or consumption' (1867 *Capital* 1, p. 44). It is in this sense that the use of a thing is a quality or property pertaining to it insofar as it satisfies human wants. It will be valueless if it does not satisfy a want, which means it can have no exchange-value. As I noted at the outset, Marx was insistent that all commodities, to be commodities, must have a two-fold character: they must have use-value (a form of substance) as well as exchange-value (a form of measured time).

As in any system of market exchange use-values are the material depositories of exchange-values, the qualitative and quantitative dimensions of a commodity always coexist. Moreover, while the only property commodities have in common for Marx is labour-power, and while this property is completely insubstantial, the transformation of labour-power into labour is none the less, and oddly, a transformation from something immaterial to something material. And if we press the definitions of labour-power a little more closely, we find it is not so immaterial after all.

In fact Marx writes expressly that 'Labour-power itself is energy transferred to a human organism by means of nourishing matter' (1867 *Capital* 1, p. 207 *n*.1)[3] and 'By labour-power or capacity for labour is to be understood the aggregate of those mental and physical capabilities existing in a human being, which he exercises whenever he produces a use-value of any description' (1867 *Capital* 1, p. 164). It is quite clear that it is the daily and generational restoration of these capabilities, or 'vital energy' (1867 *Capital* 1, p. 169), that constitute the cost of labour-power, and that labour-power only exists in a 'living vital body' (1867 *Capital* 1, p. 165, trans. mod.).

What is more, this energetic aspect of 'labour-power' is elided with 'labour' itself. This was plain enough in a passage I have just quoted, where Marx is searching for the common denominator in the exchange-value of commodities, and concludes that this 'something' is only the fact that: 'human labour-power has been expended in their production, that human labour is embodied in them' (1867 *Capital* 1, p. 46).

Labour-power and labour are alike in that they are energy, and add energy; the difference between them seems to break down in this respect. But it only seems. In other modes of production, labour retains more of its capacity for directing and/or regulating its energy in production; under capital, it loses this capacity, in that labour-power is energy acquired to be directed. In fact overall, given that labour and labour-power play precise roles in the determination of surplus-value, the use of the term 'labour' at other points in Marx's analysis makes for confusion. On the one hand, Marx's assumption that what commodities have in common is that they are all products of labour is an assumption that implies nothing about who decides to produce, whether it is their labour that is executed, or that of someone else. On the other hand 'labour' is the term reserved for the thing that adds something more

---

3 'Nourishing matter' is a standard nineteenth-century term. In *Capital* it also appears in a footnote to Sir John Gordon's 1855 report on the adulteration of bread (1, p. 171 *n*.2).

than its value in production, although it is precisely in production that labour can no longer exercise the directive or imaginative capacities that marked labour in other historical modes. As Marx was the first to point out, labour-power lost many of the capacities for making and doing that belonged to labour in those other modes; under capital, labour is alienated.

But the issue here is how labour produces (exchange) value, hence surplus-value. It does so through the 'creation of new values, because it is the objectification of new labour-time in a use-value' (1857–8 *Grundrisse*, p. 359). Now Marx is writing without any apparent regard for, having specifically extracted from, the physico-energetic alterations wrought by this objectifying power. Yet, once again, he simultaneously and tirelessly stresses that power: thus, 'Labour is the living, form-giving fire; it is the transitoriness of things, their temporality, as their formation of living time [*lebendige Zeit*]' (1857–8 *Grundrisse*, p. 361). And while, as quoted earlier, 'the equivalent for this quality (for the specific use-value of labour) is measured simply by the *quantity* of labour-time which has produced it . . . capital has brought *this quality* as part of its exchange with the worker' (1857-8 *Grundrisse*, pp. 359–60, original emphasis). The mixing in of labour-power means that there is an addition to the raw materials; it adds something which was not there before. For Marx, it is precisely this energetic addition – for the materialization of labour as he defined it must be an addition – that means the labourer raises the use-values of the raw materials entering into the commodity, so that the finished commodity had a higher (more consumable) use-value than the raw materials required to produce it. This energy addition characterizes all acts of labour. But unlike time, which is readily measurable, it does not figure in Marx's attempts at quantifying abstract labour. Labour is the term reserved for concrete useful labour, for the energy manifest in the production of specific use-values; unlike abstract labour, it cannot be quantified because of its specificity. Yet the fact that all labour-power has this energy indicates there is a common material factor which might have been quantifiable. Perhaps, in part, the difficulty lay in the idea of quantifying this additional energy, with thinking about it in the abstract rather than in terms of useful labour, and thinking this way is less foreign to these times, when the transformation of energy into matter ('material additions') is now common currency. Yet Marx almost anticipates this with expressions such as 'living time'. The more evident obstacle, as will become plainer as we proceed, was that posed by the subject-centred standpoint.

We have seen that in Marx's terms the higher use-value is the form more appropriate to subjective consumption. In our terms, it is a form more readily geared to instant gratification. The system of market exchange, and the free exchange of all things including labour-power, is beginning to come into focus as the system whereby instant gratification is realized through the consumption of substantial energy.

But to sum up thus far: it should be plain that the distinction between labour-power and labour as the 'only possible' source of additional value is problematic. It is problematic because Marx is holding that it is time, together with labour-power, that determines exchange-value, and because immaterial labour-power has a material aspect after all. I have shown this through tracing the source of surplus-value by two paths. The first led to socially necessary labour-time. The second to labour and labour-power as something that materializes or gives more of itself than it takes. The concept of 'labour-time' elides these sources, but the fact that exchange-value has a dual origin in time and energy is plain enough.

Both measurements converge in the concept of socially necessary labour-time. Socially necessary labour-time in turn determines exchange-value. How the temporal measurements distilled here fare in a value-theory without the subject–object distinction is the question pursued in the text. The next section here discusses Marx's use of the subject–object distinction as such.

## THE SUBJECT–OBJECT DISTINCTION AND THE LIVING AND THE DEAD

On the opening page of *Capital*, Marx announces that 'A commodity is, in the first place, an object outside us, a thing that by its properties satisfies human wants of some sort or another' (1867 *Capital* 1, p. 43). This obviousness is of course entirely consistent with the approach to the commodity (an object made for a subject) taken in the text, except that Marx takes this obvious subject-centred definition for granted. And why should he have not? Yet because he thinks in subject–object terms, Marx has erroneously excluded natural substances, aside from human labour-power, as sources of surplus-value. I will argue here that he has therefore overlooked that various natural forces are potentially identical to labour-power in their capacity for adding energy.

To begin drawing this argument out I turn first to Marx's analysis of the labour process, for it is here that Marx's basic suppositions about humans and nature, and the division that exists between them, are most evident. In the analysis of the labour process, as in the analysis of a commodity, Marx abstracts from certain circumstances. Here, the abstraction does not take the form of leaving certain factors aside, but of considering the labour process independently of the particular form it assumes under given social conditions (for Marx, whether they are hydraulic, feudal or contemporary does not matter). In the labour process,

> man of his own accord starts, regulates, and controls the material re-actions between himself and Nature. He opposes himself to Nature as one of her own forces, setting in motion arms and legs, head and hands, the natural forces of his body, in order to appropriate Nature's productions in a form adapted to his own wants.
>
> (1867 *Capital* 1, p. 173)

For our purposes, the important point to stress is that this independent relation between man and nature is one of opposition, wherein nature is the object to be controlled. Marx sees the original subject of labour, the earth, as existing 'independently of man' (1867 *Capital* 1: 179), as did the tools the earth provided. By virtue of this independence, the earth is comparable with the means of production of any social epoch, whether or not these means exist as raw materials and machinery; that is, natural substances which have already been mixed with labour, or as substances directly provided by nature. At the same time, Marx repeatedly acknowledges 'the ever lasting Nature-imposed condition of human existence' (1867 *Capital* 1, p. 179). He never loses track of the fact that there is no exchange-value without use-value; use-value always comes first in the sub-analyses that make up the text of *Capital*. Yet Marx, like capital, regards the nature-imposed condition of existence as if it were unconditional. This is, as it happens, remarkably similar to Lacan's assumption about energy. 'Energy begins to be of interest to us . . . only beginning with the moment in which it is accumulated, and it is accumulated only beginning with the moment when machines are put to work in a certain way' (Lacan 1956–7; see Part I). Lacan, like Marx, takes natural conditions for granted. Unlike Marx, he is also making the claim that the real is unknowable as such, and therefore impossible to 'think'. It never occurred to Marx that it might be impossible to 'think' nature. It just did not occur to him to think about it much at all.

Aside from the problem posed by ground rent,[4] Marx treats nature as an unproblematic variable, aligning it with tools or technology. Nature and technology alike are the object. Jointly they constitute the 'means of production', which Marx defines as the 'objective factors', while he defines the 'subjective factor' as labour-power (1867 *Capital* 1, p. 179).[5] As the means of production encompass both tools or technology (which are rarely living) and nature (which generally is), this means that things living as well as things dead are defined as objects counterposed to a subject.

In the capitalist mode of production, this counterposition is all the more critical, as the subjective factor, labour-power, is reckoned as the only factor capable of creating surplus-value. Marx is unequivocal.

The same elements of capital which, from the point of view of the

---

4  On Marx and rent in general, see Fine 1979. Marx treats rent not as a property of the land but of social class relations to the land. In one respect this opens out the possibility of considering land in terms of its direct exploitation in that differences in fertility lead to different returns to the same capital investment as do differences in location. Marx terms this differential rent; it applies to competition within the agricultural sector. He counterposes differential rent to absolute rent. Absolute rent is the result of competition between the agricultural sector and other sectors in the formation of surplus-value overall. The problems absolute rent poses for the always difficult question of how value is transformed into price are particularly acute, and Marx makes little headway with it in what is perhaps the most poorly revised section of *Capital* (vol 3, part VI). An analysis of Marx's writings on the question of rent would be an ideal test case for the redefinition of variable capital proposed in Chapter 4.

5  Initially, having abstracted from nature, Marx distinguishes three elements in the labour process, but the abstraction enables him to reduce the three elements to two: one subjective, the other objective. In the first place, Marx analyses the labour process by resolving it into its (three) simple elementary factors. There are '(1) the personal activity of man, i.e. work itself, (2) the subject of that work and (3) its instruments' (1: 174). These elements can be isolated in this way because the labour process is *always* 'human action with a view to the production of use-values, *appropriation of natural substances to human requirements*; it is the necessary condition for effecting the exchange of matter between man and Nature; it is the ever-lasting Nature-imposed condition of human existence, and therefore it is independent of every social phase of that existence, or rather is common to every such phase' (1: 179, emphasis added). Initially this appropriation of natural substances to human requirements is unmediated. Nature is 'man's larder and his tool house' (1: 175). Yet it is clear that even in discussing unmediated production, Marx assumes not only that the basic elements of the labour process exist independently of social forms; he also assumes a relation between these elements which is independent of social forms. Man is opposed both to the 'subject of work', or nature, and the instruments or tools. Together these become the object, or objective factors, and any tension between tools and nature disappears. Benton (1989) provides an outstanding discussion of Marx's abstraction from natural conditions, and also discusses the problems with the three elementary factors in Marx's abstraction of the labour process. This article has many overlaps with my argument. It also discusses the natural limits on use-value and capital's tendency to surpass them (see Chapter 4, 'The overall quantity of use- and surplus-value'). What Benton needs is a *dynamic* explanation of this tendency, which would make it structural.

labour process, present themselves respectively as the objective and subjective factors, as means of production and labour-power, present themselves, from the point of view of the process of creating surplus-value, as constant and variable capital.

(1867 *Capital* 1, p. 202)

As in every other epoch, under the rule of capital the subject alone creates value. This universalized subject-centred position, by virtue of a powerful abstraction, has superseded a more fundamental distinction between the living and the dead. Yet the reader will recall that it was the livingness or energy of labour-power that was critical in its ability to add value, that made it unique amongst the other commodities that entered into production. For labour adds value to the product in two senses. First, labour adds exchange-value to the product because of the difference between labour and labour-power: it is the only subjective factor in the production process. For Marx, the means of production cannot add value to the product precisely because they are objective; there is no subjective variation between the labour-time taken to produce them and the value they contribute to the finished product. This is the temporal dimension in value addition. Second, labour adds value to the product not only because it contributes more than it costs, but because this value is materialized in the product. More exactly, the materialization of living labour is inseparably tied to the transformation of the product. This is value's energetic dimension.

As the subject–object distinction subsumes other living substances, aside from labour-power, under the category 'object', we need to ascertain if there is anything in living labour that distinguishes it from these other living entities, substances, forces or sources. We need to ascertain this before we can argue that if the subject–object distinction is dropped, while the emphasis on energy, substance and time is retained, Marx's labour theory of value retains or regains some of its life. The question of what is living in Marx's theory deserves closer investigation.

Marx's argument for distinguishing 'living' labour from nature applies to all modes of production. It is a tautological argument that does no more than reiterate the subject–object premise on which it is based, but it effects this restatement by equating the subject with the living and the object with the dead. In this argument objectification is a process that stills, fixes and/or ends the life of the other, but this objectifying process is referred to as transformative or life-giving.

The notion that the process is life-giving (when it is not necessarily so) rests on Marx's definition of the objective factors, which makes no distinction between living nature and technology. Marx generally assumes that the raw materials entering into production, whether they exist as natural substances or 'raw materials proper' (that is natural substances which have already been altered by labour in that they have labour mixed in) are liable to dissolution.

> It is living labour which preserves the use-value of the incomplete product of labour by making it the material of further labour. It preserves it, however, i.e. protects it from uselessness and decay, only by working it in a purposeful way, by making it the object of new living labour power [*Objekt neuer lebendiger Arbeit macht*].
>
> (1857-8 *Grundrisse*, p. 362, trans. mod.)

Or else Marx treats natural forces and sources as he treats the instruments of production in the labour process; he treats them as if they are already dead. 'Living labour must seize upon these things and rouse them from their death sleep, change them from mere possible use-values into real and effective ones' (1867 *Capital* 1, p. 178).[6]

While Marx has 'raw materials' in mind here, it is clear that he does not distinguish between the types of raw materials entering into production (corn, for instance, is one of the objects manipulated by labour in agriculture (1867 *Capital* 1, p. 177)), or the mode of production in which those raw materials figure. In all cases it seems that the energetic act of labour preserves the instruments and the raw materials of production, and thereby preserves the labour (if any) already embodied in them. Moreover, for Marx, labour preserves substances at the same time as it consumes them; these substances are *consumed* in that they lose the material form they had prior to the production process. So Marx is aware that the labour process as he has defined it may be a process of consumption. Its constituents 'are in truth consumed, but consumed with a purpose, as elementary constituents of new use-values, of new products, ever ready as means of subsistence for individual consumption, or as means of production for some new labour process' (1867 *Capital* 1, p. 178).

Marx says of a given raw material, in the context of his argument

---

6  Marx's examples in this discussion tend towards natural substances which have already been cut out of the process of natural reproduction. The difference between natural substances which cannot re-enter natural reproduction and those which can is not discussed.

that materials are liable to decay were it not for labour, that 'it becomes extinct in one form of use-value in order to *make way for a higher one, until the object is in being as an object of immediate consumption*' (1857–8 *Grundrisse*, p. 361, trans. mod., original emphasis). So here we have the highest use-value defined in terms that are consistent with instant gratification; the more readily consumable, the higher the use-value. Here we have labour producing objects accordingly. Here too we have this transformation of something into a commodity, an object for immediate consumption, presented as an act of preservation.

## THE DIFFERENCE BETWEEN LABOUR AND NATURE

If we return to the energetic quality capital has brought as a seemingly incidental part of its exchange with the worker, it is plain that this quality at least is not one which is unique to labour. It applies equally to nature. Man

> can work only as Nature does . . . by changing the form of matter. Nay more, in this work of changing the form he is constantly helped by natural forces. We see, then, that labour is not the only source of material wealth, of use-values produced by labour. As William Petty puts it, labour is its father and the earth its mother.
>
> (1867 *Capital* 1, p. 50)

Nature, too, transforms the form of matter, and transformation, we have shown, is by nature energetic; it is a substantial embodiment of the energy used in transformation. So is there anything that really distinguishes Father Labour from Mother Nature and does so in a way that makes the difference between labour-power and labour the sole source of surplus-value? I noted that other natural substances capable of producing energy have to be made to do so. And this, it might be assumed, makes labour-power value's unique source. Yet under the rule of capital, fewer and fewer are in a position of real control, let alone ownership. It is paradoxical therefore that, apart from the palaver about living labour, the only real argument Marx gives us for distinguishing labour and nature concerns the will.

> We pre-suppose labour in a form that stamps it as exclusively human. A spider conducts operations that resemble those of a weaver, and a bee puts to shame many an architect [*Baumeister*] in the construction of her cells. But what distinguishes the worst architect from the

best of bees is this, that the architect raises his structure in imagination before he erects it in reality. At the end of every labour-process, we get a result that already existed in the imagination of the labourer at its commencement. He not only effects a change of form in the material on which he works, but he also realises a purpose of his own that gives the law to his modus operandi, and to which he must subordinate his will. And this subordination is no mere momentary act. Besides the exertion of the bodily organs, the process demands that, during the whole operation, the workman's [*Arbeiter*] will be steadily in consonance with his purpose. This means close attention. The less he is attracted by the nature of the work, and the mode in which it is carried on, and the less, therefore, he enjoys it as something which gives play to his bodily and mental powers, the more close his attention is forced to be.

(1867 *Capital* 1)[7]

To raise the structure in one's imagination, as the architect does, before erecting it in reality is to be in a privileged position in production, not at all the same as that of the workman. If one really is an architect or master builder, it is probably to be in petty-bourgeois production, where one is both boss and worker simultaneously. Generally, to realize a purpose of one's own in production is to be in a position of ownership or control. Yet although the architect example and one's 'own purpose' are crucial in the discussion of what makes labour 'exclusively human', the positions these presuppose in the division of labour in production, or a mode of production, are not discussed. Marx moves rapidly from the architect's will to the 'workman's will' as if these 'wills' had the same field of play. In fact, only the architect and others in similar positions use their imaginations, and realize their own purposes, although it can be claimed that all who work or labour use their wills. The difference is between a will that realizes one's own purpose and a will that is the vehicle for subordination to another.

---

7 The negative connotation of will conjures up the account of labour in the early Marx, particularly the Marx of the *Economic and Philosophical Manuscripts of 1844*. Labour 'is activity as suffering, strength as weakness, begetting as emasculating, the worker's own physical and mental energy, his personal life – for what is life but activity? – as an activity which is turned against him, independent of him and not belonging to him' (original emphasis, 1844, p. 67). As a minor contribution to the debate over whether there is epistomological continuity or a break between the early and later Marx, we can note that the identical sentiment, in almost identical words to those just quoted, occurs in *Capital* (see the text). In the early Marx, this negative notion of labour-as-will occurs in the context of the discussion of alienation.

As far as the uniquely human capacity of labour is concerned, the subordinated will is not far from the direction-taking machine. The difference between the machine and the docile, direction-taking worker is that the latter is capable of disputing direction, and of voluntary movement, but whether these are sufficient to make labour the sole source of surplus-value is another question. To the vast extent that capital needs portable direction-takers, to the extent that these cannot be replaced, labour-power and labour are crucial and irreplaceable in the production of surplus-value. But there is in theory nothing inevitable here. If portable direction-taking could be carried out by machines and cyborgs, if the constant capital expenditure in producing them could be kept within limits, surplus-value would still be extracted from other natural forces. The second matter to be noted is that, although there are few production processes in which all forms of productive labour are absent, there are some. There are no processes producing commodities with use- and exchange-value that take place without any energy derived from natural sources.

In fact generally, the inability of labour to impose its own will on what will be made makes for serious complications as far as Marx's definition of productive labour is concerned. The only unambiguous definition of productive labour has to exclude the work of overall design and control (Poulantzas 1968), and this raises real empirical problems. Poulantzas' definition excludes the middle class from the category of productive labour, but the middle class has expanded drastically in size in the heartlands of advanced capital. Which raises the question as to the source of the surplus lived off by the middle class, as well as the owning class.[8] It is the service sector (Renner 1953) (which caters to our instant

8   The category of productive labour has been the subject of intense debate. First, if one controls the means of production to any extent, how far one's labour is productive labour will depend on the relation between the value added in production and the wage. If the cost of the wage, the socially necessary labour-time, is commensurate with or more than the value added in production, the labour is not productive. Now of course the more one controls, the larger the wage-share. Indeed, it becomes a salary. Salaries mark the middle class, not the working class of productive labour. The separation between ownership and control characteristic of monopoly – and late capitalism – becomes widespread, and the class of controllers correspondingly so extensive, that the size of the middle class is expanded. Traditionally, the middle class is divided into two sections: the old petty bourgeoisie (small businesses such as shops and small producers) and the new middle class, the lower stratum of the class who own and control the means of production, who blend into the upper echelons of the working class. These people are technical or supervisory workers, professional groups defined by the fact that they are paid a salary, more than the amount of it. It is the new middle class that has grown in size – and this is contrary to the polarization between the working and capitalist classes predicted by Marx. Probably the most systematic attempt to define the new middle class has been that of Poulantzas (1968) who bases much of his analysis on the distinction between productive and unproductive labour. His strict adherence to the productive labour criteria makes it harder to get into the working class than to get out of it. For Poulantzas,

gratification) of the middle class which has expanded most, and this sector is definitely not productive in the technical sense. If more live off total surplus-value than produce it, or live off it more than they produce it, then there has to be another source of surplus-value.

## CENTRALIZATION, OBJECTIFICATION AND THE WILL

Marx predicted that when centralization, in the physical form of ever-larger spatial conglomerates, and the monetary form of monopolies accelerated, the worker would be reduced more and more to an adjunct of the machine. This is because increases in the size and speed of the productive forces, the technology and division of labour required to produce more and more commodities within a shorter and shorter space of time, entailed maximizing detail labour. While so many of Marx's predictions have been wrong, this one has much in it. The separation of control from the energy labour-power is capable of materializing has increased apace, leading to 'the concentration of knowledge and control in a very small portion of the hierarchy' (Braverman 1974, p. 329).[9] Energy is less and less directed by the labourers.

In this respect, Marx's theory, especially as his successors developed it, strikes its best known accord with Weber's account of rationalization. It also draws out, and this remains one of its luminous strengths, the process whereby the majority of human beings are forced into the position of 'objects', lacking the opportunity to exercise intentionality in

the old and new middle class, or petty bourgeoisie, have in common the characteristic of vacillation. They are essentially unreliable, flocking to the side of capital one minute (especially in its fascist forms), the working class the next. In the context of my analysis, however, with its emphasis on size, the role of the old petty bourgeoisie (small businesses and small producers) has to be reconsidered.

9  Cf. Harry Braverman's now classic study (1974) on the spread of detail labour into the 'mental' sphere, previously privileged over the sphere of 'manual' labour. This was the first full-length study of the division of labour within production since *Capital*. Braverman's main thesis, that capital leads to a progressive deskilling of the mental as well as manual spheres of the labour process through the spread of detailed labour, was debated in Wood (1982) and Thompson (1983) amongst others. Subsequent theoretical contributors to this debate have been limited. Overall, the deskilling thesis exacerbates the problems mental labour had always posed for the category of productive labour. Deskilled mental labours become more aligned with manual labours but their contribution to surplus-value is not direct; it takes place to the extent that mental labour is part of the 'collective worker'. This is a notion dependant on the idea of the labour process as 'a combined social process ...not of the isolated labour of independent producers'. In a combined social labour process, the producer is a collective worker who can only produce when managed (1894 *Capital* 3, pp. 383–4). Which means, in theory, and sometimes in practice, that surplus-value would be produced by those who live off it, which means that there is no disjunction between the value labour adds in production and the socially necessary time taken to reproduce labour-power. The contradiction is recognized by Carchedi, who tries to distinguish the component in salaries in relation to surplus-value, and concludes that 'whatever money is paid to the supervisor is not available for capital accumulation' (Carchedi 1975, p. 64).

production. Lukács theorized this process as irrational rationality (Lukács 1923); for Weber himself, it was instrumental, as distinct from substantive rationality. Instrumental reason, the efficient regulation of means and ends regardless of human and natural rhythms and needs has been a major theme of Adorno and Horkheimer (cf. 1947) and other members of the Frankfurt School, who see objectification as weakening the wilful resistance to capital.[10] In production, productive labourers have no goals of their own, although Marx notes that human action is always goal-oriented (cf. Mandel 1972, p. 509), and goal orientation is the keynote of being a subject.

Under the rule of capital, under the rule of time, if an object is something that lacks mindful will, productive labourers, in so far as they are reduced to an incarnation of energy which they do not themselves direct, become objects. In these ways Marx's value theory is an account of how the world is more and more a world of objects. It accounts for the solidification of the very distinction it presupposes: a world of divided subjects and objects, where the aggression and anxiety that Lacan distilled as marking out these positions is reinforced by an economic aggression that is also deadening in its effects. In that divided world human beings, as they become objects lacking the opportunity to express subjectivity, are squeezed into an alignment with nature, which has been treated as a series of discrete or potentially discrete objects all along.[11]

10 Like Weber, Horkheimer, Adorno and Marcuse thought that the origins of instrumental reason lay beyond industrial capital as such; they also accorded Protestantism a generative place in instrumental thinking. Horkheimer (1941), Marcuse (1964), Adorno (1966b).

11 Marx in his early writings had discussed this objectification in terms of alienation. Mention of the Marx of alienation perforce recalls the tired old debate about Marx's humanism, but it deserves some attention in this context. Althusser provoked that debate when he insisted that there was an 'epistemological break' between the early and later Marx. According to Althusser, the early Marx had been a humanist to the extent that he had attributed essential human qualities to human beings, and argued that the process of capitalist production alienated one from one's human essence. Alienation (*Entäusserung* and *Entfremdung*), in that it was meant to presuppose a human essence, was thus the pivotal concept in the humanism/anti-humanism debate. In turn, the main critical grounds for repudiating the notion of essence is that it presupposed some naturally given properties, and is to this extent ahistorical, asocial and thus unMarxist. The later Marx, for Althusser, had dispensed with any notion of essence, arguing that the human being of *Capital* was no more than the bearer (*Träger*) of social relations, a *tabula rasa* before their imposition. (Althusser 1964 and 1965). For our purposes it is interesting now that Marx has (at least) two notions of essence (*Wesen*) operating. One is entirely consistent with Althusser's position. 'The human essence is no abstraction inherent in each separate individual. In its reality it is the aggregate of social relations' (Marx 1845, p. 14 trans.mod.). The other notion is closest not to 'essence' but to another of the manifold meanings of *Wesen*, which is simply 'being'. Essence in the sense of being is indeed natural, but it is natural in the broadest possible sense of that term. 'That man's physical and spiritual life is linked to nature means simply that nature is linked to itself, for man is a part of nature' (Marx 1844, p. 68). No specific 'nature' is implied here, nothing is claimed for, for instance natural human aggression, competitiveness or some such. What is claimed is that the unalienated life is the life that is part of

In large-scale centralized production, these human and other natural objects are directed by subjects, but subjects they are not. Subjects are dying out.

In sum, the very logic of Marx's argument on the transition from formal to real subsumption is a logic of how the exercise of subjective will and intentionality is systematically eroded. Centralization undermines the exercise of these capacities: this criticism has been levelled at Marx and Marxists by generations of anarchist and anarcho-syndicalist theorists.[12] On the other hand, Marxists have tended to see small-scale production as an on-going form, as well as a precursor, of capital, and also see the difference in size as incidental, if not an outright handicap to the development of socialism. This is because Marx inclined to the idea that socialism was historically likely because the forces of production, involving as they do increasingly gigantic technological conglomerates, bring more and more workers into contact with one another.

This increase in concentration, or centralization, led Marx to burst forth occasionally with beliefs about increasing solidarity amongst those workers. The more they were gathered together, the more they would share a common interest. That they might also wish to get as far away from one another as possible after the day's work was done, that they might dislike those who were most like them, was not a factor that figured in Marx's often complex psychological surmises. He expected

---

nature. And whatever else we can say about the unalienated life (Marx was notoriously vague about it) we can say that it goes with nature rather than against it. What all this comes down to is that the anti-humanist issue cuts both ways. The anti-humanist *Trägers* consist of nothing but the social relations they support, and their relation to nature, their being part of nature, is somehow irrelevant. On the other hand, by this reading, productive labourers, like nature, are objectified, cut out of the nature from which they came, and in this sense they are alienated very much in the sense that Marx described. On the other hand again, they are alienated from *nature, not* from their own wills and imaginations; it is the lack of opportunity to exercise these faculties creatively that a humanist Marxism rightly berates. Thus my argument takes me towards and away from a humanist reading. It turns away from it, for it suggests Marx's reasoning became more anti-humanist than even Althusser allowed. Marx's political economy reveals that will, imagination and goal-direction cease of necessity to be the province of productive labour, to a greater or lesser extent. My position takes me towards the Marx of the alienated essence in another sense, in that it aligns the exploitation and alienation of humans with that of nature. It also emphasizes the relation between large-scale centralization and the foreclosure of opportunities for creative labour. It thus partakes of that general criticism, whose best known articulation came from the Frankfurt School, of the demise of outlets for human creativity in a system that assaults nature on the grander scale.

12  What is less well known is that anarchist political theory was also concerned with the imposition of time–space control, as much as the impositions of the state. Kern notes Conrad's dramatization of the tension between the imposition of universal public time and 'the uniqueness of private experience and private time' or 'the tension between authoritarian world time and the freedom of the individual'. Thus Conrad has the anarchist leader ask Mr Verloc to prove himself by 'blowing up the meridian' (1983, p. 34).

rather, in a welter of teleological leftovers, that the contradiction arising between the centralized, ostensibly solidarity-producing forces of production of capital, and class relations which attempted to divide and rule in the name of individual freedom, would be great enough to consign the latter to historical oblivion. Not that he was ever sanguine about the story having a happy ending. Marx's evolutionism is probably as complex in its possible outcomes as that of his contemporaries. As Gillian Beer puts it, in her uncovering of Darwin's plots,

> Evolutionism has been so imaginatively powerful precisely because all its indications do not point one way. It is rich in contradictory elements which can serve as a metaphorical basis for more than one reading of experience: to give one summary example – the 'ascent' or 'descent' of man may follow the same route but the terms suggest very diverse evaluations of the experience. The optimistic 'progressive' reading of development can never expunge that other insistence that extinction is more probable than progress . . .
>
> (1983, pp. 8–9)

One thing Marx was sure of was that the tendency of the rate of profit to fall meant that capital as a mode of production would have to end.

But it would not end, Marx stressed, without a fight. Capital would and did fight the tendency of the rate of profit to fall by the export of capital, and by (another classic Marxist term) the 'immiseration of the working class'. Simply put, this meant keeping the cost of labour-power to a minimum, even below the level of subsistence, in order to extract more surplus-value by cheating on the price of labour-power. In fact, the predicted immiseration of the working class did not occur as it was meant to do in the advanced heartlands, or it was ameliorated by unions and various forms of welfare state. But as a later generation of Marxists concerned with theories of imperialism[13] and 'Dependency' (Gunder

---

13 The best known theories of imperialism are those of Lenin, Luxemburg and Bukharin. Imperialism has both a general and a specific use in Marxist theory. Generally it refers to relations of exploitation between the advanced capitalist or metropolitan nations and the non-metropolitan or Third World countries. Specifically, it refers to a stage of monopoly capitalism (the second stage of capitalism (see n.45)), which began in the second half of the nineteenth century. This specific theory of imperialism was developed by Lenin, who defines it in terms of the export of money and productive capital in the context of capitalist accumulation. For Lenin, the accumulation of capital led to the export of capital through internal dynamics. But Luxemburg argued that a closed capitalist economy must break down; this was the spur to competition for territories.

Frank 1969)[14] pointed out: capital was not bound by the limits of the nation state; in some instances, it could extract its surplus-value under the most immiserating conditions in, say, the Philippines.

Imperialism is a process by which capital expands, and makes the world over. As an economic process, it has two aspects. It not only furthers the extraction of surplus-value; it is also demanded by the accumulation of capital, which seeks further outlets. Imperialism is pre-eminently a process of spatial expansion. But so, on a more regional scale, is capital's inbuilt need for technological expansion.

As discussed in Part I, Marx sometimes comments on how technological expansion, too, will have to occupy more natural space. It will do so literally, in the division between town and country, and in the sheer size of its sites of production. Like the size of capital's sites of production, urbanization and imperialism have received attention as spatial phenomena in themselves. The spatial impact of expanding the means for acquisition also received some, perhaps not enough, attention from Marx. At any rate more orthodox Marxism has been suspicious of analyses which forefront spatial relations.

Thus Gunder Frank's (and others') Dependency Theory of imperialism is criticized for giving too much weight to the spatial relation between centre and periphery (Laclau 1977). These critics exemplify the way in which Marxism neglects space-time (cf. Giddens 1981, 1984, 1990), although neither Marxists nor critics conceive or consider spatial factors in terms that are fundamentally integral to the production of surplus-value (with the partial exception of Harvey (1989)).[15] Space tends to be brushed to one side, like the question of the *scale* of petty commodity production. It might now be evident that the difference between the foundational fantasy in microcosm and the dynamics of capital overall is one of scale, especially where objectification is concerned. In analysing the foundational fantasy, I outlined how subjective capacities are appropriated from the other, whose agency is denied. In capital's labour process, subjective capacities are also appropriated from those subjects; as centralization proceeds, more and more people are positioned as objects.

14 Dependency theory sees the impoverishment of non-metropolitan countries as the direct result of exploitation by advanced ones. The dependency theory is exemplified in the writings of André Gunder Frank and is closely tied to the Marxist theory of imperialism.
15 This is not to say that space is being ignored in relation to surplus-value production altogether. In the new literature on socialism and the environment it is given a central place. Cf. Altvater (1987).

# Works cited

P. Adams (1988) 'Per os(cillation)', *Camera Obscura* 17, pp. 7–30.
T. Adorno (1966a) *Negative Dialectics* (tr. E. B. Ashton), New York: Seabury Press, 1973.
T. Adorno (1966b) 'Society' (tr. F. Jameson), *Salmagundi*, vols. 10–11, 1969–70.
T. Adorno (1968) 'Sociology and Psychology–II' (tr. Irving N. Wohlfarth), *New Left Review* 47, pp. 79–97.
T. Adorno and M. Horkheimer (1947) *The Dialectic of Enlightenment* (tr. John Cumming), New York: Herder & Herder, 1972.
L. Althusser (1964) 'Freud and Lacan' in *Lenin and Philosophy and Other Essays* (tr. Ben Brewster) New York and London: New Left Books, 1971, pp. 195–219.
L. Althusser (1965) *For Marx* (tr. Ben Brewster), London: Allen Lane Penguin Press, 1969.
L. Althusser and E. Balibar (1965) *Reading 'Capital'* (tr. Ben Brewster), London: New Left Books, 1970.
E. Altvater (1987) 'Ecological and economic modalities of time and space' (tr. M. Schatzscheider), *Capitalism, Nature, Socialism* 3, 1989, pp. 59–70.
T. Aquinas (1266–9) *Summa Theologiae* (ed. and tr. by T. McDermott) as *Summa Theologiae: A Concise Translation*, London, 1989.
H. Arendt (1951) *The Origins of Totalitarianism*, New York: Meridian Books, 1958.
P. Ariès (1962) *Centuries of Childhood: A Social History of Family Life* (tr. Robert Baldick), New York: Vintage Books.
Aristotle (c. 335 BCE) *The Generation of Animals* (trs. P. H. Wicksteed and F. M. Cornford) (Loeb), London and Cambridge, Mass: Heinemann, 1934.
S. Aureli Augustini (c. 400) *Confessionum* (ed. P. Knoll), Leipzig: Verlag von B. G. Teubner, 1898.
R. Bahro (1984) *From Red to Green*, London: Verso.
E. Balibar (1965) – See Althusser and Balibar 1965.
E. Baliber and I. Wallerstein (1988) *Race, Nation, Class: Ambiguous Identities*, London: Verso, 1991.
P. Baran and P. Sweezy (1966) *Monopoly Capital: An Essay on the American Economic and Social Order*, New York: Monthly Review Press.
M. Barrett (1980) *Women's Oppression Today: Problems in Marxist Analysis*, London: Verso and New Left Books.
M. Barrett (1991) *The Politics of Truth: From Marx to Foucault*, Cambridge: Polity Press.
R. Barthes (1975) *Roland Barthes*, Paris: Seuil.
J. Baudrillard (1981) *Simulacres et Simulation*, Paris: Galilée.

J. Baudrillard (1986) *America* (tr. C. Turner), London and New York: Verso.

S. de Beauvior (1949) *The Second Sex*, (tr. H. M. Parshley) Harmondsworth: Penguin, 1972.

G. Beer (1983) *Darwin's Plots: Evolutionary Narrative in Darwin, George Eliot and Nineteenth-Century Fiction*, London: Routledge and Kegan Paul.

S. Benhabib and D. Cornell (eds) (1987) *Feminism as Critique: Essays on the Politics of Gender in Late Capitalist Societies*, Cambridge: Polity Press.

J. Benjamin (1988) *The Bonds of Love: Psychoanalysis, Feminism and the Problem of Domination*, London: Virago.

W. Benjamin (1925–6) 'One way street' in *One Way Street and Other Writings*, London: New Left Books, 1979. Other writings in this volume first published between 1916 and 1937.

W. Benjamin (1938) *Illuminations* (ed. H. Arendt), London, 1970.

W. Benjamin (1939) *Charles Baudelaire: A Lyric Poet in the Era of High Capitalism* (tr. Harry Zohn), London: New Left Books, 1973.

T. Benton, (1989) 'Marxism and natural limits: an ecological critique and reconstruction' *New Left Review* 178, Nov/Dec, pp. 51–86.

P. Berry (1989) *Of Chastity and Power: Elizabethan Literature and the Unmarried Queen*, London and New York: Routledge.

L. Bersani (1990), *The Culture of Redemption*, Cambridge, Mass.: Harvard University Press.

B. Bettelheim (1983) *Freud and Man's Soul*, New York: A.A. Knopf.

H. Bhabha (1986) Foreword to Frantz Fanon *Black Skin, White Masks* (tr. Charles Lam Markmann), London: Pluto Press.

W. R. Bion (1962) *Learning from Experience*, London: W. Heinemann Medical Books.

M. Bloch (1988) 'Death and the concept of person' in *On the Meaning of Death: Essays on Mortuary Rituals and Eschatological Beliefs* (eds) S. Cederroth, C. Corlin and J. Lindström, Uppsala: Almqvist & Wiksell International, 1988, pp. 11–22.

C. Boggs (1986) 'The green alternative and the struggle for a post-marxist discourse' *Theory and Society* 15 (6) pp. 869–99.

R. Bogue (1989) *Deleuze and Guattari*, London and New York: Routledge.

M. Bookchin (1982) *The Ecology of Freedom* Palo Alto: Cheshire Books.

R. Boothby (1991) *Death and Desire: Psychoanalytic Theory from Freud to Lacan*, London and New York: Routledge.

M. Borch-Jacobsen (1989) *The Freudian Subject* (tr. Catharine Porter), London: Macmillan.

M. Borch-Jacobsen (1991) *Lacan: the Absolute Master* (tr. Douglas Brick), Stanford: Stanford University Press.

S. Bordo (1987) *The Flight to Objectivity: Essays on Cartesianism and Culture*, Albany, New York State: University of New York Press.

E. Boserup (1970) *Woman's Role in Economic Development*, New York: St Martin's Press.

T. Bottomore (ed.) (1983) *A Dictionary of Marxist Thought*, Oxford: Blackwell.

M. Bowie (1991) *Lacan*, London: Fontana.

J. Bradley and M. Howard (eds) (1982), *Classical and Marxian Political Economy: Essays in Honor of Ronald L. Meek*, London: Macmillan.

R. Braidotti (1989) 'Organs Without Bodies' *differences* 1 (1), pp. 147–61.

H. Braverman (1974) *Labor and Monopoly Capital: the Degradation of Work in the Twentieth Century*, New York: Monthly Review Press.

T. Brennan (1977) 'Women and work' *Journal of Australian Political Economy* ll (l), pp. 8–30.

T. Brennan (1988) 'Controversial discussions and feminist debate' in N. Segal and E. Timms (eds) *Freud in Exile: Psychoanalysis and its Vicissitudes*, New Haven and London: Yale University Press, pp. 254–74.

T. Brennan (1989) Introduction to *Between Feminism and Psychoanalysis* (ed T. Brennan), London and New York: Routledge, pp. 1–23.

T. Brennan (1991) 'The age of paranoia' *Paragraph*, pp. 20–45.

T. Brennan (1992) *The Interpretation of the Flesh: Freud and Femininity*, London: Routledge.

W. Brown (1991) 'Postmodern exposures, feminist hesitations' in *differences* Spring: 63–84.

S. Buck-Morss (1989) *The Dialectics of Seeing: Walter Benjamin and the Arcades Project*, Cambridge: The MIT Press.

T. Buckley and A. Gottlieb (eds) (1988) *Blood Magic: the Anthropology of Menstruation*, Berkeley: University of California Press.

J. Butler (1990) *Gender Trouble: Feminism and the Subversion of Identity*, New York: Routledge.

J. Butler (1993) *Bodies That Matter*, New York and London: Routledge.

A. T. Callinicos (1982) *Is There a Future for Marxism?*, London: Macmillan.

A. T. Callinicos (1991) *The Revenge of History*, Cambridge: Polity Press.

R. Callois (1935) 'Mimétisme et psychasthénie légendaire' *Minotaure* 7; translated as 'Mimicry and Legendary Psychesthenie' in *October: the First Decade* (ed. A. Michelson, tr. J. Shepley), Cambridge Mass.: MIT Press, 1989.

G. Carchedi (1975) 'On the Economic identification of the new middle class' *Economy and Society* 4 (1), pp. 1–86.

J. Chasseguet-Smirgel (1984) *Creativity and Perversion*, London: Free Association Books.

N. Chodorow (1978) *The Reproduction of Mothering: Psychoanalysis and the Sociology of Gender*, Berkeley: University of California Press.

A. Clarke (1919) *Working Life of Women in the Seventeenth Century*, London: Routledge and Kegan Paul, 1982.

C. Clément (1981) *Vies et Légendes de Jacques Lacan*, Paris: B. Grasset.

S. T. Coleridge (1817) *Biographia Literaria* (2 vols), J. Engell and W. Jackson Bate (eds), London: Routledge and Kegan Paul, 1984.

L. Colletti (1972) *From Rousseau to Lenin: Studies in Ideology and Context* (tr. J. Merrington and J. White), New York: Monthly Review Press.

R. W. Connell (1990) 'The state, gender and sexual politics: theory and appraisal' *Theory and Society*, 19 (5), October, 1990, pp. 507–44.

J. Copjec (1989a) 'Cutting up' in Brennan (ed.) *Between Feminism and Psychoanalysis*, London and New York: Routledge, 1989. pp. 227–246.

J. Copjec (1989b) 'The orthopsychic subject: film theory and the reception of Lacan' *October* 49, Summer, 1989.

D. Cornell (1988) 'Post-structuralism, the ethical relation, and the law' *Cardozo Law Review* 9 (6), August, 1988, pp. 1587–628.

D. Cornell (1992) *The Philosophy of the Limit*, New York and London: Routledge.

R. Cox (1987) *Power, Production and World Order*, New York: St Martins Press.

M. Dalla Costa (1973) *The Power of Women and the Subversion of the Community*, Bristol: Falling Wall.

G. Deleuze and F. Guattari (1972) *Anti-Oedipus; Capitalism and Schizophrenia* (trs. Robert Hurley, Mark Seem, H.R. Lane), London: Athlone, 1984.

G. Deleuze and F. Guattari (1980) *A Thousand Plateaus* (tr. Brian Massumi), Minneapolis: University of Minnesota Press, 1987.

C. Delphy (1977) *The Main Enemy*, London: Women's Research and Resources Centre.

J. Derrida (1965) *De la grammatologie*, Paris: Minuit, 1967.

J. Derrida (1966) 'Freud and the scene of writing' in *Writing and Difference* (tr. Alan Bass), London: Routledge and Kegan Paul, 1981, pp. 196–231.

J. Derrida (1967) *Writing and Difference* (tr. Alan Bass), Chicago: University of Chicago Press, 1978.

J. Derrida (1972) *Dissemination* (tr. Barbara Johnson), Chicago: University of Chicago Press, 1981.

J. Derrida (1972) *Margins of Philosophy* (tr. Alan Bass), Chicago: University of Chicago Press, 1982.

J. Derrida (1974) *Glas* (2 vols), Paris: Denoël/Gonthier, 1981.

J. Derrida (1980) *La carte postale: de Socrate à Freud et au-delà*, Paris: Flammarion.

J. Derrida (1986) 'The art of mémoires' in *Mémoires: For Paul DeMan* (tr. Cecile Lindsay, Jonathan Culler, and Eduardo Cadava), New York: Columbia University Press.

J. Derrida and S. Agnosti (1978) *Spurs: Nietzsche's Styles = Eperons: Les Styles de Nietzsche* (tr. Barbara Harlow), Chicago: The University of Chicago Press.

P. Dews (1987) *Logics of Disintegration: Post-Structuralist Thought and the Claims of Critical Theory*, London and New York: Verso.

D. Dinnerstein (1978) *The Rocking of the Cradle, and the Ruling of the World*, London: Condor Souvenir Press.

A. Dobson (1990) *Green Political Thought: an Introduction*, London and Boston: Unwin Hyman.

E. R. Dodds (1951) *The Greeks and the Irrational*, Berkeley: University of California Press.

A. Douglas (1977) *The Feminization of American Culture*, New York: Avon.

M. Douglas (1966) *Purity and Danger: an Analysis of Concepts of Pollution and Taboo*, New York: Praeger.

M. Douglas and B. Isherwood (1979) *The World of Goods*, New York: Basic Books.

G. Duby (1974) *The Early Growth of the European Economy: Warriors and Peasants from the Seventh to the Twelfth Century* (tr. Howard B. Clarke), London: Weidenfeld and Nicholson.

L. Dumont (1966) *Homo hierarchicus* (tr. anon), London: Paladin, 1970.

J. Dunn (1969) *The Political Thought of John Locke; An Historical Account of the 'Two Treatises of Government'*, Cambridge: Cambridge University Press.

J. Dunn (1978) *Western Political Theory in the Face of the Future*, Cambridge: Cambridge University Press.

T. Eagleton (1981) *Walter Benjamin, or Towards a Revolutionary Criticism*, London: New Left Books.

T. Eagleton (1988) *Against the Grain: Essays 1975-1985*, Oxford: Blackwell.

T. Eagleton (1990) *The Ideology of the Aesthetic*, Oxford: Blackwell.

B. Ehrenreich (1983) *The Hearts of Men: American Dreams and the Flight from Commitment*, London: Pluto Press.

N. Elias (1939) *The Civilizing Process* (tr. Edmund Jephcott), Oxford: Blackwell, 1982.

H. Ellenberger (1970) *The Discovery of the Unconscious: The History and Evolution of Dynamic Psychiatry*, London: Allen Lane.

B. J. Elliot (1991) 'Demographic trends in domestic life 1945–87' in David Clark (ed.) *Domestic Life and Social Change*, London and New York: Routledge, pp. 85–108.

R. Elliot and A. Gare (eds.) (1983) *Environmental Philosophy*, Milton Keynes: Open University Press.

E. Evans-Pritchard (1939) *The Nuer: A Description of the Modes of Livelihood and Political Institutions of a Nilotic People*, Oxford: Clarendon Press, 1940.

F. Fanon (1952) *Black Skin, White Masks* (tr. Charles Lam Markham), London: Pluto Press, 1986.

A. Fausto-Sterling (1985) *Myths of Gender: Biological Theories about Women and Men*, New York: Basic Books.

S. Feiner and B. Roberts (1990) 'Hidden by the invisible hand: neoclassical economic theory and the textbook treatment of race and gender' *Gender and Society* 4 (2), pp. 159–81.

R. Feldstein and J. Roof (eds) (1989) *Feminism and Psychoanalysis*, Ithaca: Cornell University Press.

S. Felman (1987) *Jacques Lacan and the Adventure of Insight: Psychoanalysis in Contemporary Culture*, Boston: Harvard University Press.

B. Fine (1979) 'On Marx's theory of agricultural rent' *Economy and Society* 8 (3), pp. 241–78.

J. Flax (1990) *Thinking Fragments: Psychoanalysis, Feminism, and Postmodernism in the Contemporary West*, Berkeley: University of California Press.

M. Foucault (1966) *The Order of Things: An Archaeology of the Human Sciences*, New York: Pantheon, 1977.

M. Foucault (1969) *The Archaeology of Knowledge and the Discourse on Language* (tr. A. M. Sheridan Smith), New York: Harper, 1976.

M. Foucault (1975) *Discipline and Punish: The Birth of the Prison* (tr. A. Sheridan), London: Allen Lane Penguin, 1977.

M. Foucault (1976) *The History of Sexuality*, vol. 1 (tr. Robert Hurley), 1st American edn, New York: Pantheon Books, 1978.

M. Foucault (1980) *Power/Knowledge: Selected Interviews and Other Writings 1972–1977* (ed. and tr. Colin Gordon), Brighton and Sussex: Harvester Press.

M. Foucault (1984) 'What is enlightenment?' in Paul Robinson (ed.) *The Foucault Reader* (tr. Catharine Porter), Harmondsworth: Penguin, 1991.

M. Foucault (1986) *Foucault: A Critical Reader*, David Couzens Hoy (ed.) Oxford and New York: Blackwell.

A. Frank (1990) 'Bring bodies back in: a decade review' *Theory, Culture and Society* 7 (1), pp. 131–61.

A. Gunder Frank (1969) *Capitalism and Underdevelopment in Latin America*, New York: Monthly Review Press.

N. Fraser (1990) *Unruly Practices: Power, Discourse and Gender in Contemporary Social Theory*, Cambridge: Polity Press.

S. Freud (1900) *The Interpretation of Dreams* in S. Freud, *The Complete Works of the Standard Edition of the Psychological Works of Sigmund Freud* (ed. and tr. James Strachey *et al*), London: The Hogarth Press, 1966 (hereafter SE), vol. 11, pp. 163–75.

S. Freud and J. Breuer (1895a) *Studies on Hysteria*, *SE*, vol. 2.

S. Freud (1895b) *Project for a Scientific Psychology* (*Entwurf einer psychologie*), *SE*, vol. 1.

S. Freud (1905) 'Three essays on the theory of sexuality' *SE*, vol. 7, pp. 123–243.

S. Freud (1910) 'A special type of object-choice made by men (Contributions to the Psychology of Love, I)' in *SE*, vol. 11, pp. 165–75.

S. Freud (1911) 'Psycho-analytic notes on an autobiographical account of a case of paranoia (Dementia Paranoides)' *SE*, vol. 12, pp. 9–82.

S. Freud (1912a) 'On the universal tendency to debasement in the sphere of love' *SE*, vol. 11, pp. 177–90.

S. Freud (1920) *Beyond the Pleasure Principle*, *SE*, vol. 18.

S. Freud (1925a) 'On negation' *SE*, vol. 19, pp. 235–39.

S. Freud (1925b) 'Some psychical consequences of the anatomical distinction between the sexes' *SE*, vol. 19, pp. 248–58.

S. Freud (1926), *Inhibitions, Symptoms and Anxiety*, *SE*, vol. 20.

S. Freud (1929) *Civilization and its Discontents*, *SE*, vol. 21.

S. Freud (1931) 'Female sexuality' *SE*, vol. 21, pp. 221–43.
S. Freud (1933) 'Femininity' *SE*, vol. 22, pp. 112–35.
P. Freund (1988) 'Bringing society into the body: understanding socialized human nature', *Theory and Society* 17 (6), pp. 839–64.
F. Fukuyama (1992) *The End of History and the Last Man*, London: Hamish Hamilton.
C. Gallagher (1987) 'The body versus the social body in the works of Thomas Malthus and Henry Mayhew' in C. Gallagher and Thomas Laqueur (eds) *The Making of the Modern Body: Sexuality and Society in the Nineteenth Century*, Berkeley: University of California Press, pp. 83–106.
J. Gallop (1985) *Reading Lacan*, Ithaca: Cornell University Press.
J. Gardiner (1975) 'Women's domestic labor', *Bulletin of the Conference of Socialist Economists* 4 (2).
G. Garrett and P. Lange (1991) 'Political responses to interdependence: what's 'left' for the left?', *International Organization* 45 (4), Autumn, pp. 539–64.
A. Giddens (1971) *Capitalism and Modern Social Theory; an Analysis of the Writings of Marx, Durkheim and Max Weber*, Cambridge: Cambridge University Press.
A. Giddens (1979) *Central Problems in Social Theory: Action, Structure and Contradiction in Social Analysis*, London: MacMillan.
A. Giddens (1981) *Contemporary Critique of Historical Materialism*, vol. 1, Berkeley: University of California Press.
A. Giddens (1984) *The Constitution of Society: Outline of the Theory of Structuration*, Cambridge: Polity Press.
A. Giddens (1985) *The Nation State and Violence*, Cambridge: Polity Press.
A. Giddens (1990) *The Consequences of Modernity*, Stanford: Stanford University Press.
A. Giddens (1991) *Modernity and Self-identity: Self and Society in the Late Modern Age*, Cambridge: Polity Press.
G. Gillison (1980) 'Images of nature in Gimi thought' in Strathern and Macormack, pp. 143–73.
P. Ginsborg (1990) *A History of Contemporary Italy: Society and Politics 1943–88*, London: Penguin.
M. Goldman and J. O'Connor (1988) 'Ideologies of environmental crisis: technology and its discontents' *Capitalism, Nature, Socialism* 1, pp. 91–106.
J. H. Goldthorpe (1964) 'Social stratification in industrial society', *The Development of Industrial Society*, Sociological Review Monograph, 8, pp. 97–122.
A. Gorz (1980) *Ecology as Politics* (trs P. Vigderman and J. Cloud), London: Pluto Press 1983.
P. A. Gourevitch (1986) *Politics in Hard Times: Comparative Responses to International Economic Crises*, New York: Cornell University Press.
S. Green (1993) Lectures to the Cambridge University Social Anthropology Department, March 1993.
S. Greenblatt (1980) *Renaissance Self-fashioning: From More to Shakespeare*, Chicago: University of Chicago Press.
C. Gregory (1980) 'Gifts to men and gifts to God: gift exchange and capital accumulation in contemporary Papua' *Man* 15 (4), December, pp. 626–52.
P. Grosskurth (1986) *Melanie Klein: Her World and Her Work*, New York: Knopf.
E. A. Grosz (1986) 'Irigaray and the divine', *Local Consumption*, Sydney Occasional Paper 9.
E. A. Grosz (1988) 'Space, time and bodies', *On the beach*, Sydney, vol. 13, pp. 1–12.
E. A. Grosz (1989) *Sexual Subversions: Three French Feminists*, Sydney: Allen & Unwin.
R. Grove (1990a) 'The origins of environmentalism', *Nature*, May 3, pp. 11–14.
R. Grove (1990b) 'Colonial conservation, ecological hegemony and popular resistance:

towards a second synthesis' in J. Mackenzie (ed.) *Imperialism in the Natural World*, Manchester: Manchester University Press, pp. 15–50.

F. Guattari (1984) *Molecular Revolution: Psychiatry and Politics* (tr. R. Sheed), Harmondsworth: Penguin Books.

J. Habermas (1968) *Knowledge and Human Interests* (tr. J. J. Shapiro), Boston: Beacon Press, 1971.

S. Hall, D. Held and T. McGrew (eds.) (1992) *Modernity and Its Futures*, Cambridge: Polity Press.

S. Hampshire (1951) *Spinoza*, London Harmondsworth: Penguin.

D. J. Haraway (1985) 'A manifesto for cyborgs: science, technology, and socialist feminism in the 1980s' in L. J. Nicholson (ed.) (1990) *Feminism/Postmodernism*, New York and London: Routledge, pp. 190–223.

D. J. Haraway (1989) *Primate Visions: Gender, Race and Nature in the World of Modern Science*, New York: Routledge.

G. C. Harcourt (1982) 'The Sraffan Contribution: An Evaluation' in Bradley and Howard (eds) *Classical and Marxian Political Economy: Essays in Honour of Ronald L. Meek*, London: Macmillan.

G. C. Harcourt (1993) *Post Keynesian Essays in Biography*, London: Macmillan.

S. G. Harding (1986) *The Science Question in Feminism*, Ithaca/New York: Cornell University Press.

J. Harrison (1973) 'Political economy of housework', *Bulletin of the Conference of Socialist Economists* 3 (1).

H. Hartmann (1939) *Ego Psychology and the Problem of Adaption* (tr. David Rapaport), New York: International Universities Press, 1958 (First presented 1937).

H. Hartmann (1979) 'The unhappy marriage of marxism and feminism: towards a more progressive union' in L. Sargent (ed.) (1981) *Women and Revolution: a Discussion of the Unhappy Marriage of Marxism and Feminism*, Boston: South End Press.

D. Harvey (1989) *The Condition of Postmodernity: An Enquiry into the Origins of Cultural Change*, Oxford and New York: Basil Blackwell.

S. W. Hawking (1988) *A Brief History of Time: From the Big Bang to Black Holes*, Toronto and New York: Bantam Books.

T. Hayward (1990) 'Eco-socialism – utopian and scientific', *Radical Philosophy* 56, pp. 2–14.

S. Heath (1978) 'Difference' *Screen*, 19 (3), Autumn, pp. 51–112.

G. W. F. Hegel (1787) *The Philosophy of History* (tr. J. Sibree), New York: Dover, 1956.

G. W. F. Hegel (1807) *The Phenomenology of Mind* (tr. J.B. Baillie), New York and London: Harper and Row, 1967.

M. Heidegger (1927) *Being and Time* (trs John MacQuarrie and Edward Robinson), Oxford: Blackwell 1967.

M. Heidegger (1936) 'The origin of the work of Art' in D. Krell (ed.) *Martin Heidegger: Basic Writings*, London: Routledge, 1977.

M. Heidegger (1938) 'The age of the World Picture' in M. Heidegger (1977) *The Question Concerning Technology*, New York: Harper and Row.

M. Heidegger (1947) 'Letter on Humanism' in D. Krell (ed.) *Martin Heidegger: Basic Writings*, London: Routledge, 1977, pp. 193–242.

M. Heidegger (1949) 'The question concerning technology', in *The Question Concerning Technology and other Essays* (tr. W. Lovitt), New York: Harper and Row, 1977.

M. Heidegger (1954) 'Overcoming metaphysics' in *The End of Philosophy* (ed. and tr. Joan Stambaugh), New York: Harper and Row, 1973.

M. Heidegger (1977) *Martin Heidegger: Basic Writings*, D. Krell (ed.) London: Routledge.

W. Heisenberg (1958) *Physics and Philosophy; the Revolution in Modern Science*, New York: Harper.

D. Held (1980) *Introduction to Critical Theory: Horkheimer to Habermas*, London: Hutchinson.

D. Held (1987) *Models of Democracy*, Stanford: Stanford University Press.

R. Hilton (1973) *Bond Men Made Free: Medieval Peasant Movements and the English Rising of 1381*, London: Temple Smith.

E. J. Hobsbawm (1964) *Labouring Men: Studies in the History of Labour*, London: Weidenfeld and Nicholson.

J. Hodge (1992) 'Nietzsche, Heidegger, Europe: five remarks' *Journal of Nietzsche Studies* 3, Spring, 1992 pp. 45–66.

J. Hodge (1994) 'Rethinking temporality: Heidegger, sociology, postmodernism', Working Paper 5, Institute for Popular Culture, Manchester Metropolitan University.

b. hooks (1992) *Black Looks: Race and Representation*, Boston: South End Press.

M. Horkheimer (1941) 'The end of reason', *Studies in Philosophy and Social Science* 9 (3), pp. 366–88.

G. Howie (1992) *Capitalism and Schizophrenia: a Critique of 'The Anti-Oedipus'*, Cambridge University unpublished Ph.D. thesis.

J. Humphreys (1977) 'Class struggle and the persistance of the working class family', *Cambridge Journal of Economics* 1 (3).

L. Irigaray (1974) *Speculum of the Other Woman* (tr. Gillian C. Gill), Ithaca: Cornell University Press, 1985.

L. Irigaray (1977) *This Sex Which is Not One* (tr. C. Porter and C. Burke), Ithaca: Cornell University Press, 1985.

L. Irigaray (1983) *L'oubli de l'air chez Martin Heidegger*, Paris: Minuit.

L. Irigaray (1984) *Éthique de la différence sexuelle*, Paris: Minuit.

L. Irigaray (1985) *Parler n'est jamais neutre*, Paris: Minuit.

L. Irigaray (1986) 'Divine women' (tr. Stephen Muecke), Sydney, *Local Consumption* Occasional Paper 9.

S. James (1994) 'The place of the passions in the mind' (working title) in *The Cambridge History of Philosophy: the Seventeenth Century*, Michael Ayers and David Garber (eds), Cambridge University Press (forthcoming).

F. Jameson (1977) 'Imaginary and symbolic in Lacan' in *The Ideologies of Theory*, vol. 1, Minneapolis: University of Minnesota Press, 1988.

F. Jameson (1984) Foreword to Jean-Francois Lyotard *The Postmodern Condition: A Report on Knowledge* (trs Geoff Benningham and Brian Massumi), Minneapolis: University of Minnesota Press.

F. Jameson (1991) *Postmodernism, or the Cultural Logic of Late Capitalism*, Durham: Duke University Press.

A. Jardine (1985) *Gynesis: Configurations of Women and Modernity*, Ithaca: Cornell University Press.

M. Jay (1984) *Marxism and Totality: The Adventures of a Concept from Lukács to Habermas*, Berkeley: University of California Press.

M. Jay (1986) 'In the empire of the gaze: Foucault and the denigration of vision in twentieth-century French thought' in David Couzens Hoy (ed.) *Foucault: A Critical Reader*, Oxford and New York: Blackwell, pp. 175–204.

M. Jay (1988) *Fin de Siècle Socialism and Other Essays*, London and New York: Routledge.

M. Jay (1993) *Downcast Eyes: The Denigration of Vision in Twentieth Century French Thought*, Berkeley: University of California Press.

R. Jervis (1991) 'The future of world politics', *International Security* 16 (3), pp. 39–73.

E. Fox Keller (1985) *Reflections on Gender and Science*, New Haven: Yale University Press.

P. Kelly (1984) *Fighting for Hope* (tr. Marianne Howarth), Boston: South End Press.

N. Keohane, M. Z. Rosaldo, B. C. Gelpi (1982) *Feminist Theory: A Critique of Ideology*, Chicago: University of Chicago Press.

S. Kern (1983) *The Culture of Time and Space 1880-1918*, Cambridge, Mass.: Harvard University Press.

M. Klein (1928) 'Early stages of the Oedipus complex', *International Journal of Psycho-Analysis* 11, pp. 167–80.

M. Klein (1930) 'The importance of symbol formation in the development of the ego' in *Love, Guilt and Reparation and Other Works, 1921-1945 (Collected Writings*, vol. 1), London: Hogarth Press and the Institute of Psycho-Analysis, 1985, pp. 219–32.

M. Klein (1946) 'Notes on some schizoid mechanisms', *Envy and Gratitude and Other Works, 1946-1963 (Collected Writings*, vol. 3), London: Hogarth Press and the Institute of Psycho-Analysis, 1980, c.1975, pp. 1–25.

M. Klein (1952) 'Some theoretical conclusions regarding the emotional life of the infant' in *Envy and Gratitude*, pp. 61–93.

M. Klein (1957) 'Envy and gratitude' in *Envy and Gratitude and Other Works 1946-1963: The Writings of Melanie Klein (vol. 3)*, London: Hogarth, pp. 176–235.

M. Klein (1960) 'A Note on depression in the schizophrenic' in *Envy and Gratitude*, pp. 264–267.

M. Klein (1985) *The Writings of Melanie Klein*, London: Hogarth Press and the Institute of Psycho Analysis.

A. Kojève (c. 1933 as lectures) Introduction to *The Reading of Hegel*, New York: Basic Books, 1969.

A. Koyré (1943) 'Galileo and the scientific revolution of the seventeenth century', *Philosophical Review* LII (4), July, pp. 333–48.

J. Kristeva (1974a) *Revolution in Poetic Language* (tr. Margaret Waller), New York: Columbia University Press, 1984.

J. Kristeva (1974b) *About Chinese Women* (tr. A. Barrows), London and New York: Marion Boyars Ltd, 1986.

J. Kristeva (1979) 'Women's time' (tr. S. Hand), in Toril Moi (ed.) (1986) *The Kristeva Reader*, Oxford: Blackwell, also (tr. A. Jardine and H. Blake), *Signs* 7 (1), Autumn, 1981, pp. 13–34.

J. Kristeva (1980) *Powers of Horror: An Essay on Abjection* (tr. Leon S. Roudiez), New York: Columbia University Press, 1982.

J. Kristeva (1983) *Tales of Love* (tr. Leon S. Roudiez), New York: Columbia University Press, 1987.

J. Lacan (1948) 'Aggressivity in psychoanalysis' in *Écrits: A Selection* (tr. Alan Sheridan), London: Tavistock, pp. 8–29.

J. Lacan (1949) 'The mirror stage' in *Écrits: A Selection* (tr. Alan Sheridan), London: Tavistock, pp. 1–7.

J. Lacan, (1953a) 'Some reflections on the ego' *International Journal of Psycho-analysis* 34, pp. 11–17.

J. Lacan (1953b) 'The function and field of speech and language in psychoanalysis' (The Rome report), *Écrits: A Selection* (tr. Alan Sheridan), London: Tavistock, pp. 30–113.

J. Lacan [1953–4] (1966) *Le Séminaire livre 1: les écrits techniques de Freud* (ed. Jacques-Alain Miller, Paris: Seuil) (tr. John Forrester with notes by Sylvana Tomaselli) 1975, *The Seminar of Jacques Lacan: Book 1: Freud's Papers on Technique*, (Seminar 1), Cambridge University Press, 1988.

J. Lacan [1955] (1966) 'The Freudian thing', in *Écrits: A Selection* (tr. Alan Sheridan), London: Tavistock, pp. 114–45.

J. Lacan [1955–6a] (1966) 'On a question preliminary to any possible treatment of psychosis' in *Écrits: A Selection* (tr. Alan Sheridan), London: Tavistock, pp. 179–225.

J. Lacan [1955–6b] (1981) *Le Séminaire livre III: les psychoses*, Paris: Seuil.

J. Lacan [1958a] (1966) 'The meaning of the phallus' in *Feminine Sexuality: Jacques Lacan and the École Freudienne* (eds) J. Mitchell and J. Rose, London: MacMillan, 1982 . Also translated as 'The signification of the phallus' in *Écrits* (1977), pp. 281–91.

J. Lacan [1958b] (1966) 'The direction of the treatment and the principle of its power' in *Écrits*, pp. 226–80.

J. Lacan [1958c] (1966) 'Guiding remarks for a congress on feminine sexuality' in *Écrits*, Paris: Seuil (tr. J. Rose), in J. Rose and J. Mitchell (eds), *Feminine Sexuality: Jacques Lacan and the École Freudienne*, London: Macmillan, 1982, pp. 86–98.

J. Lacan [1959–60] (1986) *Le Séminaire livre VII: l'éthique de la psychanalyse*, Paris: Seuil.

J. Lacan [1964] (1973) *The Four Fundamental Concepts of Psycho-analysis*, (ed.) J. A. Miller (tr. A. Sheridan), Harmondsworth: Penguin, 1979.

J. Lacan (1966) *Écrits*, Paris: Seuil (2 vols), Points Edition, 1971.

J. Lacan, [1972–3] (1975) *Le Séminaire livre XX, Encore*, text established by J. A. Miller, Paris: Seuil

J. Lacan, (1975) 'Seminar of 21 January 1975' (tr. J. Rose) in J. Mitchell and J. Rose (eds), *Feminine Sexuality* pp. 162–71.

J. Lacan (1977) *Écrits: A Selection* (tr. A. Sheridan), London: Tavistock.

J. Lacan and W. Granoff (1956) 'Fetishism' in M. Balint and S. Loran (eds) *Perversions, Psychodynamics and Therapy*, London: Ortolan Press, pp. 265–76.

E. Laclau (1977) *Politics and Ideology in Marxist Theory: Capitalism, Fascism, Populism*, New York: New Left Books.

E. Laclau and C. Mouffe (1985) *Hegemony and Socialist Strategy* (tr. Winston Moore and Paul Cammack), London: Verso.

P. Lacoue-Labarthe (1987) *Heidegger, Art and Politics: the Fiction of the Political* (tr. Chris Turner), Oxford: Blackwell, 1990.

J. La Fontaine (1985) 'Person and individual: some anthropological reflections' in M. Carrithers, S. Collins and S. Lukes (eds) *The Category of the Person: Anthropology, Philosophy, History*, Cambridge: Cambridge University Press.

J. Laplanche (1970) *Vie et mort en psychanalyse*, Paris: Flammarion (tr. J. Mehlman) *Life and Death in Psychoanalysis*, Baltimore: Johns Hopkins University Press, 1976.

J. Laplanche and J.-B. Pontalis (1968) 'Fantasy and the origins of sexuality' *International Journal of Psycho-Analysis* 49, reprinted in V. Burgin, J. Donald and C. Kaplan *Formations of Fantasy*, London and New York: Methuen, pp. 5–34.

C. Lasch (1978) *The Culture of Narcissism: American Life in an Age of Diminishing Expectations*, New York: Norton.

M. Le Doeuff (1986) *Vénus et Adonis suivi de gènese d'une catastrophe*, Paris: Alidades.

D. Lehmann (1990) *Democracy and Development in Latin America: Economics, Politics and Religion in the Post-War Period*, Cambridge: Polity Press.

E. Lemoine-Luccioni (1976) *Partage des femmes*, Paris: Seuil.

C. Lévi-Strauss (1963) *Structural Anthropology* (tr. Claire Jacobson and Brooke Grundfest Schoepf), New York: Basic Books.

H. Longino and R. Doell (1983) 'Body, bias and behaviour: a comparative analysis of reasoning in two areas of biological science', *Signs: Journal of Women in Culture and Society* 9 (2).

N. Luhmann (1975) *The Differentiation of Society* (tr. Stephen Holmes and Charles Larmore), New York: Columbia University Press, 1982.

G. Lukács (1923) *History and Class Consciousness* (tr. Rodney Livingstone), London: Merlin Press, 1971.

R. Luxemburg (1913) *The Accumulation of Capital*, London: Routledge and Kegan Paul, 1963.

J.-F. Lyotard (1985) *Les immateriux*, Paris: Beauborg.

D. MacCannell (1976) *The Tourist: A New Theory of the Leisure Class*, New York: Schoken Books.

J. F. MacCannell (1986) *Figuring Lacan: Criticism and the Cultural Unconscious*, London: Croom Helm.

J. F. MacCannell (1991) *The Regime of the Brother: After the Patriarchy*, London and New York: Routledge.

D. N. McCloskey (1985) *The Rhetoric of Economics*, Madison: University of Wisconsin Press.

D. Macey (1988) *Lacan in Contexts*, London and New York: Verso.

J. Mackenzie (1990) *Imperialism in the Natural World*, Manchester: Manchester University Press.

C. McMillan (1982) *Women, Reason and Nature: Some Philosophical Problems with Feminism*, Oxford: Blackwell.

B. Malinowski (1927) *Sex and Repression in Savage Society*, London: Routledge and Kegan Paul.

E. Mandel (1972) *Late Capitalism* (tr. J. De Bres), London: New Left Books, 1975.

H. Marcuse (1956) *Eros and Civilisation: A Philosophical Inquiry into Freud*, London: Routledge and Kegan Paul, 1987.

H. Marcuse (1964) 'Industrialization and capitalism in the work of Max Weber' and 'A Critique of Norman O'Brown', in *Negations: Essays in Critical Theory* (tr. J. J. Shapiro), London: Allen Lane, pp. 227–47.

E. Marks and I. de Courtivron (1981) *New French Feminisms: An Anthology*, New York: Schocken Books.

E. Martin (1989) *The Woman in the Body*, Milton Keynes: Open University Press.

K. Marx (1843) *Critique of Hegel's 'Philosophy of Right'* (tr. John O'Malley and Annette John), Cambridge: Cambridge University Press, 1971.

K. Marx (1844) *Economic and Philosophic Manuscripts of 1844* (tr. M. Milligan), Moscow: Progress Publishers, 1959.

K. Marx (1845) *Theses on Feuerbach* in K. Marx and F. Engels, *Selected Works* (3 vols), Moscow: Progress Publishers, 1969, vol. 1, pp. 13–15.

K. Marx (1852) *The Eighteenth Brumaire of Louis Bonaparte* in K. Marx and F. Engels, *Selected Works* (3 vols) Moscow: Progress Publishers, 1969, vol. 1, pp. 394–487.

K. Marx (1857–8) *Grundrisse der kritik der politischen Ökonomie*, Europäische Verlagsanstalt, 1953 (tr. M. Nicolaus), *Grundrisse*, London: NLR Allen Lane Penguin, 1973.

K. Marx (1859) *Preface to A Contribution to the Critique of Political Economy* in K. Marx and F. Engels, *Selected Works* (3 vols) (ed.) Maurice Dobb (tr. S. W. Ryazanskaya) Moscow: Progress Publishers, 1970, vol. 1, pp. 502–06.

K. Marx (1861–79) *Theories of Surplus Value* (ed S. W. Ryazanskaya) (tr. Emile Burns), Moscow: Progress Publishers, 1969.

K. Marx (1865) *Value, Price and Profit* in K. Marx and F. Engels, *Selected Works* (2 vols), Moscow: Progress Publishers, 1968, vol. 2, pp. 31–76.

K. Marx (1867) *Capital*, vol. 1 (tr. S. Moore and E. Aveling), Moscow: Progress Publishers, 1954.

K. Marx (1880) *Notes on Adolph Wagner* [*Marginal notes on Wagner*] (tr. T. Carver), in T. Carver (ed.) *Karl Marx: Texts on Method*, Oxford: Blackwell, 1975.

K. Marx (1885–1893) *Capital*, vol. 2 (tr. I. Lasker) Moscow: Progress Publishers, 1956.

K. Marx (1894) *Capital*, vol. 3 Moscow: Progress Publishers, 1971.

K. Marx (c. 1865) *Resultate des unmittelbaren produktions prozesses*, Archiv sozialistischer literatur 17, Frankfurt: Verlag Neue Kritik, 1970.

K. Marx and F. Engels (1845–6) *The German Ideology*, Moscow: Progress Publishers, 1972.

K. Marx and F. Engels (1975– ) *Karl Marx/Friedrich Engels Gesamtausgabe* (MEGA), 45 vols t.d., Berlin: Dietz Verlag

M. Mead (1950) *Male and Female: A Study of the Sexes in a Changing World*, New York: William Morrow.

C. Merchant (1980) *The Death of Nature: Women, Ecology and the Scientific Revolution*, San Francisco: Harper and Row.

M. Merleau-Ponty (1945) *The Phenomenology of Perception* (tr. C. Smith), London: Routledge and Kegan Paul, 1962.

J.-A. Miller (1977) Index, J. Lacan, *Écrits: A selection* (tr. A. Sheridan), London: Tavistock.

J. Mitchell (1974) *Psychoanalysis and Feminism*, Harmondsworth: Penguin.

J. Mitchell (1982) 'Introduction I' in *Feminine Sexuality: Jacques Lacan and the École Freudienne*, J. Mitchell and J. Rose (eds), London: Macmillan, 1982, pp. 1–27.

J. Mitchell (1986) Introduction to *The Selected Works of Melanie Klein*, J. Mitchell (ed.), Harmondsworth: Penguin.

T. Moi (1985) *Sexual/Textual Politics: Feminist Literary Theory*, London and New York: Methuen.

T. Moi (1989) 'Patriarchal thought and the drive for knowledge' in T. Brennan (ed.) *Between Feminism and Psychoanalysis*, London: Routledge, pp. 189–205.

M. de Montaigne (1580) *Essays* (tr. J. M. Cohen), Harmondsworth: Penguin, 1958.

M. Montrelay (1978) 'Inquiry into femininity' (tr. P. Adams), *m/f* 14, pp. 83–101.

T. Morrison (1988) *Beloved*, New York: New American Library.

A. G. Motulsky (1983) 'Impact of genetic manipulation on society and medicine' *Science* 219, pp. 135–40.

J. P. Muller and W. Richardson (1982) *Lacan and Language, a Reader's Guide to Écrits*, New York: International Universities Press.

L. Mumford (1938) *The Culture of Cities*, New York: Harcourt Brace.

L. Nicholson (ed.) (1990) *Feminism/Postmodernism*, London: Routledge.

F. Nietzsche (1887) *The Gay Science; With a Prelude in Rhymes and an Appendix of Songs* (tr. W. Kaufmann), New York: Bantam Books, 1974.

M. C. Nussbaum (1986) *The Fragility of Goodness: Luck and Ethics in Greek Tragedy and Philosophy*, Cambridge: Cambridge University Press.

J. S. Nye (1989) *Bound to Lead: The Changing Nature of American Power*, New York: Basic Books, 1990.

N. O'Brown (1959) *Life Against Death: The Psychoanalytical Meaning of History*, London: Routledge and Kegan Paul.

B. Pascal (1670) *Pensées* (tr. A. J. Kreilsheimer), Harmondsworth: Penguin.

C. Pateman (1988) *The Sexual Contract*, Cambridge: Polity Press.

Plato (360 BCE) *Theaetetus* (tr. A. H. Waterfield), Harmondsworth: Penguin, 1987.

Plato (370 BCE) *Phaedrus* (tr. W. Hamilton), Harmondsworth: Penguin, 1973.

V. Plumwood (1993) *Feminism and the Mastery of Nature*, London and New York: Routledge.

K. Polanyi (1945) *Origins of Our Time, the Great Transformation*, London: Gollancz.

R. Poole (1991) *Morality and Modernity*, London and New York: Routledge.

J. Porritt (1984) *Seeing Green: The Politics of Ecology Explained*, Oxford: Blackwell.

N. Postman (1985) *Amusing Ourselves to Death: Public Discourse in the Age of Show Business*, Harmondsworth: Penguin.

N. Poulantzas (1968) *Political Power and Social Classes*, London: New Left Books, 1973.

V. G. Pursel, C. A. Pinkert, K. F. Miller et al. (1989) 'Genetic engineering of livestock', *Science* 244, pp. 1281–7.

E. Ragland-Sullivan (1986) *Jacques Lacan and the Philosophy of Psychoanalysis*, London and Canberra: Croom Helm.

L. J. Raines (1991) 'The mouse that roared' in F. Grosveld and G. Kollios (eds) *Transgenic Animals*, London: Academic Press, 1992.

K. E. Read (1955) 'Morality and the Concept of the Person among the Gahuku-Gama' (peoples of Highland New Guinea), in *Oceania* 25 (4), pp. 233–82.

M. R. Redclift (1984) *Development and the Environmental Crisis: Red or Green Alternatives?*, London: Methuen.

M. R. Redclift (1987) *Sustainable Development: Exploring the Contradictions*, London and New York: Methuen.

M. R. Redclift and E. Mingione (eds) (1985) *Beyond Employment, Household, Gender and Subsistence*, Oxford: Blackwell.

J. Rée (1987) *Philosophical Tales*, London: Routledge.

J. Rée (1990) 'Timely meditations', *Radical Philosophy* 55, pp. 31–9.

K. Renner (1953) 'The service class' in T. B. Bottomore and P. Goode (eds and trs) (1978) *Austro-Marxism*, Oxford: Clarendon Press, 1978, pp. 249–52.

D. Ricardo (1817) *Principles of Political Economy and Taxation*, London: J. M. Dent, 1973

A. Rifflet-Lemaire (1970) *Jacques Lacan* (tr. David Macey), London: Routledge and Kegan Paul, 1977.

D. Riley (1983) *Am I that Name?* London: Macmillan.

R. Rorty (1979) *Philosophy and the Mirror of Nature*, New Jersey: Princeton University Press.

R. Rorty (1993) 'Anti-foundationalism and sentimentality', paper presented at Cambridge Political Thought Seminar, March 1993.

M. Z. Rosaldo and L. Lamphere (eds) (1974) *Women, Culture and Society*, Stanford: Stanford University Press, 1984.

G. Rose (1978) *The Melancholy Science: Introduction to the Thought of Theodor W. Adorno*, London: Macmillan.

G. Rose (1981) *Hegel Contra Sociology*, London: Athlone.

J. Rose (1981) 'The imaginary' in Colin McCabe (ed.) *The Talking Cure: Essays in Psychoanalysis and Language*, London: Macmillan, pp. 132–61.

J. Rose (1982) 'Introduction II' *Feminine Sexuality: Jacques Lacan and the École Freudienne*, Macmillan: London, pp. 27–57.

J. Rose (1986) *Sexuality in the Field of Vision*, London: Verso.

R. N. Rosecrance (1986) *The Rise of the Trading State: Commerce and Conquest in the Modern World*, New York: Basic Books.

G. Rubin (1975) 'The traffic in women: notes on the "political economy" of sex' in R. R. Reiter (ed.) *Toward an Anthropology of Women*, New York: Monthly Review Press, pp. 157–210.

M. Ryle (1988) *Ecology and Socialism*, London: Radius.

M. D. Sahlins (1972) *Stone Age Economics*, Chicago: Aldine-Atherton.

K. Sale (1985) *Dwellers in the Land: The Bioregional Vision*, San Francisco: Sierra Club Books.

L. Sargent (ed.) (1981) *Women and Revolution: A Discussion of the Unhappy Marriage of Marxism and Feminism*, Boston: South End Press.

D. Sayer (1984) *The Violence of Abstraction: The Analytical Foundations of Historical Materialism*, Oxford and New York: Blackwell, 1987.

I. Scheibler (1993) 'Heidegger and the rhetoric of submission: technology and passivity' in V. Conley (ed.) *Questioning Technology*, Minneapolis: University of Minnesota Press.

F. W. J. Schelling (1797) *Ideas for a Philosophy of Nature: As Introduction to the Study of this Science* (tr. E. E. Harris and P. Heath), Cambridge: Cambridge University Press, 1988.

S. Schneiderman (1980) *Returning to Freud: Clinical Psychoanalysis in the School of Lacan* (tr. S. Schneiderman), New Haven: Yale University Press.

A. M. Scott (1986) *Rethinking Petty Commodity Production, Social Analysis 20*, special issue series.

J. W. Scott (1978) see Tilly and Scott.

J. W. Scott (1992) 'Experience' in *Feminists Theorize the Political* (eds) J. Butler and J. W. Scott, London: Routledge, pp. 22–40.

A. Shaikh (1977) 'Marx's theory of value and the "transformation problem" ' in J. Schwartz (ed.) *The Subtle Anatomy of Capitalism*, Santa Monica: Goodyear, pp. 106–39.

M. Shaw (1991) *Post-Military Society*, Cambridge: Polity Press.

V. Shiva (1988) *Staying Alive: Women, Ecology, and Survival in India*, London: Zed Press.

Q. Skinner (1978) *The Foundations of Modern Political Thought* (2 vols), Cambridge: Cambridge University Press.

Q. Skinner (1985) Introduction to *The Return of Grand Theory in the Human Sciences*, (ed.) Q. Skinner, Cambridge: Cambridge University Press, pp. 1–20.

Q. Skinner (1988) *Meaning and Context: Quentin Skinner and his Critics* (ed. J. Tully), Cambridge: Polity Press.

S. Sontag (1978) *Illness as Metaphor*, Harmondsworth: Penguin, 1991.

P. Spallone (1992) *Generation Games: Genetic Engineering and the Future for our Lives*, London: The Women's Press.

B. Spinoza (1677) *Ethics*, London: J.M. Dent 1989.

G. C. Spivak (1987) *In Other Worlds*, New York: Methuen.

P. Sraffa (1960) *The Production of Commodities by Means of Commodities: Prelude to a Critique of Economic Theory*, Cambridge: Cambridge University Press, 1975.

M. Stanworth (ed.) (1987) *Reproductive Technologies: Gender, Motherhood, and Medicine*, Cambridge: Polity Press.

G. Stedman Jones (1989) 'What did Marx have against exchange?' Unpublished paper.

L. Stone (1977) *The Family, Sex and Marriage in England 1500-1800*, London: Weidenfeld and Nicolson.

M. Strathern (ed.) (1987) *Dealing with Inequality; Analysing Gender Relations in Melanesia and Beyond: Essays by Members of the 1983/1984 Anthropological Research Group at the Research School of Pacific Studies, The Australian National University*, Cambridge: Cambridge University Press.

M. Strathern (1988) *The Gender of the Gift: Problems with Women and Problems with Society in Melanesia*, Manchester: Manchester University Press.

M. Strathern (1992) *After Nature*, Cambridge: Cambridge University Press.

M. Strathern and C. MacCormack (eds) (1980) *Nature, Culture and Gender*, Cambridge: Cambridge University Press.

R. Straughan (1989) *The Genetic Manipulation of Plants, Animals and Microbes*, National Consumer Council.

R. W. Southern (1953) *The Making of the Middle Ages*, London: Cresset Library, 1978.

E. Ragland Sullivan (1986) *Jacques Lacan and the Philosophy of Psychoanalysis*, London: Croom Helm.

R. H. Tawney (1930) Foreward to Max Weber's *The Protestant Ethic and the Spirit of Capitalism*, London: Allen & Unwin, pp. 1(A)–11.

C. Taylor (1989) *Sources of the Self: the Making of the Modern Identity*, Cambridge: Cambridge University Press.

K. Thomas (1983) *Man and the Natural World; Changing Attitudes in England 1500–1800*, London: Allen Lane.

J. B. Thompson (1990) *Ideology and Modern Culture: Critical Social Theory in the Era of Mass Communication*, Cambridge: Polity Press.

P. Thompson (1983) *The Nature of Work: An Introduction to Debates on the Labour Process*, London: Macmillan.

L. A. Tilley and J. W. Scott (1978) *Women, Work and Family*, London: Methuen, 1987 (second edition).

S. Timpanaro (1974) *On Materialism*, London: New Left Books.

I. Tinker (1974) 'Women's place in development'. Summary of papers presented to the Society of International Development, Fourteenth World Conference, Abidjan, Ivory Coast, August 1974.

J. Trusted (1990) *Physics and Metaphysics: Theories of Space and Time*, London and New York: Routledge, 1991.

N. Tuana (ed.) (1989) *Feminism and Science*, Bloomington: Indiana University Press.

T. Veblen (1899) *The Theory of the Leisure Class: An Economic Study of Institutions*, London: Allen & Unwin, 1953.

M. Waring (1988) *If Women Counted: Towards a Feminist Economics*, San Francisco: Harper & Row.

M. Weber (1920) *The Protestant Ethic and the Spirit of Capitalism* (tr. T. Parsons), London: Allen & Unwin, 1930 (originally printed as an essay in 1904–5 in Archiv für Sozialwissenschaft und Sozialpolitik).

R. Weiss (1967) 'Scholarship from Petrarch to Erasmus' in D. Hay (ed.) *The Age of the Renaissance*, New York: McGraw-Hill, pp. 119–44.

M. Whitford (1990) *Luce Irigaray: Philosophy in the Feminine*, London and New York: Routledge.

A. Wilden (1968) *The Language of the Self*, Baltimore: Johns Hopkins Press.

A. Wilden (1972) *System and Structure: Essays in Communication and Exchange*, London: Tavistock.

B. Williams (1985) *Ethics and the Limits of Philosophy*, London: Fontana Press.

P. Williams (1991) *The Alchemy of Race and Rights*, Cambridge, Mass.: Harvard University Press.

R. Williams (1973) *The Country and the City*, London: Chatto and Windus.

S. Wood (ed.) (1982) *The Degradation of Work?: Skill, Deskilling and the Labour Process*, London: Hutchinson.

Y. Yovel (1989) *Spinoza and other Heretics*, Princeton: Princeton University Press.

S. Žižek (1989) *The Sublime Object of Ideology*, London and New York: Verso.

S. Žižek (1992) *Enjoy Your Symptom! Jacques Lacan in Hollywood and Out*, London and New York: Routledge.

# Index

Chodorow, Nancy 23, 58
Clarke, Alice 160, 163 (36n)
class 160–1, 163–4, 165, 184
commodity/ies 10, 16, 17, 136, 175, 213;
    compared to hallucination 118, 175–6;
    construction 176, 183– 4; defined 205;
    Departments 144, 147, 148, 164; as
    desire 90–5, 101; and labour theory
    200–4; and nature 116; two-fold nature
    19, 119, 139
communism 19–20
competition 122–3, 127, 192
Connell, Robert W. 193
Conrad, Joseph 215 (11n)
constancy 106, 108
constructed inertia 102–13, 114, 175–6;
    see also rigidity and fixed points
consumption 138–9, 144, 145, 147–8,
    161, 163–4, 205
consumptive mode of production (CMP)
    145–6, 150, 155, 158
Copjec, Joan 68 (35n)
Cornell, Drucilla 88, 177 (and 8n)
cosmic connection 80
Cox, Robert 154
cross-checking 51 (29n), 52
culture, copy of a copy 96–7

Dalla Costa, Maria Rosa 156 (28n)
Darwin, Charles 88 (7n)
Darwinian ethic 41
Dasein 94
death drive 12, 59, 64, 93, 94, 99, 103,
    106, 108–9
delay 102 (and 25n)
Deleuze, Gilles 11, 23, 24 (18n), 89; and
    Guattari, Felix 86–7, 90, 119 (4n)
democracy 193
denial 171–2, 174
dependency theory 216–17 (and 14n)
depression 186
Derrida, Jacques 15 (11n), 16–17, 21 (and
    15n), 24, 33, 88
Descartes, René 47 (27n), 85
desire 168 (2n), 169; infant 93–100,
    110–11
Dews, Peter 5 (4n)
dialogue 30–1, 51; Socratic 31, 33
distribution 152, 154
Dodds, Eric R. 84
Douglas, Ann 163 (36n)
Douglas, Mary 100 and (23n); and

Isherwood, Baron 147 (20n)
drives 64 (and 34n)
Duby, Georges 192
Dumont, Louis 83 (2n)
Dunn, John 19 (14n), 171

Eagleton, Terry 5 (4n), 187 (and 12n)
Eastern Europe 19 (and 14n), 20, 154–5
    (and 26n)
ecological crisis 27
economic scale 5, 17, 138, 173, 184,
    190–3, 214
economics 19 (12n), 44
ego 3, 30–2, 63, 65–6, 99, 108, 167, 195;
    as centre of resistance 30–1;
    construction of boundaries 82; as
    illusory representation 60 (33n);
    imaginary 49; location 105–6;
    objectification 11; opposed to
    historical understanding 37–8;
    splitting 94–5; and truth 51
ego-psychology 7–8, 27, 30, 32
ego's era 3, 7, 8–9, 14, 20, 26–75, 81, 99,
    100, 166–7; anthropomorphism of 10;
    connections in 27–9; historical origins
    of 39–49; objectification in 11; as pre-
    eminently visual 24; as psychotic 38–9
Elias, Norbert 83
Elliot, B.J. 158 (30n)
energetic connections 13, 20, 25, 27–9,
    34–5, 38, 80, 86, 115, 180, 181, 188–9,
    194
energy 16, 81, 89, 103 (26n), 104, 117,
    134, 136, 144–5; interchangeable 144;
    and labour theory 123–5, 126, 127–8,
    199–205, 206; in production 130
Engels, Friedrich 129
environment 14, 15, 20, 40, 81, 116, 119
    (3n), 126 (7n), 140 (14n), 154, 168,
    180, 181, 193; exploitation of 164–5;
    pollution of 91, 145; utopian views on
    189–90
envy 95, 98, 169
equal parenting 58
ethics 187 (12n)
ethnocentrism 26, 27, 74
Evans-Pritchard, Edward 179 (9n)
evolutionism 216
exchange-value 19, 121, 131–2, 198–203,
    208
existentialism 60 (33n)
exploitation 11; definition of 185–96